Is the State of Israel a Jewish state as envisaged by the Torah and prophets? Or is it merely a state for Jews with no particular concern as to its Jewishness? To answer this question the author presents the views of the Bible, Talmudic and medieval authorities, and modern Zionists. He criticizes both the right-wing Orthodox who refuse to recognize the State of Israel and the Israeli Government for its continued indifference to the traditions of Judaism. His fundamental thesis is that the events of the past century constitute a divine challenge to the Jewish people to create an ideal society as an example to all nations.

Religious Foundations
of the Jewish State

The Book of Temple Service (Yale Judaica Series, Vol. 12)

The Nature and History of Jewish Law (Yeshiva University, Studies in Torah Judaism, No. 9)

The Light of Redemption (Jerusalem, 5731/1971)

Beyond the Moon (A Book of Sermons, Jerusalem, 5733/1973)

Religious Foundations of the Jewish State

The Concept and Practice of Jewish Statehood
from Biblical Times to the Modern State of Israel

by

Mendell Lewittes

Ktav Publishing House, Inc.

New York / 1977

Library of Congress Cataloging in Publication Data

Lewittes, Mendell.
Religious foundations of the Jewish state.

    Bibliography: p.
    Includes index.
    1. Jews—Restoration. 2. Judaism—Israel. 3. Judaism
and state. I. Title.
BS649.J5L433   296.3'87'7095694   77-3526
ISBN 0-87068-433-7

MANUFACTURED IN THE UNITED STATES OF AMERICA

To My Beloved and Devoted Children

Joseph and Esther Lewittes
David and Betty Lewittes
Pnina and Moshe Raziel
Rhona Myra and Shalom Bar-Asher

Contents

That which we have heard and known,
And our father have told us,
We will not hide from their children,
Telling to the generation to come the praises
        of the Lord,
And His strength, and His wondrous works
        that He has done.

(Ps. 78:3—4)

Introduction

I sit down to write these words of introduction on the fifth day of Iyar, 5735 (April 16, 1975), the twenty-seventh anniversary of the establishment of the State of Israel. The mood of the country, despite the festive occasion, is sober. Though the state has achieved much over the span of little more than a quarter-century, the sanguine hopes that by now even its sworn enemies would finally recognize its right to exist in peace have not been realized. Compounding the feeling of frustration is the failure of governmental leaders in all parts of the world to understand Israel's aspirations, resulting in Israel's almost total isolation in the international political arena. It is little satisfaction that this unenviable situation is a result of submission to terrorism and economic blackmail, accompanied by a cynical indifference to justice and morality.

It is a feeling of frustration that has impelled me to undertake the task of writing this book; but my feeling stems from a different, nonpolitical, source, an internal rather than an external one. After more than twenty-five years of the existence of the State of Israel, and after Israel has triumphed on the field of battle in four major wars waged against it by superior forces, there still remain large segments of traditional Jewry indifferent to or skeptical of its religious significance. There is a whole range of negative attitudes—from outright hostility and condemnation to grudging acknowledgment of some of its virtues—manifested by Orthodox Jews who, to my mind, should be Israel's most ardent acclaimers. Our religious tradition, beginning with the Bible itself, expanded by rabbinic teaching, amplified by halakhic authorities of all ages, contains numerous references to the events which will herald the dawn of the Messianic era. These signs of Israel's redemption from Exile and Dispersion, at least in part, made their appearance concomitant with, and largely as a result of, the existence of Medinat Yisrael. Yet "Eyes have they, but they do not see." There is a refusal to see and acknowledge the redemptive character of the State of Israel. Some rabbinic authorities consider it premature and unwarranted for us to declare—as we do in the official prayer for the welfare of the State of Israel—that it represents "the beginning of the flowering of our Redemption." Others hesitantly concede that the continued existence of the state, notwithstanding the unabated warfare waged against it, partakes of the miraculous, but they still refuse to give halakhic sanction to the reciting of the traditional prayer of praise and thanksgiving, the *Hallel* with its opening benediction, on Yom HaAzma'ut, Israel's Day of Independence, a decision no doubt influenced by their ambivalent attitude toward the state. Such an innovation in Jewish practice, they fear, might imply a recognition of the establishment of the state as marking a radically new era in the history of our people.

There are two basic arguments which attempt to justify the lack of recognition of the state's redemptive significance. One is the belief held by a minority of fundamentalists that Redemption can be recognized as such only if brought about by some supernatural, cataclysmic event; and anything achieved through human effort—such effort having been forsworn by an oath administered by God Himself[1]—is ipso facto ruled out as having any eschatological implications. It would be quite futile to argue with Jews who claim on the one hand to be faithful adherents to all the teachings of the Torah, and yet on the other hand ignore one of its fundamental teachings; namely, that the history of the Jewish people is to be viewed in the light of God's Providence over His chosen people. This is the burden of the Song of *Ha-azinu* (Deut. 32), which bids us at the outset to "Remember the days of old, consider the years of generations past" (v. 7), and leads us to the conclusion that "I am He . . . I deal death and give life, I have wounded and I will heal" (v. 39). And what else is the lesson to be learned from the preaching of the Prophets, if not that God is both the Power behind the rod that smites Israel and the Guarantor of its survival. It is the acme of inconsistency that these pious Jews view the tragedy of the Holocaust as a token of God's wrath against a sinful people, but fail to view the saving of the remnant by the State of Israel as a token of God's promise, "I will remember My covenant with Jacob, and also My covenant with Isaac, and also My covenant with Abraham; and I will remember the Land" (Lev. 26:42).

The second argument advanced against the redemptive significance of the State of Israel is the twofold reality that the state is neither governed by the laws of the Torah nor are all its citizens Torah-observant Jews. Did not the Torah assert: "When all these things befall you . . . and you take them to heart . . . and you return to the Lord your God, and you and your children heed His command with all your heart and soul . . . then the Lord your God will restore your captivity. He will then bring you together again . . . to the land which your fathers occupied . . . and He will make you more prosperous and more numerous than your fathers" (Deut. 30:1–5)?

Here we are confronted with a dilemma posed already by the Sages of the Talmud, and it led to a fundamental division in the concept of Israel's Redemption. The two outstanding teachers of the generation of the *hurban* (the destruction of the Second Temple in 70 C.E.), the Tannaim Rabbi Eliezer and Rabbi Yehoshua, disagree concerning the coming of the Redemption, each of them citing Scripture in support of his opinion. The former contends: "Only if there is *teshuvah* [only if Israel first returns to God] will there be *ge'ulah* [will Israel be redemeed]; not before." Whereas the latter asserts: "There is a limit to Israel's Exile; when that limit comes to pass they will be redeemed regardless." Four generations later, the two oustanding teachers of their day, the Amoraim Rav and Samuel, were similarly divided (Talmud *Sanhedrin* 97b). And the controversy continues to this very day.

It is my firm belief that these two opinions are not mutually exclusive. They can be reconciled with each other if we view *ge'ulah* not as an instantaneous phenomenon, but as a gradual one extending over a definite period of time. *Ge'ulah* begins with a Return to the Land, continues as the signs which characterize the era of Redemption manifest themselves, but will reach its final goal, the *ge'ulah shelemah*, the complete Redemption, only after there is *teshuvah*, a return to the ways of God and Torah by the bulk of the people. *Ge'ulah* is a historical process, an unfolding and developing of Israel's divinely ordained destiny. And a Return to the Land, with the establishment of an independent Jewish commonwealth within its borders, is at one and the same time a part of the process and the instrument facilitating it. Provided, of course, that this is understood by the leaders of our people everywhere, and especially by those living in Zion.

Thus this book is both past history and future destiny. It is designed to demonstrate that a political structure and a just society are the warp and woof of Israel's Redemption; one without the other is partial and incomplete. Both those whose exclusive concern is the preservation of the State of Israel and those who are exclusively concerned with the preservation of our religious tradition and way of life must support each other and wield an influence upon each other. For this to come to pass, both will have to appreciate that the establishment of Medinat Yisrael marks a radical turning point in our history, a passing from onr epoch to another, necessitating a reexamination of once cherished attitudes and practices.

It is my humble hope that this book will help in this reexamination, enabling us to work more diligently and more passionately for the continued unfolding of Israel's destiny to be "a kingdom of priests and a holy nation."

I would like to acknowledge with appreciation and gratitude the assistance given me by my daughter Pnina, who reviewed the manuscript and made some very helpful comments out of a sense of genuine filial devotion.

Jerusalem, Iyar 5735

1

The Divine Constitution

Every commonwealth concerned with the welfare of its citizens is obliged to rule and administer the affairs of state in two areas: (1) the internal area of its social and economic life, based upon some concept of the character of the society it considers desirable; and (2) the external area of its relationships with other states or national entities, including the primary obligation of protecting the security of its people from any assault by an enemy from without.

The first area is administered by the setting up of a system of laws and statutes, and their enforcement in both public and private life by means of recognized organs of jurisprudence and internal security. The second area of national responsibility is given over to the ruling power that has the authority to conduct foreign affairs; namely, to enter into treaties with other states, to establish and mobilize armed forces when necessary, to declare war and conduct military operations.

Generally speaking, both spheres are within the competence and jurisdiction of one corpus, *the government.* This government may be constituted in one of several ways: either as a monarchy, with a king *(melekh)* or chief *(nasi)[1]* who enjoys exclusive and supreme power, even though that power may have been seized by force; or as a democracy with a group of elected representatives of the citizenry that establishes a governing administration based upon a constitution and ongoing legislation; or with varying degrees of a constitutionally limited monarchy.

The political system which the Torah has designed for the people of Israel is not quite the same as any one of the foregoing governments. According to the specific instructions of the Torah, we are commanded to establish two organs of national rule and leadership, which at first glance may seem to be independent of each other. One organ is a juridical system whose major function is to ensure domestic morality and tranquility by means of just laws, that is, the laws of the Torah; as it is written: "Judges and officers [police] shall you appoint in all your gates . . . and they shall judge the people with righteous judgment" (Deut. 16:18). Of course, the ultimate purpose of these laws was to fashion an exemplary society, "a kingdom of priests and a holy nation" (Exod. 19:6).

The other ruling organ of the Jewish state was to be the national leader known as king; as it is written: "You shall surely set over yourself a king" (Deut. 17:15). The chief function of the king was to lead the people in battle. Thus, when Moses our Teacher appointed Joshua to succeed him as the leader of the people, God said, "At his word shall they go out, and at his word shall they come in" (Num. 27:21);[2] which means, in effect, that he should lead the people in battle. And thus did our Sages interpret this expression when they laid down the law that the king has the power to declare even a war of expansion (milhemet ha-reshut), basing it upon the passage just cited.[3] This was further confirmed by the people in the days of Samuel the Seer, when they demanded from him that he set over them a king, "that our king may judge us and go out before us and fight our battles" (I Sam. 8:20). Maimonides underscores this linkage between the king and the waging of war by entitling the final section of his Code (Mishneh Torah) "Laws Concerning Kings and Their Wars."

This division of national ruling powers into two authorities is explained by Menahem ha-Me'iri as follows:[4] "In general, political leadership is entrusted to two persons; one representing the Torah [i.e., he sees to it that the people live in accord with the laws of the Torah], and he is the kohen gadol [high priest]; and one to lead in the ways of the world [i.e., in international relations], and he is the king. "Why Me'iri designates the kohen gadol as the leader representing the Torah will become clear from the ensuing discussion.

However, upon examination of the scriptural passages enjoining these two ruling authorities, we shall see that the ideal situation which the Torah proposes for the Jewish state is one in which the leadership is in the hands of one exclusive authority, a ruler who is the supreme judge and establishes a judiciary that both interprets and enforces the laws of the Torah. The judges, or their appointees, are also to serve as military officers when necessary.[5] The injunction to "set over yourself a king" and establish a monarchy would come into effect only in response to the demand of the people themselves. Consequently, the command to appoint a king did not come directly from a divine statement to Moses, as did the other commandments of the Torah, but only after the people would say, "I will set over myself a king as do all the nations about me" (Deut. 17:14). This demand first came in the days of Samuel, when the people insisted, "No, only a king shall be over us" (I Sam. 8:19), despite the dire warnings of Samuel that the king would impress them into his service and confiscate their property (I Sam. 8:11–17). This divine concession was accompanied by many restrictions, especially that the king subject himself to the laws of the Torah (Deut. 17:15–20); implying thereby that the king would be subject to the authority representing the Torah, namely the *kohen gadol*.[6]

Though the later Halakhah, following the opinion of Rabbi Yehudah, rules that it is a positive commandment of the Torah to appoint a king, one should take into account the contrary opinion of Rabbi Nehorai, who avers that there is no mitzvah to appoint a king, and "this section [of 'you shall surely set over yourself a king'] was recorded only because of the people's grievances, as it is said, 'and you will say, I will set a king over me.'"[7] It is related in the Jerusalem Talmud[8] that once Rabbi Hizkiah, while walking along the way, was accosted by a *kuthi*[9] who asked him, "Are you the chief of the Jews?" Rabbi Hizkiah replied, "Yes." Whereupon the *kuthi* said, "See what is written, 'You shall surely set over yourself a king.' It does not say, 'I [i.e., God] will set.' but 'you will set'; you yourself have set yourself."[10]

The Judiciary

Moses our Teacher, in his leadership of the Children of Israel, incorporated both authorities, of judge and of king. He was the supreme judge to whom the people repaired, as it is written, "When they have a dispute it comes before me, and I judge between a man and his neighbor" (Exod. 18:16). And as king, he was instructed to make and be in charge of the silver trumpets designed "for the calling of the congregation and for causing the camps to set forward" (Num. 10:12).[11] Thus the Sages rightly describe Moses as both king and Sanhedrin (Supreme Court of Law).[12]

Moses had been advised by his father-in-law not to bear single-handedly the entire burden of judging the people. Jethro said to him: "The thing you are doing is not right; you will surely wear yourself out, you as well as this people. For the task is too heavy for you, you cannot do it alone . . . As for you, enjoin upon them the laws and the teachings, and make known to them the way they are to go and the practices they are to follow. You will then seek out from among all the people capable men who fear God, trustworthy men who spurn ill-gotten gain . . . Let them judge over the people at all times, and it shall be that every major dispute they will bring to you, and every minor dispute they shall judge; thus making it easier for yourself by bearing the burden with you" (Exod. 18:17–22). The qualifications for judges enumerated by Jethro were incorporated in Jewish law, though it was not always possible to find men of such high moral integrity.[13]

When Moses appointed the judges, he charged them as follows: "Hear out [the disputes] among your brothers and decide justly between any man and his brother or the stranger residing with him. You shall not be partial in judgment; hear out low and high alike; fear no man, for judgment is God's; and any matter that is too difficult for you, bring it to me and I will hear it" (Deut. 1:16–17). Furthermore, the Torah repeatedly affirms: "You shall have one law for stranger and citizen alike" (Lev. 24:22; Num. 15:16). Thus was laid the cornerstone of a Jewish state; a government of law and order, with an incorruptible judicial system dispensing equal justice for all.

Later on, when Moses found the task of leading the Children of Israel through the wilderness too much for one person—they were a very discontented and contentious people—God said to him: "Gather for Me seventy of Israel's elders . . . and bring them to the Tent of Meeting. . . . And I will come down and speak with you there, and I will draw upon the spirit that is upon you and put it upon them, and they shall share the burden of the people with you, and you shall not bear it alone" (Num. 11:16−17). Israel's elders had already served in Egypt as the intermediaries between Moses and the people at large (Exod. 3:10, 12:21 ff.), and seventy elders did approach Mount Sinai with Moses before he ascended the mountain to receive the Law (Exod. 24:1). The elders continued to act on various occasions as the representatives of the people, constituting an administrative and ceremonial council rather than a legislative one. When, in a later period in Jewish history, a permanent council of elders (the Sanhedrin) was established, it assumed all governmental functions, and the number of its members was determined by the Mosaic tradition of seventy.[14]

The Priests

When Aaron and his sons were appointed to be priests ministering in the Sanctuary (Exod. 28:1), they and their children after them were also given the responsibility to be the teachers and judges of the people. Thus the command given directly to Aaron was not only to guard the holiness of the Sanctuary, "to put the difference between the holy and the common, and between the unclean and the clean"—matters that primarily affect the Sanctuary—but also "to teach the children of Israel all the statutes which the Lord has spoken unto them by the hand of Moses" (Lev. 10:10−11). When the Torah talks about the judge, it says: "You will come to the priests, the Levites, and to the judge" (Deut. 17:19); "and the man who does not hearken unto the priest who stands to minister . . . or unto the judge" (Deut. 12); and then "both the men who have the controversy shall stand . . . before the priests and the judges" (Deut. 19:17). It is apparent that the judges "who served in all your gates" were not exclusively of the priestly family;[15] rather, they were "the elders of the people," but they were under the jurisdiction and supervision of the priests who ministered in the Sanctuary. The latter were the supreme authorities "to whom you shall go up to the place which the Lord your.God shall choose, and you shall come unto the priests the Levites, and unto the judge . . . and they shall declare unto you the matter of judgment whenever there arise a matter too hard for you in judgment" (Deut. 17:18). This, for example, was the situation in the case of the *eglah arufah*, the heifer whose neck was broken. At first, "then your elders and your judges shall go out. . . . the elders of that city shall take . . . and the elders of that city shall bring down"; after that, "the priests, the sons of Levi, shall come near, for the Lord your God has chosen them to minister unto Him . . . and at their word every controversy and every plague shall be" (Deut. 21:1–5).[16]

All the days of the First Temple, until and including the period of the Return to Zion, the Torah was in the possession of the Temple priests. They were "the holders of the Torah" (Jer. 2:8), and their "lips kept knowledge, and from his mouth would they seek Torah" (Mal. 2:7). Accordingly, when King Jehoshaphat "brought the people back to the Lord, the God of their fathers . . . he set judges in the land . . . of the Levites and the priests and of the heads of the fathers' houses . . . for controversies . . . And behold Amariah the chief priest is over you" (II Chron. 19:4–11). And even in the days of the prophet Haggai, the Lord of Hosts said, "Ask now Torah of the priests" (Hag. 2:11).

The authority to judge was given over to the priests, but not the regal authority. When the time came for Moses, who in effect was the king over Israel, to depart from this world, he turned to God with the request, "Let the Lord appoint . . . a man over the congregation who will go out before them and come in before them" (Num. 27:16–17).[17] As we have seen above, the request was for an individual who would take his place as king and lead the people in battle, a position not quite suitable for a priest who ministers in the Sanctuary.[18] To indicate that the king of Israel is subject to the laws of the Torah, and consequently to the authority who represents the

Torah—namely, the high priest—Joshua was commanded: "he shall stand before Eleazar the priest, who shall inquire for him the judgment of the Urim before the Lord, he and all the children of Israel with him" (Num. 27:21).[19] The Talmud expounds this passage as follows: "*He* [the explicit pronoun] refers to the king." How do we know this? Because, as Rashi explains, "the verse is speaking of Joshua [who was a king]."[20]

The Prophet

Side by side with the leadership of the judge and the king, the Torah provides for another type of leadership in Israel, that of the prophet *(nabi)*. This leadership also stems from the position and example of Moses, who was "the master of all the prophets";[21] but differs fundamentally from the others. Even though it also arose as a response to the needs and demands of the people, it did not appear in the form of a *ruling* authority, and is completely independent of all other authorities. The prophet did not govern; nor did he legislate or reveal a new Law to the people.[22] His function was to inspire and exhort the people to fulfill God's commandments; but even more important, to clarify their basic intent, what God really demanded of His people. His calling came to him from divine inspiration and from a personal inner urge; from a consciousness within the prophet that he is called upon by God—voluntarily, or even involuntarily—to serve as God's spokesman. Therefore the prophet did not hesitate to chastise king and priest and judge alike, as well as the people as a whole.

The primary function of the prophet was to bring the word of God to the people, as God told Moses: "I will raise up for them a prophet like you from among their brothers, and I will put My words in his mouth, and he shall speak unto them all that I shall command him" (Deut. 18:18). The masses of the people, however, did not fully understand this function of the prophet. Every people, like every individual, is concerned with its fate and would like to know what the future has in store for them. For this purpose, the

ancients devised certain methods by means of which they hoped to
pierce the veil of the unknown, and have disclosed to them "what
will happen to them in the end of days." The Torah records in detail
these human attempts at divination: "an enchanter, a soothsayer, a
diviner, a sorcerer, a charmer, a consulter of ghosts and spirits, and a
necromancer" (Deut. 18:10—11). "But," the Torah adds, "whosoever
does these things is an abomination unto the Lord" (v. 12); and
therefore, "as for you, the Lord your God did not give you such
things" (v. 13). It is sufficient for the Children of Israel to hearken
to the word of the Lord, and then they can be confident that "it will
be good for them all the days of their life."

Nevertheless, the people saw in the prophet the "seer" who is
able to reveal to them where "lost asses" can be found (I Sam. 9). The
people turned to the prophet not only to inquire of the Lord whether
or not to go out into battle against the enemy (I Kings 22, inter alia),
but also to know the fate of a sick child (I Kings 14).[23] Regardless,
the prophet himself knew his function very well; to go to the people
and chastise them over their evil ways, to warn them of the dire con-
sequences if they do not change their ways, and to exhort them to serve
the Lord their God and keep His commandments. Thus is it written:
"And the Lord warned Israel and Judah by the hand of all His prophets,
every man of vision, saying: Return from your evil ways and keep
My commandments and statutes according to the entire Torah that I
have commanded your fathers and that I have sent to you by the
hand of My servants the prophets" (II Kings 17:13).

Even though our Sages say that the age of prophecy has come to
an end,[24] the institution of prophecy in Israel—besides the immortal
truths it has bequeathed to the Jewish people, and through the
Jewish people to all civilized humanity—has laid the framework for
one of the basic principles of the modern State of Israel. The Bible
tells us of the attempts made to suppress the preaching of the
prophets, even to the extent of incarcerating them or putting them to
death (I Kings 18:4; Jer. 32:2—3, 37:12—16; Amos 2:12, 7:12—13;
Neh. 9:26). Such suppression cannot be countenanced in a Jewish
state; freedom to criticize the ruling power must be an absolute right

of the citizenry. Even though the State of Israel has not yet drawn up a constitution guaranteeing this basic right, it has not only respected it, it has gone even further. We said that prophecy represented an authority independent of the authority of the state. Such an authority—though the analogy is not perfect—may be seen in the *mevaker ha-medinah*, the state comptroller, whose specific job is to scrutinize every organ of government in order to expose any malfeasance or failure to conduct its affairs properly and in accord with the law. The complexity of modern life, and the involvement of government in so many areas of the citizen's activities, makes such a system of checks and balances an absolute necessity.

The history of Israel in the period of prophecy points to another aspect of the prophet's burden which should not be overlooked. The true prophet of God had to expose and denounce the false prophet, the one "who presumes to speak a word in My name which I did not command him to speak; or who speaks in the name of other gods" (Deut. 18:20, 13:2—6; Jer. 27; Ezek. 13). Our modern sophisticated world is not free of the demagogues who would mislead their people; soothsayers "who see vain visions and speak lying divination" (Ezek. 13:7). Nor is the Israel of today free of those who speak in the name of false gods. There are the Communists, who take advantage of the freedom granted them in order to disseminate an ideology which would destroy this freedom and lead to the dissolution and disappearance of the Jewish people as a nation. And there are the Christian missionaries, who exploit the ignorance and poverty of Jewish families in order to entice the children into a faith which has falsified the teachings of Judaism and has spawned the plague of anti-Semitism. Of such false prophets the Torah has commanded us, "Do not assent or give heed to them . . . nor give them any protection" (Deut. 13:7). The enemies of the Jewish state are not entitled to its protection; those who would undermine the Law of Moses cannot be allowed the freedom to do so. This, of course, does not imply that Christians should be in any way restricted in their manner of religious worship according to the customs and traditions of their faith.

Forging the Ties of Nationhood

In the days of Moses, when the children of Israel were still journey-
ing in the wilderness, "they were dwelling tribe by tribe" (Num.
24:2). Though each tribe had its chief *(nasi)*, the comprehensive
leadership of Moses united the people into one nation. So does
Scripture testify: "There was a king in Jeshurun, when the heads of
the people gathered, the tribes of Israel were together" (Deut. 33:5).
Later, under the leadership of Joshua, the formidable task con-
fronting the tribes of conquering the land of Canaan preserved the
unity of the people. They all acknowledged Joshua's supreme
authority, as was made clear in their unambiguous response to
Joshua's first command, transmitted by the people's officers: "All
that you have commanded us we will do, and to all that you send us
we will go; as we have in everything hearkened unto Moses we will
hearken unto you . . . Any man who will rebel against your word
and not hearken unto your words in all that you command him will
be put to death; only be strong and courageous" (Josh. 1:16–18).
Joshua, in turn, fulfilled Moses' instruction to stand before Eleazar
the priest, and saw to it that Eleazar and the heads of the tribes participated with him in the distribution of the land to the several tribes
(Josh. 14:1).

We do not find in Scripture that Joshua enjoyed the title of
either "king" or "judge." Since his leadership and authority were in
direct succession from Moses, who was both king and judge, it was
not necessary to explicitly refer to him by any such title. However,
after his demise, there came about a considerable change in both the
structure and the leadership of the children of Israel. The people no
longer remained "the tribes of Israel together." Each tribe that had
not yet conquered the portion of the land destined to be its own by
the casting of the lots would go out to battle, either by itself or with a
neighboring tribe that responded to an appeal to join forces. During
this period, the period of the "Judges," the tribes did not retain the
office of chief *(nasi)* or head of the tribe *(rosh ha-mateh)*. Whenever
it became necessary to wage war, either against the ancient inhabitants of the land or against neighboring peoples, a warrior arose who

would mobilize an expeditionary force and lead his tribe in battle. This warrior was called "judge," a title which was a derivative of his readiness to lead in battle.[25] We find this phenomenon already in the second generation after Joshua, as it is written concerning Othniel ben Kenaz: "And the spirit of the Lord was upon him, and he judged Israel and went out to battle" (Judg. 3:10). Only once, with reference to Abimelech son of Jerubaal-Gideon, do we find a warrior designated as king, as is written, "And they made Abimelech king" (Judg. 9:6).

Toward the end of this period,[26] the people began to feel the lack of one chief leader who could unite the tribes into one nation. The historian of that period repeatedly laments, "In those days there was no king in Israel" (Judg. 18:1, 19:1, 21:25).[27] Apparently, it was the war of the tribes against the tribe of Benjamin which crystallized this feeling, as it is written: "The people came to Beth-El and sat there till eventide before God; they raised their voice and cried greatly and said: Why, O Lord God of Israel, did this happen in Israel that one tribe is missing this day in Israel?" (Judg. 21:2−3). It is significant to note the place where the people gathered to take counsel on how to repair the rift with the tribe of Benjamin and to unite it once again with the rest of them. The Beth-El mentioned there (see also Judg. 20:26−27) is not the city Bethel, but Shiloh, where the Sanctuary had already been established in the days of Joshua (Josh. 18:1). As long as all the tribes worshiped the Lord, the Sanctuary served as a spiritual center for the entire people and thus preserved their unity. The heads of the tribes understood this very well, and therefore they were deeply concerned lest this unity be broken when they saw the children of Reuben and Gad and half of the tribe of Manasseh, on their way from Shiloh in Canaan to the land of Gilead, build for themselves "an altar great in appearance" when they reached the Jordan (Josh. 22). The abandonment by the people of the God of Israel and their worshiping of Baal in the period of the Judges (Judg. 2:12) was the major factor in the fragmentation of the people into their respective tribal associations. At the end of this period, the Sanctuary once again became the spiritual center, and the custom was renewed "to go up once a year to worship and to sacrifice to the

Lord of Hosts in Shiloh" (I Sam. 1:3).[28] Once again the priest ministering in the Sanctuary became the judge of the entire people and its leader; hence we now find Eli the priest "sitting on his seat by the doorpost of the Lord's temple" (I Sam. 1:9).[29]

2

The Institution of Royal Rule in Israel

The period of royal rule in Israel may be said to have begun at the moment when the prophet Samuel, in his old age, gathered the people at Mizpah and said to them: "Do you see him whom the Lord has chosen, for there is none like him in all the people? And the entire people shouted and said: May the king live" (I Sam. 10:17−24).[1] This coronation of King Saul was done in conformity with the law of the Torah, which determined that in the appointment of a king two factors operate in consecutive order: God's choice and the people's acceptance. God's choice is transmitted to the people by the prophet, who presents the incoming ruler to the people and also participates in the ceremony of coronation. Thus our Sages expounded the verse "whom the Lord your God shall choose" (Deut. 17:15) as follows: "namely, by word of a prophet."[2] The people fulfill their part in the appointment of the king by their acceptance of God's choice and his rule over them. They manifested this in one of two ways: either at a public gathering, where the populace shouts the formula *yeḥi ha-melekh* ("may the king live"); or by the elders of the people making a covenant with the new ruler (II Sam. 5:3).[3] Without the assent of the entire people the kingdom is not completely legitimate. We see this both in the case of Saul and in the case of David. The first time that Samuel proclaimed Saul as king, there were wicked men *(b'nei b'liyaal)* who refused to recognize him as king, and they said, "How will this one save us?" (I Sam. 10:27). However, after his first victory against Ammon, the opposition to Saul disbanded, and it was necessary to proclaim him king once again. Therefore Samuel then said to the people, "Come,

let us go to Gilgal and we will renew the kingdom there'' (I Sam.
11:14). Such a second coronation took place with David after the
elimination of the house of Saul with the killing of Ish-Boshet (II
Sam. 4), and the conclusion of the protracted warfare between the
house of Saul and the house of David (II Sam. 3:1). Then all the
elders of Israel came to Hebron, "and they anointed David as king
over Israel" (II Sam. 5:3).

This collaboration of the prophet and the people will enable us
to resolve the dilemma posed by Nahmanides (Ramban), who asks:[4]
"If so [that the king is the chosen of God], why did the Torah find it
necessary to enjoin, 'You may not set over yourself a foreigner'?;
after all, God would not choose a foreigner." However, the situation
is as follows: Since the legitimacy of the king's rule also depended
upon the people's will, the expression of which constituted the "setting over" of the king, it was necessary to forewarn the people not to
formally accept, nor to recognize as legitimate, the rule of a foreigner
who sought to be king over Israel when there would no longer be a
prophet in Israel.[5] The people were put to this test when Agriphas
reigned, toward the end of the Second Commonwealth, as is related
in the Mishnah:[6] "When Agriphas [while reading 'the portion of the
king' in the Temple as the people were assembled, in compliance
with the ceremony of hak'hel (Deut. 31:10—13) reached the verse
'You may not set over yourself a foreigner,' he wept profusely [since
he was of non-Israelite descent].[7] But the people reassured him, saying, Do not fear, Agriphas, you are our kin." The Talmud, commenting on this incident, quotes the Tosefta: "It was taught in the
name of Rabbi Nathan: At that moment Israel committed a capital
crime, for they flattered Agriphas with an untruth."

It did not take long after the institution of royal rule in Israel for
it to become a permanent and solid feature of national life. The
authority of the king to be the supreme ruler over his people increased in strength and power. The prophet Samuel had already
described for the people the extent of the royal privileges, endowing
the king with practically unlimited power over their persons and
property (I Sam. 8:10—17). The later halakhic authorities, the Tannaim, are divided as to whether the king had a legitimate right to all

those privileges or not; some assuming that they were recounted simply in order to dissuade the people from their demand for a king.[8] There is no doubt, however, that this was the universal practice at the time, as is implied in the expression *mishpat ha-melekh* (just right of the king). The extraordinary power of the king is reflected in the fact that he could execute anyone suspected of rebelling against his kingdom.[9] Not many days went by that Solomon was king, and he sentenced Adonijah and Joab to death (I Kings 2).[10]

The Torah's assurance to the king "that he may prolong his days in his kingdom, he and his children, in the midst of Israel" (Deut. 17:20) laid the foundation for the establishment of a royal dynasty; namely, that his children and his children's children would assume the throne after him. This assurance was given directly to David by the prophet Nathan, who said to him: "When your days are fulfilled and you will lie with your fathers, I will raise up your seed after you . . . and I will establish the throne of his kingdom forever" (II Sam. 7:12–13). It also gave the king the privilege of designating which one of his children should succeed him. It was not the prophet who decided which son of David should inherit his kingdom; it was David himself who gave the instruction, "him [Solomon] I have commanded to be the chief over Israel" (I Kings 1:35). Even Adonijah, who at first aspired to succeed his father on the throne, accepted David's decision and acknowledged that "the kingdom was transferred to my brother, for it became his from the Lord" (I Kings 2:15).[11] There remained for the prophet and the people their participation in the ceremony of coronation, and therefore David instructed: "and there Zadok the priest and Nathan the prophet will anoint him as king over Israel . . . and you will say, May the king Solomon live" (I Kings 1:34).

When the kingdom of Israel was divided in two in the days of Rehoboam, and it became necessary to appoint a king not of the house of David, the prophet again appeared to announce to the people the one whom the Lord had chosen to be king over Israel. The prophet Ahijah of Shiloh said to Jeroboam the son of Nebat: "I will take you to be king . . . you will be king over Israel . . . and I will be with you and will build you a faithful house as I have built for

David" (I Kings 11:37−38), thus promising him in the name of the Lord that he will found a new dynasty. This, of course, was accompanied by the Torah's condition that he walk in the way of the Lord, "to do what is right in His eyes, to keep His statutes and commandments." Again the people did what was required of them, "And when all Israel heard that Jeroboam had returned, they sent for and called him to the congregation, and they made him king over all Israel" (I Kings 12:20).

King Versus Prophet

The superiority of the king over the prophet expressed itself again in the fact that when Nathan appeared before David "he bowed down before the king to the ground" (I Kings 1:3). It is on the basis of this token of subservience that Maimonides rules that "even the prophet standing before the king must bow down to the ground."[12] Nevertheless, despite the formal subservience of prophet to king, the latter remained dependent upon the former. Since the word of God was in the mouth of the prophet, and the king at times found it necessary to seek the word of God, he inevitably had to turn to the prophet and depend upon the latter's counsel. Thus, for example, when the king of Israel (the northern kingdom) appealed to Jehoshaphat, king of Judah, to join him in battle against Aram, "Jehoshaphat said to the king of Israel, 'Seek now this day the word of the Lord.' . . . And Jehoshaphat said, 'Is there no other prophet of the Lord that we might inquire of him?'" (I Kings 22:5−7). Furthermore, since the prophet received his instructions and mission from the Lord, the Supreme King of Kings, he did not hesitate to reprove the king and speak to him harshly when the latter strayed from the right path. Nor did he hesitate to transmit to the king the harsh fate that God had in store for him. This situation created a certain tension between the king and the prophet; to such an extent that Ahab angrily denounced Elijah as "troubler of Israel" (I Kings 18:17). On the other hand, we find that Joash, king of Israel, called the prophet Elisha "my father, my father, chariot of Israel and its horsemen" (II

Kings 13:14), the same appelation with which Elisha called out
to Elijah (II Kings 2:12). Our Sages describe such a confonta-
tion as having taken place between the prophet Isaiah and King
Hezekiah.[13] Rav Hamnuna, commenting on the verse "Who is like
the wise man, and who knows the solution of a matter" (Eccle.
8:1), says: "Who can be compared to the Holy One, blessed be He,
Who knew how to reconcile between Hezekiah and Isaiah. Hezekiah
said: 'Let Isaiah come to me, as we find that Elijah went to Ahab.'
But Isaiah said: 'Let Hezekiah come to me, as we find that Jehoram
son of Ahab went to Elisha.' What did God do? He caused Hezekiah
to become sick, and then said to Isaiah:'Go and visit the sick
[king].'"

King Versus High Priest

The institution of royal rule also brought with it a significant change
in the relationship between the king and the high priest. According
to the Torah—as we have seen above[14]—the king is required to subordinate himself to the high priest, who represents the law of the
Torah. Thus Maimonides rules:[15] "But the high priest does not present himself before the king . . . nor does he stand before the king;
rather, the king stands before the High Priest, as it is said: 'and he
[Joshua] shall stand before Eleazar the priest' [Num. 27:17]."
However, the evil deeds of the sons of Eli brought not only the
cancellation of their right to succeed their father as leaders of the
people, but also the weakening of the status of the priest and his in-
feriority to the king. The "man of God" who came to Eli with the
message that God's promise that "his house and his father's house
will walk before the Lord forever" had been revoked (I Sam. 2:30),
also indicated that the new priestly house succeeding his house "will
walk before My anointed all the days" (v. 35). That is to say, he
will be subservient to the king, who is the anointed of the Lord.[16]
From then on, the king was given the right to choose and appoint
the High Priest, as did Solomon when he removed Abiathar and appointed Zadok to take his place as high priest (I Kings 2:35).[17]
    Incidentally, the title *kohen* at that time designated not only the

descendant of Aaron who ministered in the Sanctuary but also the official who served the king; as it is written, "And Benaiah son of Jehoiada, and the Kerethi and the Pelethi, and the sons of David were *kohanim*" (II Sam. 8:18). It is also written, "And Ira the Jairite was a *kohen* to David" (II Sam. 20:26).[18] Even the vestment which ordinarily was exclusive to the high priest, the "ephod," as is written, "He chose him from among all the tribes of Israel to be My priest, to ascend upon My altar, to burn incense, to wear an ephod before Me" (I Sam. 2:28); and it is also written, "And Ahijah son of Ahitub . . . priest of the Lord in Shiloh wearing an ephod" (I Sam. 14:3), was no longer exclusive to the priest. Even the youth Samuel, who was not a priest, "ministered before the Lord girded with a linen ephod" (I Sam. 2:18).[19] King David also "was girded with a linen ephod" (II Sam. 6:14).[20]

The King and the Temple

The superiority of the king over the priest also manifested itself in matters pertaining to the Beit ha-Mikdash. The priest neither planned nor executed the plan to build "a house unto the Lord"; it was the king who did both. David himself went to bring the Holy Ark of God, first from the house of Abinadab who was in Gibeah, and then from the house of Obed-Edom in Gath, to his city Jerusalem: and he was the leader of the men "playing before the Lord" (II Sam. 6). It was King David, and not the priest and not even the prophet, who felt that the time had come[21] to build a glorious and permanent sanctuary for the Ark; and therefore he said to Nathan the prophet: "See now I dwell in a house of cedars while the Ark of God dwells within a curtain" (II Sam. 7:2). It was David who bought the threshing-floor of Aravneh the Jebusite and built upon it an altar to the Lord,[22] in accord with God's word as given to him by the seer Gad. And it was David who proclaimed: "This is the house of the Lord God, and this is the altar of burnt-offering for Israel" (I Chron. 21:18−30, 22:1). On the basis of this passage Maimonides rules:[23] "There will be no temple for all generations other than in Jerusalem and on

Mount Moriah . . . It is also said, This is 'My resting-place forever' [Ps. 132:14]."

All the planning and execution of the building of the Temple is attributed by Scripture to King Solomon; and he it was who personally conducted the ceremony of its dedication. He it was, and not the high priest, who blessed there the entire congregation of Israel; and it was he, and not the high priest, who stood before the altar of the Lord, spread out his hands heavenward, and declaimed the prayer which consecrated the Temple as a House of Prayer. He consecrated it not only for the people of Israel, but also "for the foreigner who is not of Your people Israel and comes from a distant land . . . he shall come and pray toward this house" (I Kings 8:41−42).[24] In saying further, "And they shall pray unto You toward their land which You have given to their fathers, the city which you have chosen, and the house which You [alternative reading, I] have built for Your name" (v. 48), Solomon also set the precedent for the ruling observed throughout all generations[25] that prayer one orients himself in the direction of the Beit ha-Mikdash.

The kings who reigned after Solomon saw themselves as the proprietors of the Temple's treasures, and they did not hesitate to use them for their private needs or their political affairs.[26] Thus Asa the king of Judah "took all the silver and the gold that were left in the treasures of the house of the Lord . . . and sent them to Ben-Hadad, king of Aram" (I Kings 15:18). Also concerning Jehoash it is said: "And he took all the hallowed things that his fathers, kings of Judah, had consecrated, and his own hallowed things, and all the gold that was found in the treasures of the house of the Lord . . . and sent it to Hazael king of Aram" (II Kings 12:19). Ahaz king of Judah did likewise, as it is said: "And Ahaz took the silver and gold found in the house of the Lord . . . and sent it to the king of Assyria as a bribe" (II Kings 16:8). Even Hezekiah felt compelled not only to give to the king of Assyria "All the silver that was found in the house of the Lord," but even "cut off the doors of the Lord's temple . . . and gave them to the king of Assyria" (II Kings 18:15−16).

The king also saw himself responsible for the maintenance of the Temple in good repair, as is said: "Jehoash said to the priests, 'All the hallowed money that will be brought to the house of the Lord . . . the priests shall take, each from his acquaintance, and they shall strengthen the breaches in the house'" (II Kings 12:5–6). Following this instruction, the king's scribe together with the high priest "went up and collected and counted the money found in the house of the Lord (II Kings 12:11). Similarly, Josiah, son of Amon, son of Manasseh, gave instructions to Hilkiah the high priest to "put the money brought to the house of the Lord . . . for the doers of the work . . . to strengthen the breaches in the house" (II Kings 22:4–5). As a result of this instruction, Hilkiah found a scroll of the Torah which had been hidden in the house of the Lord. He delivered the scroll to Shaphan the scribe, who read it before the king. The king was so moved by the words of the Torah, which had been neglected for generations and were like a new revelation, that he assembled "the elders of Judah and Jerusalem, the priests and the prophets and all the people both small and great; and he read in their hearing all the words of the book of the covenant found in the house of the Lord . . . and he sealed the covenant before the Lord, to walk after the Lord and to keep his commandments," and he destroyed all the altars at which Baal and other strange gods had been worshiped (II Kings 22, 23). Thus it was the king who made the people turn from idolatry to the worship of the true God of Israel, showing himself to be not only the political but also the spiritual leader of his nation.

The ruling power of the king over the Temple and the priest manifested itself in a negative way as well; in the desecration of the Temple and in the violation of the law of the Torah that forbids a non-priest to draw near and perform a service at the altar (Num. 18:3–7). Uriah the priest obeyed the command of King Ahaz and built at the side of the Temple's altar another altar, similar to the one in Damascus; and on this altar "the king offered his burnt-offering and his meal-offering, poured his libation, and he sprinkled upon the altar the blood of his peace-offering" (II Kings 16:10–13). The king continued to give instructions concerning the order of service in the Temple, "and Uriah the priest did according to all that the king Ahaz commanded" (II Kings 16:15—16). Another king of Judah, Azariah-Uzziah, committed a similar wicked act. Concerning him Scripture relates: "And by his strength he arrogated his heart to corruption; he trespassed against the Lord his God and came into the temple of the Lord to burn incense on the Altar of Incense" (II Chron. 26:16). In this instance, however, the priests demonstrated their courage and they reproved the king, "and they said to him, 'Not for you, Uzziah, to burn incense to the Lord; it is only for priests, sons of Aaron, who were consecrated to burn incense'" (II Chron. 26:18). Consequently he was punished, "and the leprosy sprouted on his forehead . . . and the king Uzziah was a leper unto the day of his death" (II Chron. 26:19—21). Apparently, if the high priest was a man of courage he could greatly influence the king to do good, as we see in the case of the king Jehoash and the priest Jehoiada, as is said: "and Jehoash did what is right in the eyes of the Lord all the days that Jehoiada the priest instructed him" (II Kings 12:3). However, after Jehoiada died the king reverted to his wicked ways and hearkened to the officers of Judah, "and they abandoned the house of the Lord God of their fathers, and they worshiped the *asheirim* [deified trees] and the idols" (II Chron. 24:17—18). Furthermore, when Zechariah son of Jehoiada "was jealous for his God" and chastised the people for their idolatrous ways, "they killed him at the command of the king in the court of the house of the Lord" (II Chron. 24:20—21).

Another instance of the royal power over priest and Temple is seen in a confrontation between a priest and a prophet. Amaziah, priest of Beth-El during the reign of Jeroboam, son of Joash king of Israel, told Amos the prophet—who had predicted the death of Jeroboam and the downfall of his kingdom—to "flee to the land of Judah . . . and prophesy there; but prophesy not any more at Beth-El" (Amos 7:13—14). It is apparent that Amaziah delivered this caustic message at the instruction of the king, whom Amaziah had informed of Amos's dire prediction, for he construed it to be a conspiracy against the king (Amos 7:10—11). The priest referred to the Temple as "the king's sanctuary," and regarded himself as an appointee of the king.

Summary and Conclusions

This brief review of the political structure in the first Jewish state, stretching almost a millennium from the days of Moses to the capture of Jerusalem by Nebuchadnezzar in 586 B.C.E., formed the general pattern of the second Jewish state established a half-century later. Furthermore, the third Jewish state, which has now been established as Medinat Yisrael, is not only an evolution from the history of the Jewish people which preceded its founding, but also must incorporate in its polity some of the basic elements of the divine constitution ordained for it by the Torah if it is to remain a *Jewish* state. From our discussion in the foregoing pages we may draw the following summary and conclusions:

The first ruler in Israel was Moses our Teacher. From his leadership there emerged three separate but interacting heads of government. The first was the high priest, who was designated to be the chief of the priests who ministered in the Holy Temple, and also the head of the people's elders, who were to judge the people according to the laws of the Torah. The second was the king, the political ruler, whose powers were quite comprehensive, but limited by the many restrictions spelled out in the Torah, "so that his heart be not lifted up above his brothers, and that he turn not aside from the commandment to the right or to the left" (Deut. 17:20). The third was the prophet, spokesman of the Lord, who both guided and rebuked the priest-judge, the king, and the people as a whole. With the establishment of the monarchy, the king assumed the supreme authority over the people, as the Sages expressed it: "There is none over him except the Lord his God."[27] Despite all the warnings of the Torah, the kings of Israel in general were no exception to the natural tendency that "power corrupts, and absolute power corrupts absolutely."

These developments brought to an end the period of the First Temple, a bitter end of destruction and exile. Nevertheless, God remembered His covenant with Israel, "and yet for all that, I have not rejected them, nor have I abhorred them, to destroy them utterly and break My covenant with them" (Lev. 26:44). After fifty years of exile in Babylon, a prophet appears with these words of comfort: "Thus said the Lord, I have returned to Jerusalem with mercy, My house shall be built therein" (Zech. 1:16). However, before we can examine the developments that took place in this new period of the "Return to Zion," we must first see what transpired during the crucial and agonizing period of the Exile.

3

A Nation Without a State, I

During the entire period of the First Temple, the three types of leadership in Israel which were delineated in the preceding chapters—king, high priest, prophet—continued to function simultaneously within their respective realms, though impinging upon each other as the circumstance required. However, with the conquest of Jerusalem in 586 B.C.E. by Nebuchadnezzar, the Jewish people became bereft of two of their three leaders; both King Zedekiah and High Priest Seraiah were exiled to Babylon (II Kings 25:6, 18—20). Fortunately, the leadership provided by the prophet remained; and it was this leadership which endowed the defeated people with the will to preserve their sense of identity as a distinct nation even though deprived of their independent government and of their homeland.

Jeremiah: Prophet of the Return

Jeremiah, who had forewarned of the destruction of the Temple and the Exile (*hurban* and *golah*), was spared any harm upon the specific instructions of Nebuchadnezzar (Jer. 39:12), and thus could continue his divine mission. He was given the option of either accompanying the exiles to Babylon or remaining "with the poor of the people who had nothing" who were permitted to remain in the land of Judah (Jer.39:10, 40:4). Jeremiah chose to remain in Judea and continue to serve as the prophet of the Lord. He urged the remnant also to remain, bringing to them, in response to their own request, the divine message, "If you will still abide in this land, then will I build you and not destroy, and I will plant you and not uproot, for I repent of the evil that I have done unto you" (Jer. 42:10). This message marked a radical change in the tone and content of Jeremiah's prophecies, conforming to the radical change which had come about in the situation of the Jewish people. The prophet of impending disaster was transformed by the dire events of the *hurban* into a prophet of impending restoration and glory. Now began a process of instilling in the people the realization that the Exile was not going to be permanent; on the contrary, the attachment of the people of Israel to the land of Israel was permanent, and could not be eroded by their being exiled from it.

Two other messages had been delivered by Jeremiah with the identical purpose of planting in the hearts and minds of a defeated people the conviction that their defeat was only temporary; that the God of Israel had by no means abandoned His chosen people. Eleven years before the destruction of the Temple, at the time of the exile of King Jehoiachin (597 B.C.E.), Jeremiah had sent a scroll "from Jerusalem to the remnant of the elders of the Exile, and to the priests, and to the prophets, and to all the people that Nebuchadnezzar had exiled from Jerusalem to Babylon" (Jer. 29:1). In the name of the Lord he advised them to establish themselves in the land of their exile, saying: "Build homes and plant gardens . . . take wives who will give birth to sons and daughters" (Jer. 29:5−6).[1] This advice was by no means intended to convey the idea that they should establish themselves in Babylon permanently, and thus abandon hope of ever returning to their homeland. On the contrary, the purpose was to encourage the exiles to avoid assimilation with the people of the host country and to retain their separate national identity through building their own communities and institutions. So doing, they would be ready to return to their homeland at the appointed time; "for thus said the Lord, After seventy years will have passed for Babylon I will remember you, and I will fulfill for you My good word to bring you back to this place" (Jer. 29:10).

Four years later, Jeremiah had occasion to despatch to the exiles in Babylon a further message, reinforcing the earlier one. He provided them with a detailed description of the disaster which was bound to befall Babylon, an event which would signal the time for the return to Zion. "In those days and in that time, says the Lord, the children of Israel together with the children of Judah . . . will seek the Lord their God. They shall inquire concerning Zion. Their Redeemer is mighty, the Lord of Hosts is His name" (Jer. 50:4–5, 34). Again Jeremiah assures the people that "neither Israel nor Judah is widowed of its God"; and he bids them: "Remember the Lord from afar, and let Jerusalem enter into your mind" (Jer. 51:5, 50).

Ezekiel: Prophet of the Restoration

Among the Jews exiled to Babylon with Jehoiachin was an inspired visionary by the name of Ezekiel, son of Buzi the priest. He dwelt in the city of Tel Aviv in Babylonia, a place where most of the Jewish exiles had settled. He was moved to prophesy to his fellow ex-patriates not long after the foregoing message of Jeremiah was delivered; and he echoed his senior colleague in the most forceful and vivid terms imaginable. Like Jeremiah, before the *hurban* he thundered against Israel's iniquities, which were bound to bring about the destruction of the Holy City; but after the *hurban* he not only prophesied the return of the dispersed to their homeland; he even foretold the restoration of the House of David, whose scion would once again reign over the reunited House of Israel.[2] The restoration would not only be a material one, a resettling of cities and a rebuilding of ruins, a replanting of waste places and an abundant yielding of fruit; it would bring with it a spiritual renaissance as well. "I will sprinkle pure water upon you, and you will be purified; I will purify you from all your uncleannesses and from all your abominations. I will give you a new heart and a new spirit in your midst; I will remove the heart of stone from your body and give you a heart of flesh" (Ezek. 36–37).

It was not a simple matter for the prophet to instill such hope in the exiled people. They were saying: "Our bones are dried up and our hope is lost; we are cut off" (Ezek. 37:11). It was not only political realism which led to this feeling of despair—who would dare predict the downfall of Nebuchadnezzar's mighty empire! The exiles were plagued by a feeling of guilt and rejection, saying: "Our transgressions and our sins are upon us, and we waste away in them; how then can we live?" (Ezek. 33:10). They even felt condemned because of the sins of their fathers, and they repeated the parable already voiced in the land of Israel, "The fathers have eaten sour grapes and the children's teeth are set on edge."[3] As did Jeremiah before him (Jer.31:28), Ezekiel reaffirmed the basic principle of God's justice and mercy; namely, "each man dies only for his own sin" and not for the sin of his father; "but if the wicked man turns from his evil ways, he will live" (Ezek. 18, 33).

Furthermore, the prophet told them that it was not for their sake that God would redeem them, but for the sake of His holy Name, which they had profaned by their iniquitous ways, "in that men said of them: These are the people of the Lord who have gone forth out of His land" (Ezek. 36:20).[4] As a result of the miracle of Israel's redemption, however, God's Name would be sanctified among all the nations. The sanctification of God's Name would be further enhanced after the ingathering of the exiles, when a mighty nation—indeed, a concert of nations—would invade the land of Israel in order to deny to the ingathered the fruits of the redemption, namely peace, security, and prosperity. These enemies of Israel, the prophet continues, will suffer total defeat in the Holy Land, "and thus I will become exalted and hallowed [vehithgadalti vehithkadashti], and I will become known in the eyes of many nations, and they shall know that I am the Lord" (Ezek. 38, 39). These words have become the classic expression of hope for the final and ultimate redemption of Israel, intoned in Israel's most hallowed prayer, the Kaddish.

To make the promised restoration of Zion more tangible in the eyes of the exiles, Ezekiel envisioned for them a detailed description of the future Temple and the sacrificial service that would be conducted therein (Ezek. 40–46).[5] He provides a central place in the Temple Service for the nasi, no doubt referring to the future high priest.[6] This is a reflection of the situation which prevailed in Judea after the days of Ezra, when the high priest was the political as well as the religious leader of the Jewish people. In addition, Ezekiel assigns to the priests who will minister in the rebuilt Temple the task of "teaching the people the difference between the holy and the profane. . . . And in a controversy they shall act as judge; according to My judgments shall they judge" (Ezek. 44:23–24).⁷ Thus he followed closely the divine instruction given to Aaron concerning the functions of the priesthood (Lev. 10:12).

Continuing to follow the example of Moses, who transmitted to the children of Israel God's instructions concerning the boundaries of the Promised Land (Num. 34), Ezekiel transmits to the exiles the word of the Lord: "This shall be the border whereby you shall divide the land for inheritance according to the twelve tribes of Israel" (Ezek. 47:13).⁸ And he adds a description of the Holy City, concluding: "And the name of the city from that day shall be 'The Lord is There'" (Ezek. 48:35).

Even though Ezekiel had been warned that the exiles, being brazen and defiant, would probably not listen to him (Ezek. 2:17), his words—added to the messages received from Jeremiah—made a profound impression upon the exiled community. The elders recognized him as the bearer of God's word, and came to his home in order to inquire of the Lord (Ezek. 20:1). On two other occasions we find them sitting before him in anticipation of a divinely inspired message (Ezek. 8:1, 14:1). Ezekiel assured them that God was with them in their exile; that even though they were scattered among the nations, God was for them even there as a *mikdash me'at*, a little sanctuary.⁹ And they are the ones—and not those who were left in Jerusalem—who will be redeemed from exile and return to the land of their fathers (Ezek. 11:14–16).

This assurance that God was with them even in their exile and after the destruction of the Sanctuary in Jerusalem was crucial for the religious loyalty of the exiled community, and consequently for their national cohesion. Among ancient peoples, exile to a foreign land implied that the emigres adopt the god of the country to which they had been exiled. Thus the peoples exiled by the king of Assyria from various eastern provinces and settled by him in Samaria were concerned because "they knew not the law of the God of the land";

namely, the God of Israel. Whereupon, the king of Assyria sent back to Samaria one of the Israelite priests who had been exiled in order to teach the new settlers how to fear the Lord (II Kings 17:24–41).[10] These new occupants of the land previously occupied by the ten tribes of the northern kingdom of Israel are the Samaritans, who later constituted a serious problem for the Jews trying to reestablish themselves in the land of their fathers. They are also known as *kuthim* (i.e., Cuthites, who came from the city of Cuth northeast of Babylon), "and though they feared the Lord, they continued to worship their idols as their fathers had done unto this day" (II Kings 17:41). The Judean exiles were an exception to this phenomenon of general history, just as Jewish history through the ages has been exceptional and unique. The vigorous preachments of Jeremiah and Ezekiel had finally made them realize that it was precisely because they had adopted the native Canaanite gods and modes of worship that they had suffered *hurban* and *golah;* and it would be folly for them now to worship the god of Babel.

Furthermore, the exiles adjusted their mode of worship to their new situation; namely, the absence of the central Sanctuary in Jerusalem, and the consequent inability to offer sacrifice therein. The prophet Hosea had already said: "Take with you words and return unto the Lord. . . . So will we render in place of bullocks the offering of our lips" (Hos. 14:3).[11] Undoubtedly, the denunciation of the prophets against those who brought sacrifices while committing injustices denigrated their value as a means of appeasing the Lord. Isaiah proclaimed: "Thus said the Lord, The heaven is My throne and the earth is My footstool; so of what significance is the house that you build for Me, and where is the place of My resting?" (Isa. 66:1). And Jeremiah, after inveighing against them who "steal, murder, commit adultery, swear falsely . . . then come and stand before Me in this house . . . and say, 'We are delivered,'" asserts: "For I have not spoken unto your fathers, nor have I commanded them on the day that I brought them out of the land of Egypt, concerning burnt-offerings and sacrifices" (Jer. 7).[12] And though the yearning for the rebuilding of the Temple in Jerusalem was and still is an integral part of Israel's prayers during the long period of its ruin, prayer as such became the essential mode of worship of the Jewish people.

Isaiah: Prophet of the Consolations

Many biblical scholars surmise the existence of a third prophet in the period of the Babylonian exile (6th cent. B.C.E.). They know nothing of his whereabouts, even his name escapes them; but since his prophecies are attached to the Book of Isaiah (chaps. 40–66), they refer to him as "Deutero (Second)-Isaiah."[13] His messages, brilliant in their oratory, constituted for the depressed exiles an additional source of encouragement and hope. Again and again he calls upon the people to arouse themselves from their despair in anticipation of the coming of their Redeemer, the Holy One of Israel, the Lord of Hosts, "for My salvation is near to come" (Isa. 56:1). He exhorts them to rejoice, "for the day of vengeance is in My heart, and the year of My redemption is coming" (Isa. 63:4). Beginning with the consoling call, "Be comforted, be comforted, My people" (Isa. 40:1), his words of solace are so compelling that seven of their chapters have been instituted as the prophetic readings in the synagogue (the *haftarot*) for the seven Sabbaths following the Ninth of Ab, the anniversary of the destruction of the Temple. And no doubt it is to them that we refer repeatedly in our daily prayers as we recite the *Kaddish* and say: "May the name of the Holy One, blessed be He, be praised . . . above all *nehemata*, all consolations." Verily could Isaiah assert: "The Lord has given me an educated tongue, to know how to sustain with words the weary one" (Isa. 50:4).

Isaiah's prophecies added a new dimension to Israel's experience of *hurban* and *golah*. Whereas the other prophets attributed these disasters solely to divine retribution for Israel's iniquities, Isaiah introduced the concept of the "suffering servant." Using himself as a symbol of his suffering people, he exclaims: "I gave my back to the smiters and my cheeks to pluckers of hair; I hid not my face from shame and spittle. For the Lord God will help me, therefore I have not been ashamed." Israel's faith in their Redeemer, despite their being "despised and forsaken of men, a man of pains and knowing sickness," will finally make their persecutors realize that "he [Israel] was wounded because of our [the Gentiles'] transgressions; he was oppressed because of our iniquities. The Lord afflicted him with the sin of all of us." And as compensation for enduring this vicarious suffering, Israel will live "to see posterity, enjoy long life, and God's purpose will prosper through him" (Isa. 53).

Thus did the prophets of Israel lay the foundation for two and a half millennia of subsequent Jewish history, a history unique and unparalleled in the annals of any other nation or people. Dispersed to the four corners of the earth, they were despised and persecuted not only by polytheistic idol-worshipers, who could not grasp a monotheism without any tangible representation of the Deity, but by the followers of their offspring religions, Christianity and Islam, as well. Without a state of their own, they clung tenaciously and stubbornly to two fundamental imperatives: Maintain your separate and distinctive character by preserving through the generations your peculiar faith and cultural heritage; and, Maintain through the generations your faith in God's promise of Redemption; namely, the Return to your ancestral land, Zion.

The first experience of Exile became the model for all subsequent exiles.[14] In this first exile it could be truthfully—though maliciously—said of them, "and their laws are different from all other people" (Esther 3:8). Four young Jewish men, though members of the royal household of Nebuchadnezzar, king of Babylon, refused to violate the dietary laws of the Torah. Daniel, Hananiah, Mishael, and Azariah spurned the king's food and drink, and subsisted on a vegetarian diet (Dan. 1). Later, when the decree went forth in Babylon that all peoples fall down and worship the golden image that Nebuchadnezzar had erected, these four stalwart Jews were adamant in their refusal to comply, even at the pain of death (Dan. 3). It was this example of *kiddush hashem*, the sanctification of God's name by readiness to give up one's very life rather than abandon faith in Him, that inspired the countless Jewish martyrs whose heroic sacrifices make glorious chapters in our millennial history. And it was this same Daniel who scrupulously observed the newly instituted practice of the exiles to pray to God three times a day with the face turned toward the Holy City of Jerusalem (Dan. 6:11).[15]

It should not be assumed that the first group of exiles—or, for that matter, any other subsequent exiles—were immune to the influence of their non-Jewish environment. On the contrary, as far as extrinsic practices are concerned, Diaspora Jews assimilated the ways of their neighbors and adopted them in their daily life. Though in the beginning it was the local official who gave Babylonian names to the Jewish youths who bore Hebrew names (Dan. 1:7), in the course of time the Jews themselves adopted non-Jewish names, either translating their Hebrew names into the local tongue or even assuming Gentile names that had no relationship to their Hebrew ones.[16] Quite readily, Jews learned to speak the language of the land in which they had settled, employing it also in their marriage and business contracts. Nay more, when the Babylonian exiles returned to Judea upon the decree of Cyrus, they brought back with them the Babylonian names of the months of the year, replacing the ancient biblical names.[17] Later, Ezra the Scribe, anxious to spread the knowledge of Torah amongst the people at large, found it necessary to replace the ancient Canaanite script in the sacred scrolls of Scripture with the popularly known square characters of the Assyrian script.[18] All these changes were accepted, as long as they did not alter or abolish the basic principles and mitzvot of the Torah.

Isaiah, Jeremiah, and Ezekiel were by no means spokesmen of a new religion, or bearers of a revolutionary message. Nor did they coin the phrase—let alone the idea—"the ingathering of the dispersed of Israel" (mekabbetz nidehei Yisrael). What they did was to affirm that the era predicted by the Torah had now arrived. "When all these things befall you—the blessing and the curse that I have set before you—and you take them to heart amidst the various nations to which the Lord your God has banished you. You will return to the Lord your God and hearken to His voice, you and your children. Then the Lord your God will return your captivity and gather you from all the nations to which He has scattered you. Even if your dispersed is at the end of heaven, from there the Lord your God will gather you. And He will bring you to the land which your fathers occupied, and you shall occupy it" (Deut. 30:1–5).

The remarkable thing was that now, for the first time in Jewish history, the words of the prophets penetrated the hearts and minds of the people and made possible, after the seeming deathblow of the *hurban*, the renaissance of Jewish life. The people returned to the Lord their God, abandoning the idolatry which had been so widespread during the days of the First Temple.[19] Israel had learned its lesson, albeit at great cost, and the time was now ripe for the Return to Zion.

4

Return and Restoration

The prophet Hosea had reminded the Jews of his day that "by a prophet the Lord brought Israel up out of Egypt, and by a prophet was Israel preserved" (Hos. 12:14). In the preceding chapter we showed how the same statement could be applied to the preservation of the Israelites in the Babylonian Exile, and to their readiness to respond—albeit in limited numbers—to the proclamation of Cyrus, king of the Persian Empire, in the year 538 B.C.E., that "whosoever there is among you of all His people, may the Lord his God be with him and let him go up to Jerusalem which is in Judah and build the house of the Lord, the God of Israel" (Ezra 1:3).[1] And once again it was prophetic exhortation that preserved the small band of returnees, they who laid the foundation for the Second Temple and ushered in a period in Jewish history which extends over five centuries, and in which were crystallized the major features of Jewish life as we see them today.[2] Two prophets appeared upon the scene, exhorting the returnees to pursue the two-fold task of rebuilding both the Temple and their statehood, despite the discouraging difficulties they encountered upon their return to Zion.[3]

Though Cyrus did not grant restored Judea complete independence, he did grant it—in accord with his general policy for the nations he conquered—complete internal autonomy. To give the returnees a sense of continuity with their formerly independent kingdom, he appointed as governor of Judea a scion of the House of David, Zerubbabel, son of Shealtiel and grandson of King Jehoiachin;[4] and as high priest Joshua, son of Jehozadak and grandson of the former high priest Seraiah. In their appointment we see restored the dual leadership of the Jewish nation described in our first chapter, the political leader and the religious leader. However, without the guidance and inspiration of the third leader, the prophet, the restored community might have foundered in face of the many economic and political hardships it encountered.

The first prophet to bring the message of encouragement and hope for better days was Haggai, whose words were specifically directed to the two new leaders, Zerubbabel and Joshua (Hag. 1:1). He exhorted them—and through them the people at large—to be strong and to proceed with the rebuilding of the Temple without delay (1:8, 2:4), predicting that "the glory of this Second Temple will be greater than that of the First" (Hag. 2:9).[5] He also promised Zerubbabel God's special protection despite the military convulsions threatening the Persian Empire (Hag. 2:22—23).

As reinforcement and amplification of Haggai's message were the prophecies of his contemporary, Zechariah son of Berechiah. Symbolizing his messages in mystical visions, Zechariah foresaw the reconstruction of Jerusalem, the rehabilitation of its citizens, and the rebuilding of the Temple under the rule of Zerubbabel. He also affirmed the authority of Joshua as High Priest, who was to work together with Zerubbabel but under his jurisdiction (Zech. 6:13). We see here a confirmation of the relative positions of king and high priest which existed in the days of the First Temple.[6] Though Zechariah underscored the centrality of the Temple in Jewish life, he reminded the people of the teachings of the earlier prophets, who had emphasized the overriding importance of establishing a righteous and compassionate society (Zech. 7:7—10). He it was who brought to Israel the eternal message that Israel's independence and glory is vouchsafed "neither by might, nor by power, but my My spirit, says the Lord of Hosts" (Zech. 4:6).

The Days of the Messiah

The most inspiring message of the prophets of Israel is contained in their vivid description of "the End of Days," the Messianic era when humanity will finally arrive at the fulfillment of its divinely ordained destiny.[7] The basic features which will characterize this idyllic era include the ingathering of the children of Israel from the far-flung corners of the Diaspora to their promised homeland; the punishment of those peoples who persecuted Israel and impeded their redemption; the recognition by all nations of the world of Jerusalem as the Holy City whence will come forth the teachings of truth and justice which will lead to universal peace and brotherhood. Zechariah saw in the Return to Zion of his day, with its modest and partial fulfillment of these prophecies,[8] a first step toward their complete realization, and he therefore proceeded to dwell upon the details of their manifestation. He repeatedly asserts that Jerusalem will be called "the City of Truth," and he exhorts the people to make it so by practicing truth, justice, and peace (Zech. 8). He bids Zion to rejoice, "for behold your king [the Messiah] is coming to you . . . a humble person riding upon an ass" (Zech. 9:9). And after those who attempt to invade the restored Jerusalem suffer defeat, God's kingdom will be established in the Holy City, "and the Lord will be king over all the earth; on that day the Lord will be One, and His name One" (Zech. 14:9).

It is impossible today to understand the Jewish people's inextinguishable aspiration, through centuries of dispersion and persecution, to reestablish its independent commonwealth in Zion, without taking into account the impact of these Messianic prophecies. Israel yearned for the restoration of its statehood because it yearned for universal peace and brotherhood. Israel prayed for its own redemption not only in order to find surcease from the persecution and abuse heaped upon it by practically the entire world, but also because it firmly believed, and continues to believe, that its own redemption will herald the redemption of all peoples from injustice, tyranny, and warfare. Israel continues to pray fervently for the rebuilding of the Holy Temple and the restoration of the sacrificial service therein, because the Temple is the visible symbol of God's kingdom upon earth. Israel adamantly clings to its sovereignty over a united Jerusalem because in its tradition a Jewish Jerusalem is the symbol of the entire world coming to recognize the eternal verities taught by its religious faith. In essence, a nationalized and unassimilated Israel endures for the sake of a universal and all-encompassing mankind.[9]

It was the timely preaching of Haggai and Zechariah—the two prophets of the Restoration and Return—that completed the process of implanting these ideals in the unforgettable consciousness of the people of Israel, thus making possible the renaissance of Jewish statehood not only in their own day and age, but in our own as well.

Land and People

A word should be said here about the numerical and territorial dimensions of this first Return to Zion, for these have their parallels in the Return to Zion of our own times. According to the biblical tradition (Ezra 2:64—65), "the whole congregation together [of *olim*, returnees] was forty and two thousand, three hundred and sixty [42,360], beside their servants of whom there were seven thousand, three hundred and thirty-seven [7,337]." It is difficult to estimate exactly what percentage of all those exiled by Nebuchadnezzar to Babylon this number represented, but it is fairly certain that it was less than half.[10] The majority of those exiled had established themselves economically and were reluctant to leave their relatively prosperous situations—gained no doubt by dint of hard labor and enterprising activity—for the impoverished economy of a defeated Judea. They were, however, among the ones of whom it is said: "And all who were round about them [about the *olim*] strengthened their hands with vessels of silver, with gold, with goods and beasts and precious things" (Ezra 2:6). Those who did go up did so out of a spirit of idealism, as Scripture testifies: "Then rose up . . . all whose spirit was stirred by God" (v. 5). Much later, the Sages were critical of the disappointing fact that only a minority had been inspired to return, and they said: "It is written: 'If she be a wall, we will build upon her a turret of silver; and if she be a door, we will enclose her with boards of cedar,' [Song of Songs 8:9]; implying that if you had made yourselves as a wall and all of you would have gone up in the days of Ezra, you would be compared to silver, which is not subject to rot [and the Second Temple would not have been destroyed]; now that you have come up like doors, you are compared to a cedar, which is subject to rot" (*Yoma* 9b). Notwithstanding this stricture, this relatively small percentage, added to the poor of the people left in Judea by Nebuchadnezzar, did manage, after a number of crises, to lay the foundation for a subsequently viable and even flourishing Jewish state.

It should also be noted that some of the *olim* returned to the Galil (Galilee), adding to the number of Jews who had remained there after the Assyrian expulsion.[11] When the borders of the Jewish homeland were later extended to include the Galil, these were added to the total population of the Jewish state, and made possible the continuity of Jewish life in Eretz Yisrael after the destruction of Jerusalem by the Romans.

Corresponding to the small number of the Jewish inhabitants of Judea was the small area in which the fledgling province enjoyed autonomy. It extended from Hebron, twenty-five miles south of Jerusalem, to Beth-El, ten miles north of the capital; from Jericho, twenty-five miles east of Jerusalem, to Lod, thirty miles west of the capital—a total of two thousand square miles (compare this with the area of the State of Israel in 1949, 7,992 square miles).[12] The Sages took note of this when they acknowledged: "Many cities were conquered by those who came up from Egypt [i.e., by the Israelites at the time of Joshua], but they were not conquered by those who came up from Babylon" (*Hagigah* 3b). Furthermore, Judea was surrounded on all sides by enemies: Edomites encroached from the Negev; the Philistines blocked off the outlet to the Mediterranean; the Ammonites and the Moabites pressed in upon them from the eastern side of the Jordan; and in the north were the threatening Samarians (Samaritans). In fact, the latter were also settled within the borders of Judea, and constituted a grave problem as to who had been given the right to self-rule in Judea, the Jewish people alone or the Jews and the Samaritans together.

In discussing the area included within the borders of the Jewish state at all periods in our history—and the present time is no exception—we must bear in mind the distinction between Medinat

Yisrael, the independent Jewish commonwealth, and Eretz Yisrael, the Promised Land which the Jewish people conceive as their rightful heritage and which possesses in Jewish law a quality of sanctity.[13] The borders of Eretz Yisrael are actually conceived on two levels: one, as an ideal reserved for "the End of Days"; and two, those set forth as the practical program for Jewish conquest and settlement. The former is spelled out in the covenant God made with Abraham, as is written: "On that day the Lord made a covenant with Abraham, saying: To your offspring I give this land, from the river of Egypt[14] to the great river, the river Euphrates" (Gen. 15:18). The latter are the borders delineated by Moses to the Israelites in the desert at the behest of the Lord just before they were to enter the land of Canaan under Joshua (Num. 34:1−12). Roughly, the borders of this Eretz Yisrael were as follows: The southern boundary ran from the southern tip of the Dead Sea, across the northern third of the Negev through biblical Kadesh Barnea (about fifty-five miles southwest of Beer-Sheva), continuing to a point where Wadi El Arish reaches the Mediterranean, thus including the northeastern sector of the Sinai Peninsula. The western border was the Mediterranean, going north beyond present-day Lebanon into western Syria, excluding its coastal region (this was the region of the biblical Hittites). The northern boundary ran through Lebo-Hamath, south of Hamath in Syria, and then veered southward to north of the sources of the Jordan (Dan-Banias). The eastern boundary ran east of the Kinnereth (Sea of Galilee), down the Jordan River into the Dead Sea.

To the above was added the area east of the Jordan River, including the northern half of today's Kingdom of Jordan, the Syrian province south of the Hermon, and the Golan Heights (biblical Gilead and Bashan), conquered in the final days of Moses and settled by the tribes of Gad and Reuben and half of Manasseh (Num. 32). This area is designated in talmudic literature as *Ever Hayarden* (Trans-Jordan).[15] Not until the time of King David, three centuries after their entry into the land of Canaan under Joshua, were the Israelite tribes able to invade and conquer all the areas delineated by Moses. David conquered most of Syria, and Solomon extended his dominion as far as the Euphrates (I Kings 5:1, 4); and we find Jews settling as far north as Lebo-Hamath (I Kings 8:65; I Chron. 13:5). Such extensive dominion did not last very long. The entire northern area was cut off from Jewish rule and settlement by the Assyrian conquest in 722 B.C.E., thus reducing the area to which the exiles returned by the grace of Cyrus to the borders of the province of Judea as delineated above.

During the period of the Second Temple, there were successive expansions of the area under Jewish rule and settlement recognized by the world powers of the time. By the time of Alexander Jannai, a century before the common era, a by now fully independent Judea comprised within its borders almost all of the land between the desert on the east and the sea on the west, though many cities within this area which had been established during the reign of the Seleucids (the Syrian Greeks) were populated by Greek-speaking Gentiles.[16] After the Romans defeated the Jews and destroyed the Temple in the year 70 C.E., Jewish life gradually became centered in the Galil, which included the area known today as the Golan Heights. (After the Israel Defense Forces captured the Golan Heights from Syria in 1967, archaeological teams of the Hebrew University surveyed the area and found the remains of numerous Jewish communities which flourished there in the third and fourth centuries, and no doubt had been settled by Jews much earlier.)[17]

Acknowledging the political and demographic realities of their time, and also taking into account the difficult economic situation,[18] the Tannaim (the Sages who flourished in the first and second centuries) defined the limits of the sanctified Eretz Yisrael as follows: "[The areas outside of Eretz Yisrael are:] From Rekem [most probably, Petra][19] eastward and Rekem itself; from Ashkelon and southward and Ashkelon itself; from Acco [Acre] and northward and Acco itself" (Gittin 1:2). They did not include the northern sectors in Lebanon and Syria which were part of the Eretz Yisrael of Moses, and which were populated by large numbers of Jews; for even though these regions had been conquered by King David they ruled that it was an unauthorized conquest ("the conquest of an individual") and therefore could not enjoy the sanctity of the Holy Land.[20] The Romans, anxious to sever the Jewish connection with

Eretz Yisrael, changed the name of this political entity from Judea to Palestine. The name Palestine stems from the Philistines, an ancient Phoenician people who had settled the southern coastal region (Gaza-Ashkelon), and with whom the Israelites battled for many centuries during the biblical period. Furthermore, in order to detach the Jewish name from the northern parts of Judea, the Romans incorporated them in the province of Syria, just as they had changed the name of Jerusalem to Aelia Capitolina.

The Arabs, sweeping in from the eastern desert, captured Palestine in the seventh century. They retained the name Palestine (Falastin) for the southern half, dividing the northern half between the provinces of Jordan and Damascus. It is interesting to note that the capital of Arab Palestine was transferred from Jerusalem to Ramlah, the only city in Eretz Yisrael actually founded by the Arabs.

We may conclude this discussion by saying that the boundaries of Eretz Yisrael are determined by two criteria: one, those specifically delineated by the Torah; and two, those under Jewish rule and *settled by Jews*. The latter criterion stems from the biblical promise, "Every spot on which your foot treads shall be yours; your boundaries shall be from the wilderness [Negev-Sinai] to the Lebanon, and from the river, the Euphrates River, to the Western Sea [the Mediterranean]" (Deut. 11:24; Josh. 1:3−4).[21]

The connection between the people of Israel and the land of Israel is expressed in legal, halakhic rulings as well as in mystical, supernatural concepts. Many commandments of the Torah, particularly those dealing with agricultural products, are applicable only in the Holy Land.[22] Nahmanides goes so far as to say that *all* the commandments, even those which Jews are obliged to observe everywhere, were intended primarily to be observed "in the midst of the land whither you are going to possess it" (Deut. 4:5).[23] Maimonides postulates that the Jewish calendar, upon which the observance of all the Festivals is dependent, could be fixed only in Eretz Yisrael, and therefore "if it were at all possible that Jews should be [totally] absent from Eretz Yisrael—God forbid that He would permit this, for He promised that He would not wipe out

signs of the nation completely, that there would not be there a
qualified Court—our reckoning of the calendar [outside of Eretz
Yisrael] would not be of any effect whatsoever."[24] Yehudah Halevi
in his *Kuzari* stresses the relationship between Eretz Yisrael and the
phenomenon of prophecy, claiming that just as certain soils are most
suitable for planting particular plants, so the Holy Land is most
suitable for communion with God and for the development of the
character of the Jewish people.[25] The inherent relationship of the
people with the land is further indicated by the fact—as is pointed
out by Nahmanides—that the Holy Land was fertile only when
cultivated by Jews; and all attempts by non-Jews to settle it have
been fruitless.[26] The intense love of Jews for Eretz Yisrael was
manifested by their kissing the ground upon entering the Holy
Land. Thus it is related of Rabbi Abba that he would kiss the stones
of Acco (the northern port of entry into Israel), and of Rabbi Hiyya
bar Gamda that he would roll in its earth, as it is written (Ps.
102:15): "For Thy servants take pleasure in her stones and love her
dust" (*Kethubot* 112a,b).

To dwell in Eretz Yisrael was always regarded by the Jew as an
unusual privilege; nay more, it was a legal right which he could impose upon reluctant members of his family (Kethubot 110b—112b).
It is related of several rabbis who had decided to leave Eretz Yisrael
that as soon as they had left they reminded themselves of Eretz
Yisrael and began to weep. They rent their garments, cited the verse
"And you shall dwell in their land" (Num. 12:29), and returned to
their homes in the Holy Land, saying, "Dwelling in Eretz Yisrael is
as important as all the mitzvot of the Torah" (*Sifre* ad loc.). When
economic conditions in Eretz Yisrael became exceedingly harsh and
many Jews were tempted to emigrate in order to alleviate their
poverty, the Sages went so far as to declare the very ground of *hutz
la-aretz* (outside of Israel) unclean (*Shabbat* 15a—b). Even the Jew
who happened to live outside Eretz Yisrael felt deeply attached to it,
and considered himself a potential resident of it. Commenting on the
verse "But of Zion it shall be said, This man and that man was born
therein" (Ps. 87:5), a Sage asserted that it includes both one born in
Zion and one who looks forward to seeing it (*Kethubot* 75a). And a

Jew who has not been privileged to dwell in Zion during his lifetime would leave instructions—as did Father Jacob—that he be buried in the Holy Land.[27]

Eretz Yisrael and the Diaspora

Because of the attachment of all Jews to the Holy Land, we must not overlook, in our discussion of the Jewish state, the contemporaneous development of Jewish community life in the Diaspora. A thriving and prospering Jewry outside Eretz Yisrael, proud of its religious and cultural heritage, is—as we shall see—vital for maintaining the viability of the Jewish commonwealth in the ancestral homeland. At the time of the Return to Zion, the major settlements of Jews outside Eretz Yisrael were in Babylonia and Egypt; but they differed considerably in their attachment to the land of their fathers and in the cultural and religious ties which bound them together.

To Babylon were exiled the elite of the kingdom of Judah, "all the princes and all the mighty men of valor . . . all the craftsmen and all the smiths; none remained save the poorest people of the land" (II Kings 24:16).[28] We have seen how the prophet Ezekiel preached to them about the moral teachings of the Torah, and spoke to them constantly of the impending Return to Zion, thus preserving in them both a love for their erstwhile homeland and a loyalty to their religious faith. Though Ezekiel had said to them, in the name of the Lord, "Although I have scattered them among the countries, yet I have been to them as a little sanctuary in the countries where they are come" (Ezek. 11:16), the Jews in Babylon did not build there a Temple for the sacrificial service prescribed by Torah, reserving that exclusive right for the Temple that would once again stand in Jerusalem. Thus they upheld the eminence of Jerusalem as the chosen dwelling-place of God's Holy Spirit, the source of religious inspiration and moral guidance for Jews everywhere. In the course of time, as rabbinic expounding of the Torah developed and schools of Torah-learning were founded in Eretz Yisrael, Babylonian Jewry sent its best sons to the academies there.[29] Furthermore, Aramaic remained for centuries the common language of the Jews in Eretz Yisrael and in Babylon. Thus the ties between Judea and the Babylonian Diaspora grew stronger and stronger, with the latter increasingly concerned with the welfare of the Yishuv, the settlers in Eretz Yisrael.

Otherwise was it with the Jewish settlement in Egypt. It had originated with the establishment of a colony of Jewish mercenaries in Elephantine, an island in the Nile, before the conquest of Egypt by the Persians. The Jews there built a Temple unto the Lord in which they conducted the sacrificial service in the manner of the Jerusalem Temple. Later, when Alexander of Macedon conquered Egypt from the Persians, he granted the Jews the privilege of establishing a settlement in Alexandria, which subsequently flourished into one of the largest and most prosperous Jewish communities in the Diaspora.[30] But they soon adopted Greek as their popular language, forgetting both their ancestral Hebrew and the Aramaic of their fathers. It was no doubt their requirements which led to the translation of the Torah into Greek, the Septuagint (ca. 250 B.C.E.).[31] They did maintain contact with the religious authorities in Jerusalem,[32] but the widening cultural and religious differences between them and the Jewish community in Eretz Yisrael led to a weakening of these ties and the ultimate disappearance of Greek-Egyptian Jewry as an element in the continuing vitality of Jewish life everywhere.[33]

In the period we are now about to examine, we shall see how the relationship between the Jewish community in Eretz Yisrael and those in the Diaspora developed into a partnership, each partner concerned with and contributing to the cultural as well as the political-economic welfare of the other. A Jewish state, which by its fundamental concept can be established only in Eretz Yisrael—all attempts to establish one elsewhere proved abortive—is thus the creation of the Jewish people as a whole, and it does not matter whether a majority of Jews live within or outside the boundaries of the Holy Land. Just as Jews outside may not—indeed, cannot—remain indifferent to the fate of the Jewish state, so Jewish citizens of the state cannot remain indifferent to the fate of Jews in any part of the globe.

Here history does and must repeat itself; the foundation of the partnership between Israel and the Diaspora laid in the period of the Second Temple is the cornerstone of Medinat Yisrael, the Jewish state of today.

5

From Prophet to Sage

It was not very long after the restoration that the Jewish state in Judea had to depend upon its partner, Diaspora Jewry, to save it from the danger of total collapse. Already at the very outset, when the returnees began to build the Temple, "the adversaries of Judah and Benjamin," the Samaritans (see above, p. 33), attempted to frustrate the reconstruction. They harried the builders in Jerusalem, and they wrote a hostile letter to the Persian authorities accusing the men of Judea of preparing a rebellion against the empire (Ezra 4). Only the encouragement provided by the prophets Haggai and Zechariah, and the steadfast determination of the leaders Zerubbabel and Joshua, enabled the work of reconstruction to continue unabated (Ezra 5).

It is difficult, when recapitulating the events of that era, not to notice the striking parallel to the events of our own times; the harassment and hostility of the Arabs to the restoration of the modern State of Israel and its continued development. And it is sad to contemplate that while in the sixth century B.C.E., the response of King Darius to the insinuations of Judea's enemies was to reaffirm the decree of Cyrus granting the returnees the right to build the Temple, and even to assist them with material goods (Ezra 6), in the twentieth century C.E. the United Nations did nothing to uphold its resolution calling for the establishment of a Jewish state in Palestine when the fledgling state was attacked from all sides by the Arab hordes. *O tempora! O mores!*

There is no written record of what transpired in Judea for more than half a century after the governorship of Zerubbabel; but much can be surmised from what is revealed in the words of Malachi, the

50

last of the prophets.[1] The enthusiasm with which the dedication of
the Second Temple had been welcomed by the returnees was by now
dissipated. The priests treated the Temple Service with contempt,
and they neglected their duty to teach the Torah and serve as the
spiritual guides of the people. Furthermore, instead of upholding the
purity of Jewish family life, as they had been particularly charged
by the Torah (Lev. 21:7), they, together with the people at large,
divorced their Jewish wives and married the daughters of idol
worshippers. As a result, the priests were held in contempt by the
people, who neglected to pay the tithes and the heave-offerings due
those who officiated in the Temple. Immorality and injustice were
widespread, the people justifying their waywardness by asserting
that no good comes from serving the Lord.

Malachi minced no words in chastising the priests, reminding
them of the holy mission for which their tribe had been chosen. He
also warned the people at large of the dire punishment they would
soon suffer for their treacherous deviation from the exemplary life
for which Israel had been chosen by God from amongst all the other
peoples of the earth. Those who remained loyal to God's word
would be spared on the day of retribution, and thus would be
demonstrated to all the difference "between those who serve the
Lord and those who do not serve Him." The only hope that Israel
would escape from ruin lay in its adhering to the Torah of Moses,
the servant of the Lord. This hope, the prophet assured the people,
would surely be realized because God will send His "prophet Elijah
before the coming of the great and awesome day of the Lord, to turn
the heart of the fathers to their children and the heart of the children
to their fathers" (Mal. 3). It is this prediction of Malachi which is the
source of the deep-rooted tradition in Judaism that Elijah will appear
to herald the coming of the Messiah and the dawn of the Messianic
age.[2]

It was not long after Malachi's prediction that there appeared in
the streets of Jerusalem a dedicated Jew from Babylon, whose
avowed purpose was to spread the knowledge of the Torah of Moses
and thereby institute the Torah way of life in Judea. News of the
spiritual deterioration which had developed in Judea had reached the

Jewish community in Babylon, where the laws of the Torah were both studied and practiced. Outstanding among the disseminators of Torah knowledge was a priest by the name of Ezra, described in the biblical book which bears his name as "a diligent scribe [sofer] in the law of Moses . . . who had set his heart to expound the law of the Lord, and to do it, and to teach in Israel statutes and judgments" (Ezra 7:6, 10).

Ezra now set his heart to go up to Jerusalem to see what could be done to stem the tide of religious and ethnic assimilation which was engulfing the community there. Armed with a letter from King Artaxerxes granting him the authority to introduce all measures that he deemed necessary, including the right to punish any who refused to comply, Ezra made the five-month journey in the year 458 B.C.E., accompanied by over a thousand co-religionists, and carrying with him much gold and silver donated by the king and others for the Temple Service. Soon after his arrival in Jerusalem he summoned all those who had married foreign women and made them resolve by solemn oath and covenant to dismiss their idolatrous wives and the children born from them (Ezra 10).

Building Under Siege

In the letter of authorization given by King Artaxerxes, Ezra had been empowered "to appoint magistrates and judges . . . and to teach the laws of your God to him who knows not" (Ezra 7:25). However, before he could proceed with this essential task with full vigor, the situation of Jerusalem's security took a turn for the worse, and all activities had to be diverted to the defending of the Jewish position in the capital. The hostility of the Samaritans to the Jewish rebuilding of Jerusalem, which began in the early days of the Return to Zion (see above, p. 50), flared up again, no doubt exacerbated by the dismissal of the non-Jewish wives and children. The Samaritans rallied round them the neighboring Ammonites, Ashdodites (Philistines), and Arabs who had settled in the Negev, and attacked Jerusalem, breaching its walls and burning its gates. Reports of this precarious situation reached the royal cupbearer in Shushan, a patriotic Jew by the name of Nehemiah. As did Ezra thirteen years earlier, Nehemiah requested and received from the king permission for a temporary leave of absence in order to go up to Jerusalem and help restore its defenses. Given the power of governor, Nehemiah organized the Jews of Jerusalem into a building force, and in several weeks the breaches in the walls of the city were repaired. Whereupon, the Samaritans, heaping abuse upon the efforts of Nehemiah, attacked the city again, compelling Nehemiah to organize the builders into a military force as well (Neh. 1–4).

Once again the ancient history we are recapitulating has a familiar ring. As one reads the description of these events in the Book of Nehemiah, one cannot fail to see the similarity between what happened then in the middle of the fifth century B.C.E. and what is happening now in Medinat Yisrael twenty-five centuries later, though contemporary events are spread over a much wider area and involve nations both near and far. Building activity and defense measures had to be pursued simultaneously then as well as now. Thus we read; "Building the wall, one hand does the work and the other hand holds a weapon . . . And the builders every one had his sword girded on his hips and was building . . . The night was for guard duty and the day for labor" (Neh. 4:11–16). With such heroic efforts, and with the help of the Almighty, the evil designs of Israel's enemies were temporarily frustrated, then as well as now.[3]

With the security of Jerusalem established, Nehemiah was able to call upon Ezra to proceed with his educational mission. At a public assembly held on Rosh Hashanah, Ezra stood upon a raised platform in the plaza facing the Temple gate[4] and "read from the scroll of the Torah of God distinctly, giving meaning, and they understood the reading" (Neh. 8:8). Several weeks later, the people were again assembled, and after hearing a lengthy resume of Jewish history[5] stressing God's providence over Israel and Israel's many backslidings, a covenant was signed, with an oath "to walk in God's Torah which was given to Moses the servant of God, and to observe and to do all the commandments of the Lord . . . that we would not give our daughters unto the [non-Jewish] people of the land . . . and that we would not buy on the Sabbath or on a Holy Day" (Neh. 9–10). The people also agreed to maintain the Temple Service properly, and to offer the required first-fruits and tithes.

In all this, it is significant that there was complete cooperation between Nehemiah, the political leader, and Ezra, the religious leader. Indeed, it is Nehemiah who claims for himself the credit for stopping the desecration of the Sabbath by ordering the closing of Jerusalem's gates every Saturday so that no merchants might enter on the day of rest (Neh. 13).

New Directions in Jewish Life

One cannot overestimate the far-reaching implications of Ezra's activity. Our Sages were not employing hyperbole when they stated: "When the Torah was forgotten from Israel, Ezra came up from Babylon and established it" (*Succah* 20a); and they went so far as to compare him with the great lawgiver, Moses (*Sanhedrin* 21b). For Ezra generated two revolutions in Jewish life and thought, giving Judaism new directions in which to steer the course of Jewish nationhood amidst the turbulence of massive political and cultural upheavals yet to come: (1) he transferred the revelation of God's word to His people Israel from the mouth of the prophet to the dictum of the sage;[6] and (2) he removed the Torah from the exclusive possession of the priesthood into the domain of the people at large. Moses had once said: "Would that all the Lord's people were prophets, that the Lord put His spirit upon them" (Num. 11:29); but from Ezra's day onward, the hope of Israel was: "Would that all the Lord's people were scholars, that the Lord put His understanding in them."[7]

The generation of Ezra thus marks the end of the age of prophecy.[8] The chief function of the prophets was to clarify the basic purpose and spirit of Mosaic monotheism—namely, social justice and the brotherhood of man under the fatherhood of God—to a people emerging in a polytheistic and idolatrous world, where pagan worship was based upon myth and manifested itself in immoral rites. With the experience of the *hurban*—the destruction of the First Temple, the elimination of Jewish independent sovereignty, and the dispersal of the bulk of Jewry from its homeland—the people of Israel finally took to heart the messages of the prophets. They came to realize that Jewish nationhood was something unique; that its continuity did not depend upon the usual trappings of statehood, but upon the adherence of its people to their unique heritage and the quality of the society that it fostered. Now that this lesson had been learned and Jewish statehood was being revived, what the hour required was a reconstitution of fragmented Jewry into a community expressing a specific way of life which would embrace all Jews with a common law and tradition. And, of course, of foremost importance was the center from which would radiate to all Jewry both instruction and inspiration, and which all Jewry in turn would look upon as the source of their religious faith and their kinship with the Jewish nation.

For this to be accomplished, teachers rather than preachers were required; teachers who would be able to *expound* the law and explain in detail how its many provisions were actually to be carried out. Furthermore, they would determine the conditions under which the laws of the Torah apply, and they would introduce new norms appropriate to the new times. This the prophets as such could not do, for such matters do not call for Divine revelation, which speaks in eternal accents, but for the human search for the contemporary meaning which inheres in God's unchanging words.[9] Thus did our Sages understand the function of prophecy when they said: "It is written: 'These are the commandments, [Lev. 27:34], whence we learn that from now on [i.e., from the time that Moses transmitted the laws of the Torah] a prophet is not permitted to innovate anything" (*Shabbat* 104a).[10] With respect to scholars, however, the statement is made: "Many are the things which are expounded from Scripture" (J. *Pe'ah* 2:4[17a]), and "Even that which a trained disciple in the future will teach in the presence of his master has already been said to Moses on Sinai" (ibid.). Which means that the inferences drawn from Scripture by the Torah scholars of all ages derive their sanction from a tradition of interpretation beginning with Moses himself.

The difference between prophet and sage can best be illustrated by what is related in the Jerusalem Talmud (*Megillah* 1:5[70d]). We read: "Eighty-five elders, of them thirty and some prophets,[11] were unhappy about Mordecai and Esther's request that the holiday of Purim be instituted. They argued: 'It is written, "These are the commandments which the Lord commanded Moses"; thus did Moses say to us, "No other prophet will in the future innovate anything for you from now on," and yet Mordecai and Esther seek to innovate something!' They did not leave arguing the matter back and forth until the Holy One, blessed be He, illumined their eyes and they found [sanction for] it in the Torah. For it is written, 'Inscribe this as a reminder in the book,' [Exod. 17:44], and 'in the book' refers to [and thus sanctions] the Book of Esther." We can now well understand why the Talmud asserts: "A scholar is superior to a prophet" (*Baba Bathra* 12a).[12]

With the transition from prophet to sage, the latter replaced the former as the spiritual leader of the Jewish people. Whereas in First Temple days it was the *nabi* who, as God's spokesman, chastised king and priest and people alike, in Second Temple days it was the *hakham* who fulfilled that function. When the First Temple was destroyed and king and priest were banished from Israel, the prophet assumed the whole burden of leadership (see above, p. 28); but when, six and a half centuries later, the Second Temple was destroyed and again king and priest were banished, the chief scholar was able to assume the whole burden of leadership for a vanquished but surviving people. Thus R. Simon could now say that in Israel "there are three crowns: the crown of the Torah, the crown of the priesthood, and the crown of kingship" (*Abot* 4:13); and another Sage could add: "Torah is greater [in its emoluments] than the priesthood and the kingship" (*Abot* 6:5).

This assumption of leadership on the part of the scholar became the cornerstone of democracy in Jewish life. Whereas kingship and priesthood are a matter of lineage, the eminence of scholarship is open to all. Thus we read: "If you were to say, 'There are the sons of the elders, there are the sons of the great ones, there are the sons of the prophets,' Scripture teaches us, [Deut. 11:22], 'If then you keep diligently all this commandment, telling us that all are equal in Torah.[13] And it likewise says, 'Moses commanded us the Torah as the heritage of the congregation of Jacob, [Deut. 33:4]; it is not written here 'the heritage of priests, Levites Israelites,' but 'of the congregation of Jacob'" (Sifre to Deut. 11:22). And in the scale of importance for Judaism, the Sages ruled, "A scholar of illegitimate birth precedes an ignorant high priest" (Mishnah Horayot 3:8). Furthermore, in matters of Torah learning even one's official position does not determine the importance or validity of what he says. Thus we read, "If one hears a matter [of Torah] from the mouth of a disciple it is as if he had heard it from the mouth of an ordained scholar; from the mouth of an ordained scholar, as if from the mouth of the Sanhedrin; from the mouth of the Sanhedrin, as if from the mouth of Moses; and from the mouth of Moses as if from the mouth of the Holy One, blessed be He" (Sifre to Deut. 11:13).

The Jewish Legislature

To produce such revolutionary changes in Jewish life, Ezra and his associates instituted many practical measures, most of them remaining permanent features of Jewish life down to this very day. First of all, he convoked an assembly of elders and invested them with the authority to enforce their resolutions upon the people. Thus is it written: "A proclamation was made throughout Judah and Jerusalem unto all the children of the Exile [i.e., the returnees] that they should gather together at Jerusalem; and whosoever will not come within three days in accord with the counsel of the nobles and elders, all his wealth will be confiscated and he himself excommunicated from the congregation of the Exile" (Ezra 10:7−8). This act of Ezra in convoking an assembly of elders led to the establishment of a regular Assembly which met from time to time in order to proclaim takkanot, regulations affecting the entire House of Israel.[14]

The members of this Judean parliament were known as *Anshei K'nesset ha-Gedolah*, "Men of the Great Assembly," who received from the prophets the tradition of Judaism based upon the Torah of Moses (*Abot* 1:1).[15] From this body, the parliament of the modern State of Israel, the Knesset, derives both its name and the number of its members, 120.[16] Basing themselves upon the powers vested in the first Knesset, the Sages ruled that *hefker beit-din hefker*; namely, a court of law—and particularly a court of religious law—has the power to declare a person's property removed from his possession even retroactively. This ruling has wide ramifications, and has been applied in numerous practices in Jewish life.[17] Also, the penalty of excommunication (*herem*) in the proclamation of Ezra became the most effective measure for the enforcement of rabbinic decisions in later Jewish life.[18]

Among the many *takkanot* instituted by the Knesset of Ezra's time, and no doubt under his leadership and initiative, the following are the most significant:

1. *Fixing the text of the Daily Prayer* (the eighteen benedictions of the *Shemoneh Esreh*; *Megillah* 17b). Though thrice daily devotions were already practiced before the Return to Zion (see above, pp. 34 and 36), it was necessary to adjust the text of the prayer to the new circumstances in Jewish life, especially as far as the restored Temple Service was concerned.[19] Maimonides offers the following explanation for the need to fix the text of prayer at that time.[20] "When Israel was exiled in the days of the wicked Nebuchadnezzar, the Israelites mingled [with the people] in Persia, Greece, and other nations. Children were born to them in those Gentile lands and their language became mixed . . . For that reason, when they wanted to pray their language was inadequate for the supplication of their wants, or for expressing praise of the Holy One, blessed be He, in the sacred tongue without mixing in foreign expressions. As soon as Ezra and his Court of Law saw this, they instituted eighteen benedictions in an ordered sequence . . . so that they be arranged for everyone who would learn them, and thus the prayer of the faulty of speech would be perfect like the prayer of those who possess a pure tongue."

This common language of prayer was an important factor in strengthening the unity of the Jewish people through the centuries, despite their dispersal to the four corners of the earth and their speaking different languages. It must be remembered, however, that this fixing of the text of our prayers did not negate the halakhic ruling that prayer may be recited in any language (Mishnah *Sotah* 7:1). Any additional supplications which an individual may want to recite, or even, for that matter, any supplementary prayers which a congregation may want to add, need not be recited in the sacred tongue. Thus, for example, the *Kaddish* is recited in Aramaic because that was the language spoken by the majority of the Jewish people at the time of its composition.[21]

2. *Redaction of the Pentateuch and the Prophets.*[22] Ezra was called *ha-sofer*, the Scribe, and accordingly his associates and the Torah expounders of the generations succeeding him are designated *soferim*. The Talmud says that they were so designated because "they would count all the letters of the Torah" (*Kiddushin* 30a), thus sanctifying their edition of the Torah as the authentic one for both public and private use.[23] The Talmud also speaks of *Mikra Soferim* and *Ittur Soferim* (*Nedarim* 37b), most probably referring to their fixing the text of Scripture where they found two or more versions of the same passage, and deciding where to adopt the "full" or the "deficient" spelling. They even made slight emendations of the text in order to conform to the literary style of the day. The Sages ruled that certain words in the Pentateuch should be written with dots over them. They attribute this ruling to Ezra, made when he encountered words about which he was doubtful whether or not they should be included in the text. We read in *Abot D'Rabbi Nathan* (34:5) as follows: "Thus said Ezra, 'If Elijah will come and ask me why I have written these words [that do not belong], I will reply that I have placed dots over them [to indicate their doubtful inclusion]. And if he tells me that they do belong, I will remove the dots from them.'" Subsequent generations exercised scrupulous care that the exact wording of Scripture be preserved free from error, and even if one letter in a scroll of the Torah is found to be incorrect it is invalid for public reading until corrected. And one who

permits a scroll to remain uncorrected for more than thirty days ignores the admonition in Job (11:14): "Let not unrighteousness dwell in your tents" (Kethubot 19b). As a result, today, after many centuries of scribal transmission, we have a uniform text of Scripture free from the variant readings which plague other traditional literatures.[24]

3. *Substituting the contemporary Assyrian script of the Hebrew letters*, in place of the ancient Canaanite script current in the days of the First Temple (Sanhedrin 21b; see above, chap. 3, n. 18). It is this Assyrian script which is in use today and required by the Halakhah for Tefilin, Mezuzot, and scrolls of the Torah.

4. *Periodic public readings of a section of the Torah.* Ezra and his Court of Law instituted that a section of the Pentateuch be read in public on Monday and Thursday mornings, and on Sabbath mornings and afternoons (Baba Kamma 82a).[25] The statutory readings for Festival mornings, comprising the section dealing with the respective Festival (Mishnah Megillah 3:5), had previously been introduced by Moses (Megillah 32a), though we have no written testament that this was actually practiced in First Temple days. Originally, the Torah was divided into small sections, each section called a *sidrah*, so that the reading of the entire Pentateuch was completed in approximately three years (Megillah 29b). Later, in Babylonia, the portion read on each Sabbath was expanded so that the Pentateuch was covered in one year.[26] In the post-talmudic era, the day on which the annual cycle of Torah-reading was completed, the ninth day of the Succot Festival (actually, the second day of Shemini Atzeret, celebrated only in the Diaspora), began to be celebrated as Simhat Torah with much singing and dancing. Ezra's *takkanah* of regular Torah-reading made the *Humash*, the Five Books of Moses, an open book whose contents became familiar even to the humblest Jew in the community.

5. *Recitation of the Targum;* that is, to recite the Aramaic translation of the Hebrew Scripture at all statutory readings of the Torah. Thus did our Sages interpret the expression *meforash* (distinctly) in the verse which recounts Ezra's reading of the Torah at the public assembly (Neh. 8:8). Rules were formulated as to the

manner in which the recitation of the Targum should accompany the Torah-reading (Mishnah *Megillah* 4:4, 5, 10), and even the individual at home was required to review the weekly portion together with the Targum, reciting each verse in the original Hebrew twice and its Aramaic translation once (*Berakhot* 8a—b). Later halakhic authorities (the Rishonim of the early Middle Ages) relaxed this last requirement, ruling that since Aramaic was no longer the Jewish vernacular one may substitute Rashi's commentary in place of the Targum.[27] Nevertheless, all standard editions of the *Humash* printed today include the Targum of Onkelos, and we are urged by the *Shulhan Arukh* (Code of Jewish Law) to continue even nowadays the practice of reading the Targum. Until recently, the Jews of Yemen retained the ancient practice of reciting the Targum at public statutory readings.[28]

6. *That courts of law should conduct regular sessions in towns on Mondays and Thursdays* (Baba Kamma 82a).[29]

Social and Economic Legislation

The Talmud ascribes to Ezra several more *takkanot*, mainly of a social and economic nature (*Baba Kamma* 82a). We must bear in mind that a substantial part of the Torah's legislation is of such a nature, designed specifically to protect the dignity and welfare of the indigent, and to prevent their being exploited by the wealthy. Man's greed—aphorized so pointedly in the rabbinic statement,[30] "If a man has one hundred shekels, he wants to increase it to two hundred"—is so dominating that the restraints put upon it by the Torah need constant reinforcement. The prophets of Israel thundered against man's lust for wealth and power, and the Sages of Israel applied the pressure of their decrees in order to channel man's greed into socially beneficial activities.

Nehemiah was no exception to this responsibility of Jewish leadership. When he heard the cry of the poor Jews oppressed by their own brethren in Judea, he became incensed. He summoned the nobles and rebuked them for seizing the mortgaged fields and selling their brethren as slaves because of the non-payment of high-interest loans. He made them swear that they would relinquish the oppressive debts and return the seized fields and vineyards. For these economic reforms also, he asked God to remember him for good, "for all that I have done for this people" (Neh. 5).

Long before this, when the tribes of Israel were about to settle in Eretz Yisrael, Joshua distributed the land on certain conditions of economic cooperation (*Baba Kamma* 80a). The institution of practical measures regulating the economic affairs of the community, in accord with the needs of the times but inspired by the social legislation of the Torah, is a prime function of a Jewish state. The primary purpose of such measures must be what our Sages call *tikkun ha-olam*; namely, ordering society in such a manner so that the interests of one member or one class will not clash with the interests and welfare of the members of the community as a whole.[31] In accord with the spirit expressed in the verse "Its ways are ways of pleasantness, and all its paths are peace" (Prov. 3:17), rabbinic legislation was also designed to promote peaceful relationships in the community and encourage good neighborliness even with the non-Jews in our midst (Mishnah *Gittin* 5:8–9).

Religious authorities have the added power to rule that certain economic laws of the Torah were meant to apply only under particular conditions, and therefore are no longer in effect under the prevailing conditions. Thus the law of the Jubilee Year (Lev. 25:8–28), which ordained that any patrimonial land which had been sold reverts to the original owner at the Jubilee Year, was declared to be no longer in effect at the time of Ezra because then the settlement of the land did not include all the tribes of Israel (*Arakhin* 32b).[32] And with the abeyance of the law of the return to the land, the law of the *ebed ivri*, the Hebrew slave (Exod. 21:2–11), also fell into desuetude, though some important sections of that law are still relevant today.[33]

Furthermore, when certain laws of the Torah for the protection of the poor were circumvented by the rich, *takkanot* were introduced to ensure that the poor should not suffer. Thus Hillel the

Elder, who lived in the second half of the first century B.C.E.,
instituted that one who had sold his house in a walled city—he no
doubt was forced to sell because of a burdensome debt—could exercise the right granted him by the Torah to repurchase it at the ex-
piration of one year (Lev. 25:29) despite the attempt of the buyer to
deny him the right (Mishnah *Arakhin* 9:4). Hillel was also the
author of the more famous *takkanah* of the *pruzbol*, a document
which obviated the law of the Torah that all debts are to be cancelled
in the Sabbatical Year (Deut. 15:1—3). Thus we read in the Mishnah
(*Shebiit* 10:3): "*Pruzbol* is one of the things that Hillel the Elder instituted when he saw that the people had stopped lending money
and transgressed what is written in the Torah, 'Beware lest you har-
bor a base thought, etc.' [Deut. 15:9—10]."

From the foregoing we can see that the division between the
religious and the secular domains which exists in other com-
monwealths need not exist in the Jewish state. The religious
authorities, the sages and elders in a Jewish community, whether
that community comprises only the inhabitants of a small village or
embraces all the citizens of an entire country, did not consider any
facet of communal life outside the sphere of their jurisdiction. As
the Talmud expresses it: "All the affairs of a community must be the
concern of the scholar living there" (*Mo'ed Kattan* 6a). It is this
comprehensive concern and jurisdiction of the *hakham* of a community which made possible the continuity of organized communal
institutions for the Jewish people despite the loss and absence of an
autonomous political state.

In this connection, it is pertinent to point out a basic proposition
of religious-juridical authority in Jewish life posited by the Sages.
The Mishnah (*Rosh Hashanah* 2:9) states: "The names of the elders
[in the days of Moses—Exod. 24:9] were not expressed in order to
teach us that every court of three set up to judge Israel are equal in
authority to the court of Moses." And the Talmud there adds the
familiar phrase, *Yiftah bedoro kishmuel bedoro*—Jephtah, a leader
of the Israelites in the period of the Judges (Judg. 11), who was of illegitimate birth and dubious character, commands the same

authority in his generation as did Samuel the Seer in his generation. This is a lesson which regrettably has yet to be properly understood and put into practice in our days.

As we pointed out at the very beginning of our discussion of Jewish statehood, the ideal administration designed by the Torah for the Jewish polity consists of one jurisdictional body dealing with all matters of political as well as economic and social concern. But no people lives in an ideal world, and therefore it cannot govern itself ideally. The complexity of society, the division of humanity into separate peoples and classes, demands a division of powers; a political-secular authority and an ideological-religious authority. The Torah granted such a dual administration for Israel by providing for a king in addition to a judiciary, but it insisted that both be guided by the same set of rules; namely, the laws of the Torah. Only in such a situation can we approach the ideal, when there abides harmony and cooperation between the two governing powers. The vicissitudes of Jewish history are largely a reflection of the existence or absence of such cooperation. The Jewish people were able to reconstruct their national life after the Return to Zion from the Babylonian Exile because Ezra and Nehemiah, the religious leader and the political leader, worked harmoniously for the attainment of a common goal. To what extent this harmony existed in the five centuries remaining to the period of the Second Commonwealth we shall investigate in the next chapter.

6

A Democratic Theocracy

There is no period in Jewish history which has been the subject of such critical scrutiny and analysis as that of the Second Temple; and rightly so. First of all, there exist more contemporary literary records of both Jewish and non-Jewish origin which supply grist for the mills of the historians than of any previous period. Secondly, this is the period in which new trends appeared in Jewish life which have had a lasting influence upon subsequent Jewish generations. This is the period in which the Jewish people came into contact with the Greek and Roman civilizations, which are the forebears of our modern Western civilization. In this period began that intensive development of the *Torah she-be-al-peh*, the Oral Law, which is the source of the traditional religious practices of Jews today. Furthermore, the ideological controversies surrounding the various interpretations of Judaism which persist to this day—in different terms, perhaps, but essentially reflecting the same theological and philosophical differences of opinion—have their roots in the sectarian divisions which arose in Jewish Palestine over two thousand years ago. And finally, the close of this period marks the birth of Christianity, and Christians today, desirous of learning the milieu in which their religious faith was conceived, must perforce study this particular period of Jewish history.[1]

This book is not a review of Jewish history as such, and we are not concerned at the moment with the details of the history of the Second Temple period, which can be found in the multifarious texts on the history of the Jewish people. Our particular concern is with the forms of self-government which characterized Jewish life in the course of its long history, and with the basic ideas which influenced the structure of Jewish society in its varying circumstances. It is our hope that such concern will assist in giving direction to the lives of Jews everywhere, and especially those guiding the destiny of the modern State of Israel.

The Torah's Form of Government

One of the main sources, though not always the most reliable, of our knowledge of the events which transpired during the several centuries preceding the destruction of the Second Temple by the Romans in the year 70 C.E. are the prolific writings of Josephus Flavius, who himself was personally involved in the events surrounding the fall of the Second Jewish Commonwealth. Josephus not only wrote a history of his times (*Wars of the Jews*), but also other works whose major purpose was to defend the character of the Jewish people, and the laws of the Torah which governed them, from the anti-Semitic slanderers of Judaism among the Greek and Roman literati (*Antiquities of the Jews; Against Apion*).[2]

In attempting to describe for the non-Jewish world of his day, in whose eyes Jews and Judaism seemed strange and peculiar, the nature of the government ordained for the Jewish people by the Torah, Josephus wrote the following significant words: "Some peoples have entrusted the supreme political power to monarchies, others to oligarchies, yet others to the masses. Our lawgiver Moses, however, was attracted by none of these forms of polity, but gave to his constitution the form of what may be termed—if a forced expression be permitted—a *theocracy*, placing all sovereignty and authority in the hands of God" (*Against Apion*, II, 165).[3]

Now there is no doubt that Judaism emphasized, in its classical sources, the "kingship" of God, which is stressed both in the prophetic writings and in the ritual of prayer;[4] but this in no way was intended to exclude a human king ruling over Israel.[5] Indeed, generations of Jews, beginning with the prophets of the Exile, looked forward to the reestablishment of the Davidic dynasty with the coming of the *melekh ha-mashiach*, the anointed king, while at the same time predicting the coming of the Lord to reign over His people in Zion, and eventually to reign over all the earth.[6] Thus one cannot assert that a monarchy, albeit a constitutionally limited one, is excluded—as, in fact, it has not been excluded—from the forms of government ordained for the Jewish people.

However, what is true is that the Jewish people can and did govern themselves satisfactorily for centuries without a monarchy. From the day of the Return to Zion under Zerubbabel until the day Aristobulus, the son of Johanan Hyrcanus, proclaimed himself king of Judea, a period of four hundred years, the Jewish people were under the sovereignty of foreign kings, first Persian and then Greek. Nevertheless, Jews governed themselves and retained their national identity as long as they were granted religious and cultural autonomy by their overlords. The Maccabees waged war against Antiochus Epiphanes, not in order to restore a Jewish monarchy or to gain independent sovereignty, but in order to regain the religious autonomy which Antiochus attempted to deny them by force. In fact, "those Jews who were willing to fight for the free exercise of their religion recoiled, now that the struggle was over, from the more and more pronouncedly secular character of the dynasty founded by Johanan Hyrcanus."[7]

This is so because our lawgiver Moses gave to his constitution the form of what may be termed—if I be permitted a forced expression—a *nomocracy*; that is, placing all sovereignty and authority in the Law. Indeed, the sovereignty of God is usually associated in the Prophets and the Psalms with His manifestation as the Divine Judge. Hence the supplication in the *Shemoneh Esreh* for the restoration of "our judges as at first" is coupled with the prayer that "You God reign over us alone in kindness and mercy" and concludes, "God the King Who loves righteousness and justice." The Sages of the Talmud maintain that even God Himself, the giver of the Law, is subject to its rulings and heeds its commandments.[8] Thus when Rabbi Eliezer disputed a certain ruling of his colleagues and called upon a voice from heaven to corroborate his opinion, Rabbi Yehoshua declared: "*It is not in heaven* [Deut. 30:12]," and Heaven is obliged to follow the majority opinion in accordance with the

Law.[9] For the rule of the Law in Judaism is absolute, encompassing the Most High with the lowliest of humans, prince and pauper alike.

Judaism and Monarchy

The ambivalent attitude of halakhic Judaism toward the institution of monarchy may be sensed in the following legendary conversation between God and King David, as related in the Talmud (*Sanhedrin 107a*). "David said: 'Master of the Universe, why do they recite [in the daily *Shemoneh Esreh* prayer] *the God of Abraham, the God of Isaac, and the God of Jacob,* but not *the God of David?'*[10] God replied: 'They [the Patriarchs] successfully withstood tests of their faith.' Whereupon David countered: 'Then put me to the test.' God said: 'All right, I will test you with a woman' [Bath-Sheba]." And since David failed this test, he did not merit to have his name associated with God's name. Nevertheless, David did receive some recognition in our prayers, as we find in another statement of the Talmud (*Pesahim* 117b). "In the daily prayer [for the flourishing of David's kingdom] we conclude the benediction *God who makes the horn of salvation flourish* [without mentioning David's name]; in the *haftarah* [the reading from the Prophets] we conclude one of the benedictions *God the Shield of David.*"[11]

What theological attitudes may we see reflected in these talmudic statements? Each of the Patriarchs expressed his devotion to God in a distinctive manner. Abraham is known as *amud ha-hesed*, the pillar of lovingkindness; he served God by acts of kindness toward his fellow-men. Isaac is *amud ha-avodah*, the pillar of worship, he served God in offering himself as a sacrifice. Jacob is *amud ha-Torah*, the pillar of the Law; he served God in his diligent study of the Torah.[12] These Patriarchs, however, served God *before a king reigned in Israel*, before Israel became a people and required a form of government. By the time David reigned there had been added a fourth pillar to Judaism, *amud ha-malkhut*, the pillar of kingdom. In founding a House of Royalty, a dynasty which received God's blessing and affirmation (II Sam. 7:16; Ps. 89:20−38), David added another avenue of devotion and service to God. David argued: What the individual in isolated acts of kindness or sacrifice or study of Torah may not be able to achieve in establishing God's kingdom on earth, which is the ultimate goal of Judaism, may be achieved through establishing a human kingdom which, by virtue of its special powers of enforcement, can create a righteous society.[13] This was David's fervent prayer: "O God, give the king Your judgments . . . that he may judge Your people with righteousness, and Your poor with justice" (Ps. 72:1–2). David's ideal was to found a dynasty that would lead the people of Israel to its divinely ordained purpose, "to be to God a kingdom of priests and a holy nation" (Exod. 19:6). And the Jewish people expresses its faith in this ideal in its unwavering belief in the coming of the Messiah, whose kingdom will be the human instrument for bringing about the universal recognition of God's undivided sovereignty over all nations and principalities.

The history of the Second Commonwealth—like the history of the First Commonwealth (see above, p. 26)—demonstrates that a monarchy in Israel, free to wield its extraordinary powers without restraint, failed the challenge sought by King David. The Hasmonean kings after Johanan Hyrcanus were involved in one intrigue after another, and their hands were sullied with the blood of members of their own family. Instead of upholding the religious traditions for which their forefathers fought and laid down their lives, they adopted the aristocratic manners of the Greeks, and they murdered or banished members of the High Court, the Sanhedrin, incurring thereby the hatred of the common people. They sought to curry favor with the Roman emperors, inviting them to become involved in their military escapades designed to expand their powers and hegemony, a tactic which ultimately led to the end of their kingdom and of Jewish political independence.

Judaism and Democracy

The prophet Hosea predicts that after the return from Exile "the children of Israel will seek the Lord their God and David their king . . . in the end of days" (Hos. 3:5). But even before "the end of days" Israel has sought and has now established an independent democratic government in the land of its fathers. As we have seen above (p. 17), the appointment of a king requires the assent of the people at large; and therefore any government—and the modern State of Israel is no exception—which has received its mandate from the people has all the authority which Jewish law and tradition has placed in the person of the king. Thus the first chief rabbi of Israel, the late Abraham Isaac Hakohen Kook, asserted that "at a time when there is no king, all royal prerogatives are transferred to the nation in general, since the rights of a kingdom includes that which concerns the general situation of the nation," and therefore "when a leader of the nation is appointed by the people at large, he assuredly stands in place of a king with respect to the royal prerogatives that concern the welfare of the people."[14] Nay more, the acts of a monarch in Israel acquire validity only if done in accord with the will of the majority, which can be expressed through its elected representatives. Thus a medieval authority rules that "only those lands are endowed with the sanctity of Eretz Yisrael if they were conquered by a king of Israel or a judge or a prophet *with the consent of a majority of Israel.*[15]

Democratic procedures expressing the will of the people are basic in Judaism not only for the national government but for local authorities as well. The Sages of the Talmud ruled (*Berakhot* 55a): "An officer [*parness*] of the community may not assume office unless he has the approval of the community." In Second Temple days the populace expressed its will vociferously, in one case demanding the dismissal of a high priest who conducted the Temple Service in a contemptuous manner, and in another case demanding the appointment of a high priest who met with their favor.[16] And the people gathered in the Temple Court on Succot did not hesitate to pelt with their *ethrogim* (citrons) a priest who refused to perform the service as determined by the Sanhedrin (Mishnah *Succah* 4:9). On these and related phenomena of the period, the late Solomon Schechter commented: "The bulk of the nation, far from being affected by the apostasy of their political leaders, arrayed themselves in organised resistance, determined to defend their religion against all attacks from within and without."[17] And he attributes this "strange phenomenon" to the spiritual forces opposed to the priestly aristocracy.

Let us examine, then, the position of the priesthood in those days, to determine which spiritual forces arose in opposition, and why. For this we must return to Josephus' appellation of the Jewish form of government.

The Jewish Theocracy

Josephus was undoubtedly correct when he applied the term *theocracy* to the Jewish government of the Second Temple period prior to the establishment of the monarchy. For in the four hundred years mentioned above (p. 67), the religious leader of Judea and its political leader were combined in one person, the high priest. The sovereign rulers of both the Persian and Greek Empires recognized the high priest as the titular head of the Jewish people, granting him the right to mint coins and to tax the people, exacting through him the tribute due them from a subject nation. They even recognized the high priest in Jerusalem as the head of those Jews residing outside the borders of Judea; and in the period under discussion their numbers and the extent of their settlements in the further regions of the respective empires increased. Thus Alexander of Macedon granted the request of the high priest that the Jews of Babylonia and Medea be permitted to observe the laws of their faith. It is in accord with this ancient tradition that the leaders of the State of Israel today voice their concern over the fate of Jews in the Diaspora (in Russia and Syria in particular) who are subjected to discrimination and oppression.

The esteem in which the high priest was held by the foreign overlords is demonstrated in the following incident, recounted both by Josephus and the Talmud.[18] When the Samaritans sought from Alexander the right to destroy the Temple in Jerusalem, he granted their request. When the news of the emperor's decision was brought to the high priest Simon the Just,[19] he donned the priestly vestments and went with the nobles of Jerusalem to intercede with Alexander. Upon their arrival at Antipatris, Alexander saw Simon, descended from his carriage, and bowed down before him. Whereupon Alexander's courtiers remonstrated, "A great emperor like you should bow down before this Jew!" He said to them, "When I go out to battle I see this man's countenance and I am victorious." And Alexander reversed his decision and permitted the Jews to destroy the temple of the Samaritans.

Another high priest by the name of Simon, who lived one hundred years later, was held in great esteem by a contemporary author, Ben Sira, who wrote as follows: "The highest among his brothers and the glory of his people, Simon son of Johanan the priest . . . He is concerned for his people against the spoiler, he fortifies his city against the enemy. How glorious is he as he emerges from the Temple, as he goes out from within the Curtain" (Ben Sira, chap. 50).[20] Here again we see the high priest both as officiant in the Temple and protector of his people's security.

Yet another Simon, high priest and prince, enjoyed the esteem of both his own people and of foreign emperors. This was Simon son of Mattathias the Hasmonean, last surviving brother of Judah the Maccabee. Under his forceful but benevolent leadership Judea gained complete independence from foreign domination, and was recognized as a sovereign state by Rome. Reminiscent of the popular acclamations at the coronation of kings in the First Temple (see above, p. 17), Simon was formally installed at a public ceremony as high priest and prince (nasi) of Judea (140 B.C.E.). Simon refused the title "king," as he felt that it is reserved for a scion of the House of David.[21] In his day it was instituted that the dating of all documents should read "in the nth year of the high priest, minister to God Most High [El Elyon]," in place of the previous practice of dating documents to the reign of the Greek king.[22] Of this Simon's times the historian writes: "The people were happy in the freedom to live their own life, material prosperity increased, strict justice was to be had in the courts, apostasy was suppressed, the laws of the Jewish religion were faithfully obeyed."[23]

The Decline of the Priesthood

Unfortunately, the aforementioned high priests were by no means typical of the other chief officiants who served in the Second Temple. More appropriate to the great majority of them is the condemnation voiced in an earlier age by the prophet Micah (3:11): *"and her [Zion's] priests teach for a price."* The office of high priest, instead of it being reserved, as the Halakhah requires, for a distinguished son inheriting his distinguished father,[24] was taken over by scheming members of priestly families who paid the most tribute to the foreign overlord. It all began when Antiochus Epiphanes seized the throne of the Syrian kingdom and Judea became a province subject to his hegemony (175 B.C.E.). This is the Antiochus who attempted to impose by force the Greek way of life upon the Jews by enactment of severe decrees against the observance of the Jewish religion. And he found ready allies in those Jews in Judea who were lured by the lavish and unrestrained manners of the Greek aristocrats, their cultivation of the body, and their athletic contests which were associated with the rituals of Greek paganism.

The first priestly son who prostituted the exalted office of high priest because of his affinity for Greek manners was Joshua, son of the Simon praised by Ben Sira and brother of the incumbent high priest, Honio (Onias). This Joshua, who adopted the Greek name Jason, promised Antiochus huge sums of money from the Temple treasury if the emperor would oust his brother and appoint him as high priest. He also sought and obtained from Antiochus permission to set up a gymnasium in Jerusalem and register the young participants as Antiochites; namely, citizens of a Greek city.[25] After serving a short while, he in turn was replaced by another brother by the name of Menelaus. The high priesthood changed hands so often that the Talmud is constrained to comment: "It is written: 'the fear of the Lord prolongs days, but the years of the wicked shall be shortened' [Prov. 10:27]; *the fear of the Lord prolongs days* refers to the First Temple, which stood 410 years and only eighteen priests served therein; whereas *the years of the wicked shall be shortened* refers to the Second Temple, which stood 420 years[26] and more than three hundred high priests served therein" (*Yoma* 9a). It should be mentioned, however, that there was one high priest who received his appointment because of money paid to the king and yet served his people well. Joshua ben Gemala was appointed high priest because his wife Martha, daughter of Boethus, gave King Agriphas II three hundred *dinarim*, but he is remembered for good for the great educational reform that he instituted; to wit, that there should be teachers in every community for children from the age of six (*Yebamot* 61a, *Baba Bathra* 21a).

In fact, the priests in general were quite an undisciplined group, and several measures had to be taken to restrain their aggressiveness.[27] The Mishnah (*Yoma* 2:2) relates: "It once happened that two priests ran up the Altar Ramp at the same time to perform the service of clearing the Altar [of its ashes at the beginning of the daily service], and one of them pushed his fellow priest so that he fell and broke his leg. When the Court[28] saw that the priests, if left unregulated, can endanger themselves, it instituted that the clearing of the Altar should be assigned by lot." The Talmud (*Pesahim* 57a), quoting the Tosefta, relates that at first the skins from the animal sacrifices, which were emoluments of the ministering priests, were distributed every evening, but the aggressive priests would seize them for themselves by force, and therefore it was instituted that the skins be distributed only once a week, when all the priests of the weekly contingent would be present.[29] The lack of discipline was so frightful that one observer bemoaned: "Woe unto me from the House of Yishmael ben Piabi and their violence; they are high priests, their sons are treasurers, their sons-in-law are superintendents, and their slaves beat the people with sticks" (*Pesahim* 57a).

Hellenism Meets Judaism

We have indicated that it was the desire on the part of members of the priestly aristocracy to assimilate the Greek way of life that led to the degradation of the priesthood. The assumption of these Hellenists was that Hellenism and Judaism are incompatible, and that in order to adopt the former it is necessary to reject the latter. Was this assumption correct; are Greek culture and the way of life enjoined by the Torah mutually exclusive?

Three centuries before Mattathias the Hasmonean raised the banner of revolt against the tyranny of Antiochus with the rallying cry, "Who is unto the Lord, let him join forces with me!" Greece had already attained its cultural zenith, its most glorious period of esthetic and intellectual achievment. This was the age of Pericles the statesman, Phidias the sculptor, and Socrates the philosopher; figures who to this very day loom before us as giants of politics, art, and mind. How, we may ask, could such beauty of form and keenness of logic produced by these figures represent a danger to the truths taught by the Torah? Did not the Greek philosophers come to the conclusion that there is One Supreme Being, One Creator or Prime Mover, as God is referred to in their philosophical jargon? Did not the great Jewish teacher Maimonides more than a thousand years later demonstrate by irrefutable argument that Aristotle's propositions do not negate the fundamental teachings of Judaism? Many historians see in Judaism and Hellenism the two most potent forces for the progress of humanity, the two most valid approaches to the understanding of man and the world in which he lives. Such an estimation may be seen in a *midrash* of the Rabbis. From the blessing which Noah gave to his children Japhet and Shem (Gen. 9:27), our Sages expressed the hope that "the beauty of Japhet dwell in the tents of Shem" (*Megillah* 9b), implying thereby that the culture of Greece, the outstanding progeny of Japhet, be welcome in the houses of learning of Israel, the outstanding progeny of Shem. If only Hellenism and Judaism had joined forces, had found a common meeting ground and mutual understanding, each accepting the fundamental teachings of the other, then the world would truly have been blessed, sparing itself centuries of misery and darkness, of sterile conflict and senseless warfare.

What are the outstanding features and basic motivations of these two civilizations, Hellenic and Judaic? Both believed in the dual nature of man, his physical nature and his rational-ethical nature, but Greek thought stressed the former, whereas Hebrew thought stresses the latter. Not only man's body fascinated the early Greeks, hence their sculpture and gymnastics, but man's physical environment as well. Ancient Greek culture is the basis of the science of physics, a science which has revealed to man the forces inherent in matter which can be harnessed to man's advantage. What concerned the Jewish teachers, however, was man's moral behavior, his social relationships, his very humaneness. Though Greek philosophers spoke of justice as a principle of government, for Judaism justice, when tempered with mercy, is the very foundation of human society. The ideal of Judaism, as it is expressed by the Psalmist, is: "Mercy and truth are met together; righteousness and peace have kissed each other" (Ps. 85:11). Judaism calls upon man to reconcile his dual nature; to adjust his physical needs and drives to moral and ethical imperatives—a difficult task, perhaps, but certainly not an impossible one. Is it not then, possible for Hellenism to dwell in the tents of Judaism? And if so, why could they not dwell together in Judea two thousand years ago?

To understand this we have to understand a basic sociological fact. Every civilization or culture exists on two levels: one, that of the elite; the other, that of the masses. Philosophers are one thing, ordinary people another. The abstract propositions of the Greek thinkers, their search for truth, their ideal of human happiness, were far removed from the thoughts and habits of the masses. Greek thought did not penetrate into the consciousness of the average citizen; nor did it fashion the character of Greek society. The masses persisted in their paganism and superstition, their hedonism and immorality, their worship of the body and its needs combined with their ignorance of the soul and its demands.

Such a dichotomy, a conflict between the ideal and the real, did indeed exist among the people of Israel in the early stages of their history. In the days of the First Temple, we had the towering giants of the spirit, the Hebrew prophets, who heard the voice of God and knew what God demands of His people. But the people were still steeped in idolatry and superstition, practicing the abominations of Canaan, unaware of the moral and ethical teachings of the Torah. The Torah, however, is not a book for prophets alone; it was and is designed for the people at large. Thus in the course of time the gap between prophet and people was narrowed, and the teachings of the Torah began to shape the character and influence the social and religious life of the average citizen. The efforts of Ezra and the *soferim* to make the Torah *morashah kehillat Yaakov*, the heritage of every Jew, bore fruit in the determination of the bulk of the nation, when put to the test, to defend their religion against all attacks from within and without (see above, p. 71).

The attack from within, endangering the vital spirit of Israel, came when Hellenism in its crassest form, the Hellenism of the masses with its exaggerated emphasis on the bodily form and its complete lack of social responsibility, began to fascinate many Jews who were beguiled by its glitter and supposed sophistication. This pseudo-sophistication particularly attracted the priestly families in Judea, the aristocratic nobles who had little in common with the average Jewish villager tending his farm and adhering to the traditions of his ancestors.

The foregoing analysis not only illumines a significant period in our history; it also should serve to make us aware of the serious religious and social problems which challenge Jewry today, and especially that part of Jewry which resides in and is building the future of the State of Israel. Israel today cannot, nor need it, isolate itself from the dominant civilization of our times, the so-called Western civilization. But it must be acutely conscious of the dangers to our national renaissance which this civilization represents. What are the major ideals which have helped develop the Western world to what it is today? I might say that there are chiefly two: scientific or technological progress, and democratic principles of government. Judaism has nothing to fear from these ideals. But there is also a mass culture of Western society, the civilization of the average man and woman, which is far removed from the noble principles to which they subscribe. It is characterized by status-seeking, pleasure-seeking materialism, excessive permissiveness, and a widespread indifference to religion. These are the new "principles" which have brought the alarming increase in violence and terrorism; and the people of Israel are by no means immune to these manifestations of modernity.

Against these morally corrosive influences Israel must protect itself if it is to remain a *Jewish* state. Not against science per se must we defend ourselves—as some extremists in the Torah world advise their students—nor against the humanistic ideals of democracy; but against the mass culture of the New Left in all its ugly shapes and forms. With the absence from the elementary educational system in Israel of a genuine program for *toda'ah yehudit*, a knowledge of and a love for traditional Judaism, a large percentage of Israeli youth are practically defenseless against the inroads of moral corruption. Only the conviction that the State of Israel is called upon to preserve the special moral quality of the Jewish people will give its citizens the strength required to withstand the designs of its enemies to destroy its independence.

This is the lesson we must learn from the history of the Maccabean era. Who knows? Perhaps the State of Israel was established so that the Jewish people may realize their prophetic destiny to become the *or la-goyim*, the light unto the nations, and save Western civilization from corruption and doom, as did the few Maccabees, who by their heroic stand saved for the world at large the Hebraic legacy of universal peace and justice.

Pharisees and Sadducees

The Maccabean revolt was, in a sense, a civil war, an uprising of the traditionalists in the community who wanted to preserve their ancestral ways against their fellow-Jews who were abandoning the old ways for the new ones introduced by the spread of Hellenism. This division within the Jewish community led to the sectarian cleavage between the *Perushim* (Pharisees) and the *Zadokim* (Sadducees), which persisted for the more than two centuries from the rededication of the Temple by Judah the Maccabee in 165 B.C.E. to its destruction by the Roman legions in 70 C.E.

Much has been written about these two parties in order to explain their origins and what actually were the different ideologies which divided them. Some historians see in them the natural division between liberals and conservatives, though there is argument as to which party was liberal and which conservative. Others place all the emphasis upon the different outlooks engendered by the differences in economic status—the rich landowners and merchants versus the poor peasants. Some emphasize the differences in political views, the Sadducees maintaining the crucial importance of the independent sovereignty and power of the state, whereas the Pharisees maintained the crucial importance of religious and cultural autonomy even under a foreign sovereign. Others contend that differences in religious and theological doctrines were the basis for the sectarian cleavage. There is even little agreement among historians as to the origin of the names given to the two parties; what the term *Perushim* means, and why the others were called *Zadokim*.[30]

Principles of Faith

In the contest between the Zadokim and the Perushim for the support of the people at large, the Perushim were the victors. Their leaders were the chief officers of the Sanhedrin, whose decisions and doctrines became the accepted norms in Jewish life not only for the Jews in Judea, but also for the vast number of Jews in the Diaspora who looked to Jerusalem for religious guidance. It therefore behooves us, for a proper understanding of traditional Jewish belief and practice, which we hope will continue to be the basis for Jewish life in the developing future, to examine the basic doctrines of the

Perushim and their interpretation of Judaism as taught by the Torah.

The popularity of the Perushim was, no doubt, due to their avoidance of extremist views and positions. They did not set too high a standard of holiness and spirituality for the people, fully aware that "the Torah was not given for ministering angels";[31] but they were not unmindful of the moral discipline and ritual observances which membership in a godly people must impose.[32] Their choice of the golden mean between asceticism and permissiveness they illustrated in the following parable: "This Torah is comparable to two paths, one of fire and the other of snow. If one inclines to the first he will perish in the fire; if he inclines to the second he will perish in the snow. What, then, should one do? One should walk in the middle" (J. *Hagigah* 2:1 [77a]). Thus, on the one hand, the Perushim tempered the harshness of the biblical penal code;[33] but on the other hand, they administered extra-biblical punishments when moral or religious laxity threatened to become widespread.[34]

The age-old and perpetually vexing problem of theodicy, which prompted one of the Sages to remark, "It is beyond us to explain the well-being of the wicked or the sufferings of the righteous" (*Abot* 4:15), exercised the minds of the Perushim. The Torah does promise a reward for observing its commandments, and predicts dire punishment for those who transgress its commandments, and yet reality seems to contradict these assertions. To reconcile the principle of reward and punishment with this reality, the Perushim postulated the principle that the promises of reward and the predictions of punishment are fulfilled in the afterlife.[35] Hence we have the cardinal doctrine of human immortality, that the human soul—which is a spark of the Divine—endures beyond death, and it either enjoys the delights of Paradise or suffers the pangs of Gehenna in accord with Divine justice. The Perushim went further. The only appropriate reward for a person who strove during his lifetime to make this mundane world a perfect world is to actually live in such a perfect world. Hence follows the doctrine of the resurrection of the dead (*tehiyat ha-meithim*), as is stated in the Book of Daniel (12:2): "And many of them that sleep in the dust of the earth shall awake;

some to everlasting life and some to reproaches, to everlasting abhorrence."[36]

One of the early teachers of Pharisaic doctrine, Antigonus of Socho, advised his disciples: "Be not like slaves who serve their master on condition that they receive a bounty; rather, be like slaves who serve their master on condition that they do not receive a bounty" (Abot 1:3).[37] In Abot de-Rabbi Nathan, chap. 5, we read the following commentary to the foregoing statement: "Antigonus of Socho had two disciples who used to study his words. They taught them to their disciples, and their disciples to their disciples. These proceeded to examine the words closely and demanded: 'Why did our ancestors see fit to say this thing? Is it possible that a laborer should do his work all day and not take his reward in the evening? If our ancestors had known that there is another world and that there will be a resurrection of the dead [where the reward will be paid], they would not have spoken in this manner.' So they arose and withdrew from the Torah, and split into two sects, the Sadducees and the Boethusians; Sadducees named after Zadok [progenitor of the high priest], Boethusians after Boethus."

The Tannaim, the teachers of Judaism in the century following the destruction of the Temple, who were the true disciples and spiritual heirs of the Perushim, insisted that the promise of the resurrection of the dead is rooted in the Torah, and that he who denies this forfeits his portion of the world-to-come; i.e., in the spiritual delights experienced by the souls of the righteous after they depart from this world.[38] Thus tehiyat ha-meithim and the belief in reward and punishment from which it stems are dogmas of traditional Judaism incorporated in our daily prayers and in the articles of faith drawn up by medieval Jewish philosophers.[39] In the course of time, these concepts were the subject of much elaboration and fanciful interpretation;[40] but we may leave this subject with the following quotation from Maimonides: "The order in which these future events will come to pass and all their details are not fundamental in our religion. One should not occupy himself with all the legends and spend much time with the homiletic interpretations of these matters, for they do not bring one to the fear or the love of

God. Rather, one should believe in these principles in a general way."[41]

The Oral Law

The most significant achievment of the Perushim lay in their con-firming for the Jewish people the authority and authenticity of the *Torah she-be'al-peh*, the Oral Law, coexisting with and constituting the authentic interpretation of the *Torah she-bikhtav*, the Written Law; namely, the Pentateuch. Thus it is related that when a certain non-Jew interested in converting to Judaism asked Shammai, "How many Torahs do you [Jews] have?" he was told, "Two, the Written Torah and the Oral Torah" (*Shabbat* 31a). The Oral Law was con-ceived as an unwritten tradition originating with Moses accompany-ing and clarifying the Written Law, and both of them were revealed by God at Sinai.[42] The Sages of the Talmud, the direct descendants of the Perushim, found confirmation for this basic principle of faith in the following Biblical verse: "It is written: 'And God said to Moses, Come up to Me on the mountain and be there, and I will give you the stone tablets and the Torah and the Mitzvah which I have written, to teach them' [Exod. 24:12]; *Tablets* refers to the Ten Commandments, *Torah* refers to the Pentateuch, *Mitzvah* refers to the Mishnah, *which I have written* refers to the Prophets and the Writings, *to teach them* refers to the Gemara [the talmudic exposi-tion of the Mishnah]; thus teaching that all were given to Moses at Sinai" (*Berakhot* 5a). Indeed, the Sages insisted that the Oral Law is more precious than the Written Law, since it is a token of God's special relationship with the people of Israel, who are the sole pos-sessors of the Oral Law. The other peoples of the earth possess the Written Law, since the Bible has been translated into practically every language on earth, but the true understanding of it lies beneath the surface of its literal meaning and has been revealed only to the *hakhamim*, the Sages of Israel.[43]

The Oral Law, we said, is based on an unwritten tradition; and the Perushim acknowledged that many of the *halakhot* which they enjoined upon the people had no basis in Scripture (Mishnah *Hagigah* 1:8). For example, they insisted, against the opposition of the Zadokim, upon the performance of certain ceremonies in the Temple Service during the Festival of Succot even though they are not mentioned in the Torah, on the grounds that they are *halakhah le-Moshe mi-Sinai*, a ruling handed down by Moses from Sinai.[44] The later Sages, however, sought to link the *halakhot* of the Oral Law with the text of the Written Law by finding in the latter some oblique reference to the former.[45] The earlier Sages, the *hakhmei ha-perushim*, led the way to this development in their method of biblical exegesis, which in itself was a development and expansion of the work of Ezra and the *soferim* in expounding the Torah (see above, p. 55). It is obvious that no written code of law suffices in actual practice, and its injunctions have to be clarified in greater detail by the scholars of the law. For example, the Torah commands, "You shall not do any work on the Sabbath" (Exod. 20:10), but does not specify, with two or three exceptions, exactly which activity is prohibited on the Sabbath. This specification is within the competence and jurisdiction of the *hakhmei ha-masoret*, the scholars of the oral tradition. Furthermore, the law has to be applied in a way appropriate to the exigencies of the times, which may vary from one generation to another; and we have already seen the necessity for the enactment of *takkanot* or new regulations for the welfare of the community (above, pp. 57f.).

Hillel was the first to formulate rules of biblical exegesis (*middot she-ha-Torah nidreshet bahen*, hermeneutics), seven in number; and these were later expanded into thirteen by the Tanna Rabbi Yishmael.[46] In fact, it was the application of two of these rules by Hillel which earned for him the office of *nasi*, head of the Sanhedrin. The story, as related in the Talmud (*Pesahim* 66a), is as follows: Once the fourteenth [of Nisan] occurred on a Sabbath, and they [the *benei Betheira*, who then occupied the office of *Nasi*] did not know whether or not the Passover sacrifice is offered on a Sabbath. They were told that there was a person who had come up from Babylonia and served [was a disciple of] the two great men of their generation, Shemaiah and Abtalyon [the previous heads of the Sanhedrin], and he knew the law. Whereupon they sent for Hillel and asked him the law. He answered: "Is there, then, only one Passover sacrifice during the year that supersedes the Sabbath; there are many more than two hundred Passover sacrifices during the year [i.e., the daily and additional offerings similar to the Passover sacrifice] which supersede the Sabbath." "How do you know this?" they asked him. He said to them: "It is written, *in its appointed time* [Num. 9:2] concerning the Passover sacrifice, and it is written, *in its appointed time* [Num. 28:2] concerning the daily sacrifice; now just as in the latter instance the sacrifice supersedes the Sabbath, so does it in the former instance [an inference from the rule of *gezerah shavah*, a similarity of phrases]. Furthermore, we can also deduce the law from the rule of *kal va-homer* [the inference from minor to major]." Then and there, Hillel was seated at the head of the Sanhedrin and was appointed *nasi* over them.[47]

Houses of Biblical Exposition

The process of *midrash halakhah* employed by the Perushim, and the Tannaim who succeeded them, was neither arbitrary nor the result of hastily conceived expediency. It was forged out of the deliberations of scholars and the teachings of masters to their disciples. Thus the Perushim founded academies where oral traditions were transmitted and new interpretations (*hiddushim*)[48] were submitted for consideration. If the latter were accepted by the majority of scholars present, they were incorporated into the Oral Law and taught to subsequent generations of disciples. Originally, there was one large academy in Jerusalem to which students flocked not only from other cities in Judea but from Babylonia as well. Thus Hillel himself came from Babylonia to study under Shemaiah and Abtalyon (*Yoma* 35b). This pair of scholars had another outstanding disciple by the name of Shammai (*Abot* 1:12), but he differed so much in temperament from Hillel (*Shabbat* 31a) that each attracted a separate group of scholars, and thus the famous schools of Beit Shammai and Beit Hillel were founded.

Among any group of serious-minded men, controversy and difference of opinion is bound to exist, for "just as men's features differ one from another, so do their opinions differ one from another." Indeed, this is a praiseworthy phenomenon, for only out of discussion and the expression of all opinions can a proper conclusion be arrived at.[49] That is why our Sages say, concerning the disputes of Beit Shammai and Beit Hillel, "These and these are the words of the Living God" (Erubin 13b); and even minority opinions which were not accepted as the Halakhah were nevertheless recorded in the Mishnah and thereby incorporated in the body of the Oral Law (Eduyot 1:4—6).

This is all well and good, provided two things are present: one, that the scholars engaged in the discussion regard each other with mutual respect; and two, that the participants are well schooled and express an opinion after having received the proper education. In the beginning, the disciples in the two schools of Shammai and Hillel treated each other with affection and friendship (Yebamot 14b), but subsequently the Shammaites employed physical force in order to impose their opinions upon their contenders (J. Shabbat 1:4 [3c]). This was, no doubt, due to the fact that many of the disciples "had not served their masters sufficiently." This sad fact also led to an inordinate increase in the number of opposing halakhic opinions, with each side stubbornly maintaining its particular point of view to such an extent that the danger existed of another schism in Jewish life.[50] To prevent this, the Sages in Yavneh shortly after the destruction of the Temple, when unity was so essential for the continuity of organized Jewish life, adopted the rule that in all matters disputed between Beit Shammai and Beit Hillel the Halakhah is according to the opinion of Beit Hillel.[51]

The Sanhedrin

The Torah itself foresaw the probability of "matters of dispute in your gates" (Deut. 17:8), and therefore provided for the highest instance, a Supreme Court, whose decision would be binding upon all

Israel. The Torah commands: "You shall act in accordance with the law they instruct you, and carry out the verdict they announce to you . . . Do not deviate from the ruling that they hand down to you either to the right or to the left" (Deut. 17:11). It is from this verse, incidentally, that we derive that mitzvot of rabbinic origin—such as kindling the Sabbath candles or reading the Megillah on Purim—are on a par, at least as far as the benediction for their performance is concerned, with mitzvot of the Torah.[52]

According to a talmudic tradition, the procedure of bringing matters of dispute to the Supreme Court was as follows: "If someone required a ruling [halakhah], he would go to the court [beit din] of his town. If there was no court in his town, he would go to the court nearest him. If the court there had heard the law,[53] they would tell him; if not, he and the outstanding member of the court [mufla][54] would repair to the court on the Temple Mount. If they had heard, they would tell them; if not, they would all go to the Great Court in the Chamber of Hewn Stone,[55] before whom the question was presented. If they had heard, they would tell them; if not, a count was taken [of the members of the Great Court]. If the majority said 'unclean,' it is unclean; if the majority said 'clean,' it is clean. From there the ruling goes out and extends to all Israel. From there also a committee would be sent [to the various communities] to examine candidates for a judgeship; anyone who is a scholar and is humble, who fears sin, enjoys a good reputation, and is pleasing to people, is appointed judge in his city. From there he could be promoted and given a seat in the Chamber of Hewn Stone" (Tosefta Sanhedrin 7:1).

In the foregoing source, the Supreme Court is called Beit ha-Din ha-Gadol, and it consisted of seventy-one members (see above, p. 9). In other sources, which unquestionably refer to the same Court, it is called "the Great Sanhedrin," or simply "Sanhedrin," though Sanhedrin may also refer to a court of twenty-three empowered to judge capital cases.[56] The Great Sanhedrin was not only a court of religious law; it was a Council of Elders, as is indicated by the Greek origin of its name, and acted in administrative capacities, as in the appointment of judges to the lower courts and in the supervision of the Temple Service.[57] It also was a legislative body, enacting *takkanot* for the regulation of civil as well as religious procedures. During the rule of the Hasmonean kings, the Sadducees contended with the Pharisees for the control of the Sanhedrin, and sought the help of the kings for this purpose.[58] The kings no doubt had their own Sanhedrins or Councils of Elders for political purposes, and occasionally convened their Council to regulate certain procedures in the Temple. There also was a Court of Priests, which dealt primarily with the day-to-day running of the Temple Service.

We have time and again pointed out the two major divisions of authority which necessarily co-exist in a Jewish state, the political, under the jurisdiction of the king, and the religious, under the jurisdiction of the judges. An eminent medieval halakhic scholar explained this division as follows: "The purpose of the judges and the Sanhedrin was to judge the people with the laws of the Torah which are absolute truth and justice, and these would raise them to be godly; but since these laws might not be sufficient for civil order, the Torah provided for the rule of the king."[59] Such a division, though necessary, is bound to create a serious conflict, as it is impossible to draw an exact line of demarcation between the two jurisdictions and a clash between the two is quite likely. We shall have occasion in a later chapter to discuss this problem as it has arisen in the modern State of Israel. Nevertheless, we have seen how in the absence of a kingdom the religious authorities are able to assume the responsibilities of political leadership. The medieval scholar quoted above recognized this in the following statement: "When there is no king in Israel, the judge assumes both authorities, that of the judge and that of the king." This fact saved the Jewish people from disintegration after the second *hurban*, the collapse of the kingdom of Judea and the destruction of the Second Temple by the Roman legions under Titus. How this came about is treated in the next chapter.

7

A Nation Without a State, II

Tish'ah B'ab, the ninth day of the month of Ab, is the national day of mourning of the Jewish people. It is observed—in addition to a twenty-four-hour abstention from food and drink—in the manner of one who is sitting *shiva*, mourning the death of a member of the family. The scriptural reading prescribed for the day is *Megillat Eikhah*, the Book of Lamentations, written by the prophet Jeremiah after the destruction of the First Temple, for Tish'ah B'ab commemorates the destruction of both the First and Second Temples, each destruction marking the end of a Jewish kingdom and of the independent sovereignty of the Jewish people in its homeland.[1]

It should be borne in mind, however, that the situation of the Jewish people at the time of the second catastrophe was quite different from that at the first. At the time of the earlier *hurban*, those exiled to Babylon were "all Jerusalem, and all the nobles, and all the mighty men of valour . . . and all the craftsmen and the smiths; none remained save the poorest of the people of the land" (II Kings 24:14). But at the time of the second *hurban*, though many were taken to Rome as slaves and the city of Jerusalem was utterly destroyed, most of Israel's leading citizens were permitted to remain in Judea. Furthermore, this time there were many well-established Jewish communities in the Diaspora, ready both to render assistance to the defeated Judeans and to guarantee the continued existence of a vital, traditional Jewish way of life. And above all, after the experience of the first Exile, which did not spell the end of Jewish nationhood but rather led to its reconstitution after a comparatively short period, the second Exile was not quite as traumatic; and the hope for a speedy second reconstitution of Jewish nationhood burned brightly in the hearts of the people. Thus, the end of the kingdom and of the Temple Service was not viewed as a complete break in Jewish history calling for a revaluation of the basic tenets of Judaism, but rather as a time for adjustment to the new circumstances in which Jewry now found itself.[2]

An outstanding religious leader of the time, whose bold and foresighted leadership enabled the people to make the necessary adjustments to their new situation, was Rabbi Yohanan ben Zakkai. He had had the privilege as a youngster to sit at the feet of the great Hillel, and no doubt learned from him to make *takkanot* when the times required it. When the Temple still stood, Rabbi Yohanan, though not the *nasi* of the Sanhedrin, played a prominent role as a leader of the Pharisees; and it was he who argued the validity of their interpretations against the Sadducees, even employing biting sarcasm.[3] His studiousness and vast knowledge of Torah became legendary; and his disciples were the outstanding scholars of their generation.[4]

The first thing Rabbi Yohanan ben Zakkai did in order to ensure the continuity of Jewish national life was to establish in Yavneh, a town near Ashdod, an Academy and a Beit ha-Din which would assume the functions of the Sanhedrin of Jerusalem. The manner in which he accomplished this is related in the Talmud (*Gittin* 56a) as follows: When Jerusalem was under siege by the Romans and the city was ravaged by hunger, the Rabbis wanted to make peace with the Romans but the rebels (the war party) would not allow them. So Rabbi Yohanan met secretly with his nephew Abba Sikra, who was head of the rebels, and said to him, "Find some way in which I can get out of the city; maybe I can salvage something out of our predicament." Abba Sikra advised him to spread the word that he (Rabbi Yohanan) was sick, and then to feign death. Whereupon, two of his disciples carried him out of the city as if he were a corpse, and took him to Vespasian, commander of the Roman legions. Rabbi Yohanan requested of him permission to go with his disciples to Yavneh. There he established his Academy and Beit Din; and after the Temple was destroyed he proceeded to institute certain regulations which would enable the Jewish people to adjust themselves to the absence of the central Sanctuary. He decreed, for example, that the shofar may be blown on Rosh Hashanah which falls on a Sabbath wherever there is a *beit din*, a performance previously restricted to the Temple in Jerusalem.[5] He saw to it that the proclamation of the New Moon, essential for the observance of the Festivals, be in the hands of the central *beit din* even though it no longer met in Jerusalem. Other regulations were designed to keep alive the memory of the Beit ha-Mikdash and instill the hope that it would speedily be rebuilt.[6]

May the Temple Speedily Be Rebuilt

It was Rabbi Yohanan ben Zakkai who explained to his disciples that the absence of the Temple Service, even though it was one of the three pillars upon which the world stood, did not bring with it the absence of God's grace for His people Israel. On the contrary, the other two pillars, the study of Torah and acts of lovingkindness, can fulfill the functions of the Temple offerings. It is related that Rabbi Yohanan was once walking by the Temple ruins, followed by his disciple Rabbi Yehoshua. Seeing the ruins, Rabbi Yehoshua cried out: "Woe unto us that the place where the iniquities of Israel were atoned for is laid waste," Whereupon Rabbi Yohanan responded: "My son, be not grieved; we have another atonement as effective as this, acts of lovingkindness, as it is said, 'For I desire mercy and not sacrifice' [Hos. 6:6]." It was also taught, "It is said, 'and the knowledge of God more than burnt-offerings' [Hos. 6:6], teaching that the study of Torah is more beloved by God than burnt-offerings."[7] Indeed, the Sages assert that "he who studies the laws [Torah] of the sacrifices is as if he had actually offered them" (*Menahot* 110a); and two of the tractates of the Talmud, *Zebahim* and *Menahot*, deal with these laws at great length and in great detail.

This is by no means to imply that the Jewish people gave up hopes of rebuilding the Temple. The exact dimensions of the second structure on the Temple Mount and the order of services conducted therein were faithfully recorded, to be later incorporated in the

Mishnah, Tractates *Middot* and *Tamid*, and its being rebuilt became the symbol of Israel's hopes for redemption. There is no regular prayer in our liturgy which does not include a petition for the rebuilding of the Temple and the restoration of the sacrificial service therein.[8] The only prayer recorded in the Mishnah is one for the rebuilding of Jerusalem (*Abot* 5:20);[9] and no description of "the days of the Messiah" is complete without the fulfillment of the twice-expressed prophecy, "Many peoples shall go and say, Come and let us go up to the mountain of the Lord, to the house of the God of Jacob . . . for out of Zion shall go forth the Law, and the word of the Lord from Jerusalem" (Isa. 2:3, Mic. 4:2). Jerusalem, the Temple structure, and the celebrations conducted in it were described in glowing terms in order to deepen the consciousness of the severe loss sustained by its destruction, and to increase the yearning for its rebuilding. Thus we read: "Who did not see the rejoicing at the ceremony of the Water-Drawing [Beit ha-Sho'evah, held in the Temple on Succot], has never in his life seen joy; who did not see Jerusalem in its glory, has never in his life seen a beautiful city; who did not see the Beit ha-Mikdash standing, has never in his life seen a glorious edifice" (*Succah* 51a).

Signs of mourning were introduced into every Jewish household to serve as constant reminders of the *hurban*, though Rabbi Yehoshua counseled the people not to mourn excessively. Affirming the oath taken by the exiles of the first *hurban*, "If I forget thee, O Jerusalem, let my right hand forget its cunning; let my tongue cling to the roof of my mouth if I remember thee not, if I set not Jerusalem above my chiefest joy" (Ps. 137:5−6), ashes would be placed on the head of every bridegroom (*Baba Bathra* 60b). On Tish'ah B'Ab, preachers would select as their text verses from the Book of Lamentations and dwell upon the enormity of the disaster befallen Israel because of the *hurban*; how Israel had fallen "from a lofty roof to a deep pit."[10] It was even said that "every generation in whose days the Temple is not rebuilt is as if they had destroyed it" (J. *Yoma* 1:1 [38c]). And the four fast days instituted after the first *hurban* were once again added to the Jewish calendar.[11]

The hopes for the speedy rebuilding of the Beit ha-Mikdash

seemed about to be transformed into a reality less than fifty years after its destruction. When Hadrian became emperor in 117 C.E., he gave a vague promise to allow the Jews to resettle in Jerusalem and rebuild the Temple. However, the ancient enemies of Israel, the Samaritans, persuaded Hadrian to rescind his promise; and there is no doubt that the Christians, whose numbers in the Holy Land were slowly increasing, and whose newly formulated theology averred that the Jews had been rejected by God because of their rejection of Jesus as His divinely begotten son, were also urging Hadrian to change his attitude toward the Jews. At any rate, Hadrian's erstwhile moderation turned into intense hatred, and he decreed severe penalties for any Jew who observed the practices of his faith, especially the study of Torah. These evil decrees fanned the spirit of revolt against Rome and led to the short-lived attempt of Bar Kochba to reestablish an independent kingdom in Judea. We shall see later how the crushing defeat of Bar Kochba affected the hopes of the Jewish people that "speedily will the Beit ha-Mikdash be rebuilt."

The Restoration of Jewish Autonomy

Not many years after Rabbi Yohanan had established the Sanhedrin in Yavneh, a scion of the House of Hillel, son of the *nasi* at the time of the *hurban*,[12] was able to assume the position of titular head of the Sanhedrin and become the recognized leader of the Jewish people. Once again the vacuum created by the absence of king and high priest was filled by the religious leader. He was able to provide for the nation deprived of its independent state the necessary leadership which made possible the continuation of Israel's national identity even in a situation described as *galut*.[13] This salvation of Jewish leadership was again due to the foresight of Rabbi Yohanan. When he had appeared before Vespasian (see above, p. 89), he had not only requested "Give me Yavneh and its sages," but also that the family of Rabbi Gamaliel" be spared (*Gittin* 56b).[14]

It appears that the procurator of the province of Syria extended official recognition to Rabbi Gamaliel's position as *nasi*,[15] and the latter proceeded to exercise his authority as such and consolidate the organ of self-government set up by Rabbi Yohanan. One of the first things Rabbi Gamaliel did, something which to this day has been a unifying force in Jewish life, was to call upon a rather obscure member of the Sanhedrin[16] to fix the text of the daily prayer in the proper order (the significance of this order will be discussed in a later chapter). This prayer comprises the eighteen benedictions of the weekday *Shemoneh Esreh Amidah*, which, with slight variations, has remained the official prayer of every Jewish community in every part of the globe. Prayer was once again established as the recognized substitute for the sacrificial service of the Beit ha-Mikdash (see above, p. 34).

The text of one of the benedictions, the one calling for the downfall of the wicked, did not satisfy Rabbi Gamaliel, for it did not specify a group of Jews who had become a special menace to both Judaism and the Jewish people; namely, the Jewish Christians.[17] He therefore called for a volunteer from among the members of the Sanhedrin to revise the text and include a malediction against the *minnim*, the sectarians who could no longer be considered a sect *within* Judaism.[18] In the course of time, the censors in Christian countries eliminated the word *minnim* from the prayer book; and only recent editions of the Siddur have restored it to its proper place. It is interesting to note that the word which replaced *minnim* is *malshinim*, slanderers. Indeed, Christians, especially in the Middle Ages, have distinguished themselves as slanderers and defamers of the Jewish people, branding them Christ-killers, poisoners of wells, and bloodthirsty murderers of Christian children.

Another ruling of Rabbi Gamaliel which consolidated his position as *nasi* provided that the fixing of the calendar by intercalation (*ibbur ha-shanah*, adding an extra month to the year—*Adar Sheni*—in order to equalize the lunar year of 354 days with the solar year of 365 days) must receive the approval of the *nasi*.[19]

On more than one occasion Rabbi Gamaliel was quick to assert his authority over the members of the Sanhedrin. The Mishnah (*Rosh Hashanah* 2:8—9) relates that Rabbi Dosa ben Hyrcanus disputed the ruling of Rabbi Gamaliel fixing the New Moon of the month of Tishrei and consequently the day of Yom Kippur, the tenth of Tishrei. Rabbi Yehoshua agreed with Rabbi Dosa's ruling. Whereupon, "Rabbi Gamaliel sent a message to Rabbi Yehoshua, 'I sentence you to come to me with your staff and your money on the day which is Yom Kippur according to your reckoning.' Rabbi Akiba went and found Rabbi Yehoshua distressed, but he said to him, 'I can learn [by inference from Scripture] that whatsoever Rabbi Gamaliel has done is done' [i.e., has to be accepted]. Rabbi Yehoshua then went to Rabbi Dosa, who said to him, 'If we come to question the decision of Rabbi Gamaliel's court, then we would have to question the decisions of all the courts which stood from the days of Moses.' So Rabbi Yehoshua took his staff and money on the day which was Yom Kippur according to his reckoning and went to Yavneh, to Rabbi Gamaliel. Whereupon Rabbi Gamaliel stood up and kissed him on his head and said to him, 'Come in peace, my master and my disciple; my master in wisdom and my disciple that you have accepted my decision.'"

Rabbi Gamaliel's assertion of his authority did in one instance overstep the bounds of reasonableness, and brought about his temporary demission from the office of *nasi*. Again it was a dispute with Rabbi Yehoshua, this time concerning the obligation to recite the evening prayer. Rabbi Gamaliel embarrassed Rabbi Yehoshua by demanding that he stand all during the lecture, and this was not the first time that he had done this. The members of the Academy would no longer tolerate such overbearing conduct and removed Rabbi Gamaliel from office, appointing the young Rabbi Elazar ben Azariah in his stead.[20] That day, we are told, there was another victory for democracy. Rabbi Gamaliel had severely restricted the number of students permitted to enter the Academy, admitting only those of proven probity; whereas the new administration opened the doors wide to all who wished to enter. According to one tradition, four hundred benches were added to take care of the influx of new students; according to another tradition, seven hundred were added. Subsequently, Rabbi Gamaliel went to appease the angry members, who reinstated him but retained Rabbi Elazar as his assistant

(*Berakhot* 27b—28a). This was very fortunate, indeed, for thus the office of *nasi* remained the prerogative of the House of Hillel, and this subsequently led to the appointment of Rabbi Gamaliel's grandson Judah, who added great luster and great achievement as the most renowned *nasi* in Israel.

The Jewish Courts

One of the most important factors in assuring the continuity of Jewish national identity after the *hurban* was the continuation of the Jewish judicial system. At the very beginning of this book we delineated the fundamental position of the judiciary in Jewish statehood and its responsibility to judge the people righteously, in accord with the laws of the Torah. With the loss of sovereignty in the first century of the common era, the Sages who assumed the task of maintaining Jewish autonomy as far as Roman imperial domination would allow—and even beyond that—insisted upon the maintenance of Jewish courts of law under the control of the central authority, the Sanhedrin.

The Roman administration had set up courts of its own which dealt both in criminal and civil matters. Thus the Mishnah (*Gittin* 1:5) speaks of "all legal documents drawn up [registered] in the courts of the Gentiles." Perhaps typical of the judges who served in these courts is the following story related in the Talmud (*Shabbat* 117a-b). Rabbi Gamaliel and his sister, Ima Shalom, the wife of Rabbi Eliezer, wanted to demonstrate how corrupt one of the Gentile judges was. Ima Shalom sent him a golden lamp and then appeared before him in court, petitioning him to divide her father's estate between herself and her brother. The judge, prompted by the gift, acceded to her petition and ordered the division. When Rabbi Gamaliel then protested that according to Jewish law a daughter does not inherit together with a son (Num. 27:8), the judge said, "From the day you [the Jewish people] have been exiled from your land, the law of Moses has been replaced by another code which says that a son and a daughter share equally in their father's estate."

On the morrow, Rabbi Gamaliel gave the judge a Libyan ass and appeared again in court. Now the judge said, "I have read the concluding paragraph of the new code and there it is written, 'I have not come either to subtract from or add to the Law of Moses,'[21] and there it says that a daughter does not inherit when there is a son." Whereupon Ima Shalom said (to remind him of her gift), "Your light will shine like a lamp"; but Rabbi Gamaliel countered, "The ass has kicked over the lamp."

This demonstration by Rabbi Gamaliel and his sister was no doubt designed to reinforce the severe ban decreed by the Tannaim against Jews resorting to non-Jewish courts. Typical is the statement of Rabbi Tarfon, a contemporary of Rabbi Gamaliel. He said, "Wherever you find courts of Gentiles, even though they may judge according to Israelite law, you are not permitted to have recourse to them; for it is said, 'And these are the judgments that you shall set before them' [Exod. 21:1]; before them, and not before Gentiles" (Gittin 88b).[22] This ban was reiterated in even more forceful terms by Maimonides in his concluding statement to the laws of Sanhedrin. "Anyone who presents his case before Gentile judges and their courts, even though their laws are like the laws of Israel, is a wicked person, and is as if he had abused and blasphemed and raised his hand against the Torah of our teacher Moses."

The Jewish courts in the various cities of Judea and Galilee were set up by the Sanhedrin in Yavneh, which appointed the judges who served in the local courts.[23] However, the Sanhedrin itself, once it was removed from its seat within the Temple precincts, was circumscribed in its judicial powers; it could no longer exact the death penalty.[24] In this connection, we should note the differences of opinion concerning capital punishment among the Tannaim who flourished at that time. The Mishnah (Makkot 1:10) reports: "A Sanhedrin that executes one person in seven years is called 'destructive.' Rabbi Elazar ben Azariah says, 'One person in seventy years.' Rabbi Tarfon and Rabbi Akiba say, 'Were we in the Sanhedrin, no man would ever be executed.' Rabbi Simon ben Gamaliel says, 'If so, they would increase the number of murderers in Israel.'" This reluctance to sentence criminals to death has now become widespread, and most Western countries, including the State of Israel, have abolished the death penalty. One wonders, witnessing the increase in willful homicide today, if the contention of Rabbi Simon ben Gamaliel is not being proved to have been the correct one.

The resolve to carry on the Jewish system of justice as enjoined by the Torah, to "hear the disputes between your brothers, and judge righteously between a man and his brother and the stranger with him" (Deut. 1:16), necessitated the regulation of judicial procedures; the number of judges required relative to the particular matter before the court; the qualifications, competence, and authority of the judges; the laws to guide them in making their decisions. With the written code of Jewish Law, the Pentateuch, as the basis for their discussions, the Tannaim in their respective academies ruled for almost every conceivable case of monetary claims, damages, property both movable and immovable, employer-employee relations, domestic relations, inheritance, and the like. All this—what is usually termed *bein adam la-havero*, between man and his fellowman—in addition to the regulation of ritual observances—*bein adam la-Makom*, between man and his Maker—laws concerning agricultural activities and their produce, Sabbaths and Festivals, ritual cleanness and uncleanness, and the laws concerning the Temple Service, which—as we pointed out above—served as a substitute for the actual service itself. Such a host of statutes and judgments, ordinances and penalties, rules and regulations, remained unwritten law, committed to the memories of the Tannaim in accord with their own ruling that "things which are oral may not be spoken [i.e., taught in a halakhic discourse] from a written text," just as "things which are written [i.e., Scripture] may not be taught orally" (*Gittin* 60b).

The Generation of Religious Persecution

As long as the Sanhedrin remained in Yavneh under the vigorous leadership of Rabbi Gamaliel, the central authority could maintain some uniformity in Jewish practice amidst the welter of discussion and opinion among his contemporaries. However, the harsh decrees of Hadrian against the practice and dissemination of Torah posed a serious threat to the continuity of Jewish tradition, and consequently to Jewish national identity. This was the generation referred to in talmudic literature as *doro shel shemad*, the generation of the attempt to destroy Israel through religious persecution. Commenting on the verse in the Song of Songs (8:6), "For love is strong as death," the *Midrash Rabbah* says that it refers to the love of God of the generation of *shemad*, as it is said, "But for Your sake are we killed all the day" (Ps. 44:23).

A heavy price was paid by this generation for the survival of Judaism and the Jewish people. Tradition speaks of "The Ten Martyrs of the [Roman] Kingdom," giants of the human spirit. Outstanding among them was Rabbi Akiba. His determination to teach Torah at the risk of his life he explained by a well-known parable. A fox was walking by the bank of the river and noticed the fish jumping from one place to another. Asked the fox of the fish, 'From what are you fleeing?' They answered, 'From the nets that humans spread to catch us.' Said he to them, 'Would it please you to come up to dry land; we can then dwell together.' Whereupon they said to him, 'They say that you are the wisest among the animals. You are not wise; you are stupid. If in the habitat which sustains our lives we nevertheless fear death; how much more so, in the place where we perish.' 'Our situation is similar,' continued Rabbi Akiba. 'Now that we occupy ourselves with the study of the Torah, concerning which it is written *for it is your life and the length of your days* [Deut. 30:20], we are nevertheless exposed to death; how much more so, were we to cease its study'" (*Berakhot* 61b).

Another of these sainted martyrs is the person credited with making possible the continuation of the chain of religious authority in Israel which derives from the very first authority, Moses our Teacher. The Talmud relates: "Yet let that man be remembered for good, and Rabbi Judah ben Babba is his name; for if not for him the judgments imposing fines [which require ordained judges] would have ceased in Israel. For it happened that the wicked kingdom [the Roman emperor Hadrian] decreed that both he who ordains and the ordainee shall be put to death, and the city where the ordination took place shall be destroyed. What did Rabbi Judah ben Babba do! He went to a place between two great mountains, between the cities of Usha and Shepharam [in Galilee, to which places the Sanhedrin moved after leaving Yavneh] and ordained there five elders—Rabbis Meir, Judah, Simon, Jose, and Elazar ben Shamua. He bid them to leave him and flee for their lives; and he was pierced with three hundred iron spears until his body became like a sieve" (*Sanhedrin* 13b—14a).

This generation suffered another great national tragedy, the fall of Betar, the garrison town ten kilometers southwest of Jerusalem. This defeat put an end to the attempt of Bar Kochba and his followers to regain Jewish sovereignty in Judea, a sovereignty which the Jewish people did not recover until the establishment of the modern State of Israel, a stretch of 1,814 years. The fall of Betar, where the number of victims was so great that "their blood flowed to the Mediterranean, a distance of forty miles,"[25] was a crushing blow to the Jewish hopes for Redemption. In fact, the Mishnah (*Taanit* 4:6) includes it among the five great tragedies which befell the Jewish people on Tish'ah B'ab.

The Mishnah

Remarkable, and unique in the annals of nations, is the ability of the Jewish people to recover after catastrophe. Their faith in God's promise never to break His covenant with Israel (Lev. 26:44) did not waver, despite the great suffering and harrowing losses they endured. How true to history is the declaration we make once a year as we celebrate our first redemption from bondage "Blessed is He who keeps His promise to Israel . . . It is this which has stood by our fathers and us; for not one alone rose against us to annihilate us . . . but the Holy One, blessed be He, saves us from their hand" (*Haggadah shel Pesach*).

Following the example set by Rabbi Yohanan ben Zakkai, the sages who had been ordained by Rabbi Judah ben Babba proceeded to reestablish the central authority in Israel as soon as the new emperor, Antoninus Pius, revoked the decrees of Hadrian (140 c.e.). Their first act was to fix the calendar, so essential for the observance of the Jewish Festivals. Here is what they did, as related in the Jerusalem Talmud (*Hagigah* 4:1 [78d]): "Seven elders gathered in Bik'at Rimon to intercalate the year. Those who had a robe [the vestment of an ordained elder] cut it in half and gave a half to those who did not have a robe. Each one was called upon to deliver a homiletic discourse. As they were about to leave they said, 'Let us leave a mark of what we have done.' Nearby there was a marble rock. Each one took a nail and set it in the rock as if it were a piece of dough; and the rock became known as 'the rock of nails.'"

They next went to Yavneh to reconstitute the Sanhedrin. There they issued their first *takkanah*; they preserved the memory of the victims of Betar by adding a fourth benediction to *Birkat ha-Mazon*, the grace after meals (*Berakhot* 48b). How seemingly paradoxical a commemoration this was; to recite a blessing to God that "He is good and does good to us" after dashing our hopes for Redemption! But the Sages realized that the times called for, not another token of mourning after a defeat, but a token of encouragement to a harassed people. They could not, however, remain in Yavneh; the devastation in Judea was too great. So they transferred the seat of the Sanhedrin to the town of Usha (about twelve kilometers east of Haifa), issuing a call to all scholars to gather there.[26] Rabbi Simon, the son of Rabbi Gamaliel, assumed his position as *nasi*, and under his leadership they proceeded to issue a series of regulations, known as *takkanot Usha*, to help restore the social and economic life of the community. They fixed the financial obligations of husbands to their wives, and of parents to their children (*Kethubot* 49b–50a); divorce procedures to promote the stability of family life; and commercial procedures "for the improvement of society" and "for the ways of peace" (*Gittin*, chaps. 4–5).

The son of Rabbi Simon and his heir in the office of *nasi* was the illustrious Rabbi Judah who because of his legendary piety became known as *Rabbenu ha-Kadosh*, our holy master, or simply Rabbi. He moved the Sanhedrin from Usha to Beit She'arim (about midway between Haifa and Nazareth), where he was subsequently buried, thus sanctifying it as a place of burial for thousands of Jews in the third and fourth centuries. From there Rabbi Judah moved the Sanhedrin to Sepphoris (Tzippori, ten kilometers northwest of Nazareth), from the valley to the heights, because of his health. Among his disciples were Abba Arikha, known simply as Rav, who founded the Academy of Sura in Babylonia, which remained a center of Jewish learning and guidance for all Israel of the *golah* for almost a millennium; and Rabbi Yohanan bar Napha,[27] who founded the Academy in Tiberias, and whose disciples' teachings comprise the bulk of the Jerusalem Talmud. Thus the foundation was laid for the corpus juris of the Jewish people, the Talmud, the basis of Jewish self-government during the long period of *Galut Edom*, the Exile which began when Rome overpowered Jerusalem.[28] Rabbi Judah enjoyed the esteem and affection of the emperor Antoninus,[29] and during his days the Jews in Eretz Yisrael enjoyed a full measure of autonomy. Perhaps because of this Rabbi Judah desired to curb the excesses of mourning on the seventeenth of Tammuz and the ninth of Ab.[30] He conducted his position as *nasi* with authority and pomp, bolstered by his great wealth;[31] though he himself lived modestly and utilized his means to encourage the penurious scholars who flocked to his Academy.[32] The greatest achievment, however, of Rabbi Judah's career was the compilation of the Mishnah. It is for this work that he stands out as one of the great luminaries of Jewish history, and for which Judaism is everlastingly indebted to his foresight and enterprise.

We have stated above (p. 67) that the Jewish government is a "nomocracy," a rule of law; and the law in this case is the law of the Torah as expounded by the Sages in all generations. By the time of Rabbi Judah, the law had become quite complex and the opinions of the teachers quite diverse. Furthermore, the community in Babylonia had become autonomous, with its own institutions of learning and authority.[33] It was, therefore, necessary to collect the teachings which had accumulated over the centuries, sift them through, and put them in order as far as their subject matter was concerned (see above, p. 97). Rabbi Judah supervised this process of collection and arrangement, out of which emerged the Six Orders of the Mishnah, the Code of Jewish law which remained the basis for all subsequent expositions of Torah and halakhic decision. Rabbi Judah himself, for the most part, did not make the law rigid and definitive, but included in the Mishnah the diverse opinions of the Tannaim.[34] The later sages, the Amoraim, or Speakers, based their studies and decisions on the Mishnah, but also took into consideration statements of Tannaim not included in the Mishnah and therefore designated *Baraitot*, namely, outside sources. These extraneous sources are derived from other Tannaitic compilations, such as the *Tosefta* (additional material), and the *Mekhilta, Sifra*, and *Sifrei* (rabbinic exegesis of Exodus, Leviticus, Numbers and Deuteronomy, respectively). The discussions of the Amoraim, their homiletic discourses (*aggadah*) as well as their legal arguments and decisions (*halakhah*), are incorporated in the Gemara, i.e., a study of transmitted law. The Mishnah and the Gemara together comprise the Talmud, which consists of sixty-three Tractates (*Mesikhtot*).[35]

Throughout subsequent ages, the Talmud has been the subject of constant study and analysis, and the literature based upon it is "longer than the earth and broader than the sea" (Job 11:9). In fact, one usually refers to its contents as "the sea of the Talmud."[36] For our discussion of Jewish self-government, however, suffice it to say that the Talmud became the chief preoccupation of Jewish religious leaders up until modern times, made possible the autonomy of Jewish communities in the far-flung corners of the Diaspora, and preserved Jewish national identity throughout the long and precarious Exile. One may say without exaggeration that *the Talmud was the Jewish State in Exile.*

8

The Rise and Fall of
Jewish Autonomy in Exile

In Eretz Yisrael

The peak of Jewish self-government after Israel's loss of independent sovereignty in the year 70 C.E. was achieved in Eretz Yisrael[1] in
the reign of Rabbi Judah I as *nasi* (175–219). His vigorous
leadership of the Sanhedrin and the Academy of Torah scholars,
combined with his lavish estate and the esteem in which he was held
by the Roman authorities, enabled him to fill his exalted position in
all its power and glory. The Talmud, with its characteristic hyperbole, expresses it this way: "We do not find combined in one person
eminence in both knowledge of Torah and high office from the days
of Moses till the days of Rabbi" (*Gittin* 59a).[2]

The best sons of thriving Babylonian Jewry flocked to Rabbi
Judah's Academy to receive from him the authority to act as the
religious leaders of their respective communities. Even three generations later in Babylonia, when Rabbah the son of Rav Huna would
argue with those who received their commission from the exilarch
(reish galutha), he would say to them: "My authority does not
proceed from you; I have received authority from my father, my
father from Rav, Rav from Rabbi Hiyya, and Rabbi Hiyya from
Rabbi" (*Sanhedrin* 5a).

It was this Rabbi Hiyya, the most prominent colleague of Rabbi
Judah, of whom the Talmud asserts: "When the knowledge of
Torah was forgotten in Israel, Rabbi Hiyya and his sons came up [to
Eretz Yisrael] from Babylonia and reestablished it" (*Succah* 20a).

Rabbi Hiyya tells us how he accomplished it: "I went and planted flax, from which I wove nets and trapped deer. I gave their meat to orphans, and made parchment from their skins on which I wrote five scrolls of the Pentateuch. I went to a place [where there was no teacher] and taught each of five youngsters one of the scrolls. I also taught each of six other youngsters one of the six orders of the Mishnah. I said to the youngsters: 'Before I return I want each of you to teach what you have learned from me to your companions.' Thus I saw to it that the Torah should not be forgotten in Israel." Whereupon Rabbi Judah exclaimed: "How great are the deeds of Hiyya" (Baba Metzia 85b).

Another incident which indicates the crucial importance with which the Sages regarded the appointment of teachers—and which incidentally reveals the origin of the name adopted by the most extreme wing of Orthodox Jewry today—is related as follows:[3] "Rabbi Judah the Nasi sent Rabbi Hiyya, Rabbi Asi and Rabbi Ami to pass through the towns in Eretz Yisrael in order to set up teachers of Scripture and Mishnah. They came to one place and did not find any teacher. They said to the leaders of the community: 'Bring to us the neturei karta [Aramaic for "guards of the city"].' They brought them the sentries of the city! Whereupon the Rabbis exclaimed:: 'Are these the guards of the city. These are the destroyers of the city! And who,' they were asked by the townspeople, 'are the real neturei karta?' The Rabbis answered: 'The teachers of Scripture and Mishnah'" (J. Hagigah 1:7, [76c]).

The impact of Rabbi Judah's and Rabbi Hiyya's activities on behalf of religious education was so strong and their influence so lasting that the later Sages compared them to the great men of previous ages whose heroic deeds brought salvation to Israel from its many crises (Megillah 11a). Salvation from a crisis of survival was indeed necessary at the time. The Jewish community in Eretz Yisrael, which had suffered so much as a consequence of Bar Kokhba's ill-fated rebellion, was struggling under a heavy burden of taxes imposed by the none too friendly imperial government. In fact, in order to grant some relief to the impoverished populace, Rabbi Judah decreed that the area of Beit She'an was to be considered outside the sanctified boundaries of Eretz Yisrael so that its produce would be exempt from the requirement of tithing (*Hullin* 6b). And not much later, Rabbi Yannai proclaimed throughout Eretz Yisrael that it was permitted to work the fields during the Sabbatical year of Shemitta since the government demanded that the taxes (a percentage of the yield) be paid even then (*Sanhedrin* 26a). This was a cancellation of a privilege which Jews had enjoyed for centuries, ever since the days of Alexander the Great.

Rabbi Judah was concerned that the authority of the *nasi* be not diminished after his demise. Before he died, he summoned the Sages of Israel and said to them: "Though my son Simon is the [greater] scholar, my son Gamaliel will be the *nasi*."[4] He then called in Gamaliel (the third patriarch of that name) and instructed him in the ways of the patriarchate. He advised him to conduct his position with great dignity and wield his authority over the disciples with severity (*Kethubot* 103b). Rabbi Gamaliel's term of office did not last very long, nor was he as distinguished as his father. The true leaders of the Jewish people, exercising their leadership both as heads of their academies and as members of the Sanhedrin, were the scholars who flourished at the time.

The situation of the Jews in Eretz Yisrael found some temporary improvement during the reign of the benevolent Alexander Severus, but took a great turn for the worse after he died (235). At this time, Rabbi Judah II, son of Rabbi Gamaliel III, succeeded his father as *nasi*. He is referred to in the Talmud as Rabbi Judah *Nesiah* (the Aramaic form of *nasi*) in order to distinguish him from his more illustrious grandfather.[5] He strove to conduct the patriarchate in all its dignity and authority, but the worsening economic and political conditions made this difficult. We are told that when Rabbi Simon ben Lakish visited him, Rabbi Judah said: "Pray for me, for this kingdom is very wicked"; and Rabbi Simon advised him not to accept any gifts from anyone so that he would not have to give anything in return. However, as they were sitting a woman came in bearing a platter with a knife and Rabbi Judah took the knife, thus compromising his dignity (*Bereishit Rabbah* 78:15). Rabbi Judah II moved the seat of the Sanhedrin from Sepphoris to Tiberias, its last

seat before it was finally suppressed for all time about a century later
(that is, until its still-hoped-for restoration). About this final move
the Talmud comments: "Tiberias is the lowest of all [other seats of
the Sanhedrin], lowest not only in the geographical sense, but in the
extent of its authority. However, Rabbi Yohanan assures us that
therefore the Redemption of Israel will begin from Tiberias" (Rosh
Hashanah 31b).

After the death of Rabbi Judah II, the Sanhedrin ceased to wield
universal authority over all Israel, both in Eretz Yisrael and in the
Diaspora. In Eretz Yisrael there developed two centers of Jewish life.
One was in Tiberias, where Rabbi Yohanan headed the Academy.
He continued to attract disciples from Babylonia, but most of them
remained only for a short period, long enough to bring back to their
native country the halakhic traditions learned in Eretz Yisrael. Rabbi
Yohanan's fame as a scholar was so great that he was regarded in the
same category as a Tanna; and Maimonides attributes to him the
compilation of the Jerusalem Talmud even though its final editing
took place more than a century later.

The other center was in Caesarea, where Rabbi Abbahu, a disciple of Rabbi Yohanan, headed the academy. Caesarea, a city of
mixed Greek and Jewish population, was the seat of the Roman
governor, who regarded Rabbi Abbahu as the leader and champion
of his people. The Talmud relates that when Rabbi Abbahu would
go from his academy to the palace of the governor, the latter's
maidservants[6] would greet him with song and say: "Master of his
people, leader of his nation, lamp of light, may your coming be blessed with peace" (Kethubot 17a).[7] Rabbi Abbahu also attracted many
scholars to his academy, and they are referred to in the Jerusalem
Talmud as "the rabbis of Caesarea."[8] One of the well-known takkanot of Rabbi Abbahu, subsequently adopted by all Israel, is the
manner in which the shofar should be sounded on Rosh Hashanah
(Rosh Hashanah 34a). His forte, however, was Aggadah, homiletical
discourse and interpretations of Scripture, many of them designed
to refute its Christological interpretations.

Aggadic preaching was now more popular than Halakhic instruction. It is related that Rabbi Abbahu and his colleague Rabbi Hiyya bar Abba came to a certain community and both were invited to preach. Rabbi Abbahu preached Aggadah, whereas Rabbi Hiyya bar Abba preached Halakhah. Everybody left Rabbi Hiyya and went to hear Rabbi Abbahu, causing the former to become very disheartened. Whereupon Rabbi Abbahu said to him: "I will tell you a parable. To what can our experience be compared? To two hawkers who come to a town, one selling precious stones and the other household articles. Who has the most customers, if not the one selling the household articles!" (Sotah 40a). The popularity of Aggadah over Halakhah was in itself an indication of the deteriorating conditions in Eretz Yisrael. The Midrash states: "In the past, when money was plentiful, people longed to hear a word from the Mishnah, Halakhah, and Talmud; now that money is scarce, and especially that people are oppressed by the subjugation to foreign rule, they long to hear words of blessing and consolation" (Shir ha-Shirim Rabbah 2:4)[9]

At the beginning of the fourth century the emperor Constantine embraced Christianity, thus placing vast secular power in the hands of Christendom. Almost immediately, Christendom began to utilize this power in order to commit matricide; namely, to extinguish the Judaism out of which it sprung. Decrees were promulgated restricting the observance of Torah and mitzvot, exceeding the harshness of the Hadrianic gezeirot. In the course of the century, the academies in Tiberias and Caesarea languished, the Jewish courts were deprived of all authority, and synagogues were forcibly converted into churches. The doom of the Sanhedrin as the central authority for all Israel emanating from Eretz Yisrael was, under such circumstances, inevitable.

The Origin of the Present-day Jewish Calendar

We have previously mentioned that one of the main functions of the Sanhedrin, which endowed it with universal authority, was its right to fix the Jewish calendar and thus determine the dates for the celebration of the Festivals. There were two methods by means of which the Sanhedrin in Eretz Yisrael communicated its monthly declaration of a new month to the dispersed communities of Israel: first, by means of torches waved on the peaks of mountains, and later, by the dispatching of messengers (Mishnah *Rosh Hashanah* 2:2–4).[10] Those communities which were two weeks or more distant from the seat of the Sanhedrin would have no way of knowing by the fifteenth of the month which day had been declared to be the first day of Nisan or Tishri, and thus could not know which day was to be the beginning of the Passover or Succot Festivals, which commence respectively on the fifteenth of the months mentioned. As a result, they would celebrate the Festival for two days in place of the one enjoined by the Torah. (A month could be either twenty-nine or thirty days, no more and no less, hence the doubt was in only one day.) It was particularly the large Jewish community in Babylonia which would not make its own calendrical calculations—even though it had scholars competent to do so—and depended upon the Sanhedrin in Eretz Yisrael. Thus the custom arose in Babylonia, and from there subsequently in all other parts of the Diaspora, to celebrate what is called *yom tov sheni shel galuyot*, the second day of the Festival for the Diaspora. (Since Rosh Hashanah occurs on the very first day of the month of Tishri, even the Jews in Eretz Yisrael celebrated two days of Rosh Hashanah; *Betzah* 5a.)[11]

By the middle of the fourth century, conditions in Eretz Yisrael were so difficult that it became impossible for the Sanhedrin to communicate its decisions concerning the calendar to Babylonia. Once, for example, the messengers sent from Tiberias to announce the intercalation of a month were intercepted by the Romans, and the message had to be transmitted in code (*Sanhedrin* 12a). Therefore, the *nasi* at the time, Hillel II, promulgated a calendar for all time, fixed in accord with certain rules and regulations that were known even in Babylonia. Nevertheless, the Jews in Babylonia were instructed by the authorities in Eretz Yisrael to continue the custom of their fathers and observe the second day Yom Tov (*Betzah* 4b). This is the calendar, and this is the custom, followed to our present day. It is the final heritage left to the entire Jewish people by that glorious institution, the Sanhedrin, which for centuries guided the destinies of Israel as "one people in the Land" (II Sam. 7:23).

A brief respite from discrimination and persecution, and the restoration of many of its rights of self-government, was given to the community in Eretz Yisrael during the short reign of the emperor Julian. He repudiated Christianity and rejected its persecution mania. He voided the harsh decrees against Judaism, befriended the Jews, and honored their *nasi*, Hillel II. He wrote an epistle of encouragement to all the Jews of the Roman Empire, promising them to rebuild the Temple in Jerusalem (why this promise did not become a reality will be explained in a subsequent chapter). Unfortunately, Julian died during the war against the Persians, and the community in Eretz Yisrael reverted to its miserable condition. In the year 425, the office of *nasi* was completely abolished, bringing to an end the rule of the Sanhedrin as well.

This is not to imply that religious creative activity ceased in Eretz Yisrael with the disappearance of the patriarchate. Scholars in Tiberias in the sixth and seventh centuries gave us a system of vocalization for Hebrew Scripture and produced a standard text of the Bible known as the Masoretic text.[12] Poets in Eretz Yisrael known as *payyetanim* produced liturgical poems, *piyyutim*, which were added to the Sabbath and Festival prayers. But no longer could one say, "For out of Zion comes forth the Torah, and the word of the Lord from Jerusalem." In fact, as the source of religious instruction moved from one country to another, Jews would substitute the names of local cities in place of the Zion and Jerusalem of the verse.

Attempts to Revive the Sanhedrin

Two attempts were made in the course of time to revive the authority of the Sanhedrin in Eretz Yisrael. At the beginning of the tenth century, there appeared in Eretz Yisrael a scholar by the name of Ben Meir who claimed to be a descendant of the House of Hillel. In a dispute with the Gaon Saadia concerning the date of Rosh

Hashanah, he insisted that his decision should be followed since it emanated from Eretz Yisrael, the only true source of determining the Jewish calendar. However, his contention was challenged and defeated by the gaon, whose authority stemmed from the Academy in Babylonia, which had already for several centuries superseded that of Eretz Yisrael.[13]

The second attempt was made at the beginning of the sixteenth century, when a large group of scholars were living and teaching in Safed. The Jewish community there consisted mostly of Sephardi Jews, refugees from the Spanish expulsion and Inquisition. Eretz Yisrael at that time was under Turkish rule, and the Jewish community enjoyed relatively broad autonomy for its own religious adherents. A renowned scholar by the name of Jacob Berab, who settled in Safed in his old age, decided to restore the ancient practice of *semikhah*, the conferring of the right to act as religious judge in all cases, thus making it possible for those receiving the *semikhah* to constitute themselves as a Sanhedrin, with all the universal religious authority that that implied. He failed, however, to receive the cooperation of the chief rabbi of Jerusalem, Levi ibn Habib—such cooperation was indispensable for the reconstituting of *semikhah*— and the whole plan had to be abandoned.

One of the younger ordainees of Rabbi Berab was Joseph Karo. In a way, his great achievement, the compilation of the *Shulhan Arukh*, or Code of Jewish Law, which serves to this day as the basis for rabbinic decision, was a kind of Sanhedrin. It was intended to provide a central authority in Jewish law, a unifying factor for Jewish life stemming from the Holy Land. But one cannot compare a written code with a body of living men who possess, and are ready to exercise, the authority to interpret the written code and revise its regulations as the changing circumstances warrant; just as Jewish law could not have continued to guide the Jewish people through the vicissitudes of the ages had it consisted solely of the *Torah she-bikhtav*, the Written Law, and not had the *Torah she-b'al-peh*, the Oral Law, as well.

The time was really not ripe for the reconstitution of a central authority in Israel. The Jewish community in Eretz Yisrael was too small to be able to wield an influence upon the much stronger communities in the Diaspora. Even the *Shulhan Arukh* of Karo had to be amended for Ashkenazic Jewry, a task effectively accomplished by Rabbi Moses Isserles of Cracow. Furthermore, the migration of Jews from one country to another was still more centrifugal than centripetal. The reestablishment of a Sanhedrin can only come about when Eretz Yisrael becomes the *tel talpiyot*, "the eminence to which all faces are turned" (*Berakhot* 30a).

The dwindling of Jewish life in Eretz Yisrael in the fourth century fortunately did not spell the end of self-rule for all Jewry. By this time, Babylonian Jewry, with its great scholars and academies, and with its political head, the *reish galutha*, or exilarch, was strong enough to assume the role of universal authority for all Jewry. Based upon the passage in Kohelet (1:5), "The sun rises and the sun sets," the Sages aver: "A righteous man does not depart from this world until there is born a righteous man to replace him" (*Kiddushin* 72b). Similarly, a center of Jewish life does not disappear before another center appears to take its place. And why was Babylonia destined to take the place of Eretz Yisrael? One rabbi of the Talmud explained it as follows: Rabbi Hiyya taught: "That which is written, 'God understands the way thereof, and He knows the place thereof' [Job 28:23], indicates that the Holy One, blessed be He, knew that Israel would not be able to endure the brutal *gezeirot* of Edom [Rome], therefore He exiled them to Babylon" (*Pesahim* 87b).

In Babylonia

The peak of Jewish self-government outside Eretz Yisrael was reached in Babylonia about the time the Patriarch Judah I was the *nasi* in Eretz Yisrael, and continued with some interruptions for almost eight centuries. The Jews in Babylonia had enjoyed religious freedom ever since the days of Cyrus, and therefore they were able to pursue their private and communal life with ease of mind (*Menahot* 110a). In half a dozen cities the population was overwhelmingly Jewish; thus in Pumbeditha, for example, it was

ruled that if thieves entered a wine-cellar and helped themselves to
the wine, the wine remained kosher because "most of the thieves are
Jewish" (*Abodah Zarah* 70a). Babylonian Jews were very conscious
and proud of their long history. They pointed with pride to ancient
synagogues which purportedly contained stones brought from the
ruins of the First Temple and served as the resting place for the
Shekhinah (the Divine Presence) in Exile (*Megillah* 29a).[14] They also
were very proud of their lineage, claiming that the purity of their
descent from ancient Jewish families was superior even to that of the
Jews residing in Eretz Yisrael. (*Kiddushin* 69b, 71a). Such pride inevitably led to self-confidence and independence, enabling them to
assume the leadership of Klal Yisrael when the decline of the center
in Eretz Yisrael made it necessary.

We have made frequent reference to the vitality of the Jewish
community in Babylonia, and to the significant contribution of its
citizens to the vitality of Jewish life and institutions in Eretz Yisrael.
By the time of Judah I there had already been appointed a titular
head of the Babylonian Jewish community, known as *reish galutha*,
or exilarch, and recognized as such by the Persian government. Now
the exilarch emerged as a rival to the hegemony of the patriarch in
Eretz Yisrael. When, for example, Rabbi Judah asked Rabbi Hiyya
whether his high office put him in the category of the *nasi* mentioned in the Torah (Lev. 4:22−26), he was told: "Behold your rival
is in Babylonia" (*Horayot* 11b); that is, the exilarch there exercises
his authority over his community independently of the *nasi* in Eretz
Yisrael, and thus the authority of the patriarch is not over *all* Israel.
According to one version, the authority of the exilarch exceeded that
of the patriarch, for the former "ruled Israel with the scepter" (symbol of royalty), whereas the latter was "the lawgiver who teaches
Torah to all" (*Sanhedrin* 5a, referring to Gen. 49:10).[15] Furthermore,
the exilarch claimed descent from the male line of King David,
whereas the patriarch could only claim descent through a female
forebear (J. *Kilayim* 9:4 [32b]).

Side by side with the political leadership of the *reish galutha* was
the religious leadership of the *reish methivta*, the head of the
Academy. In fact, two great academies flourished in Babylonia from

the days of the first Amoraim to the end of the period of the
Geonim. (After the period of the Talmud, the heads of the academies
were given the title *gaon*).[16] The Academy of Sura was founded by
Abba Arikha, called Rav because of his preeminent erudition, and
the Academy of Nehardea (transferred from there to Pumbeditha in
the year 259) was founded by Samuel, famous as physician and
astronomer as well as talmudist. The founders of these academies
were recognized as great teachers by their contemporaries in Eretz
Yisrael (*Hullin* 95b), and their successors commanded the respect
and authority of Jewish communities throughout the Diaspora. All
questions of Jewish law and practice were addressed to the heads of
the Yeshivot in Babylonia, and it was sufficient for the latter to respond: "This is the practice in our Yeshivah" for it to be accepted as
binding Halakhah. Twice a year Jews would assemble in the thousands at one of the academies to hear the head of the academy expound the laws of the Festivals. These semi-annual gatherings were
called *kallah*, and our prayer book still carries a blessing for *reishei
de-kallah*.[17] The honor accorded the head of the *kallah* was so great
that Rav Ashi (one of the compilers of the Babylonian Talmud, first
quarter of the fifth cent.) was constrained to remark: "The Gentile
inhabitants of Matha Mehesia [the temporary seat of the Academy
of Sura] must be terribly stubborn; they witness the great honor
given to the Torah twice a year and yet not one of them converts to
Judaism" (*Berakhot* 17b).[18]

Even though the rabbis in Babylonia could not have conferred
upon them the traditional *semikhah*, a privilege reserved only for
members of the Sanhedrin ordained in Eretz Yisrael, they
nevertheless considered themselves the legitimate heirs and
representatives of the earlier authorities in administering Jewish law
(*Baba Kamma* 84b). They did not hesitate to institute *takkanot*, or
new regulations, many of which are adhered to this very day. For
example, Rav instituted the version of the Rosh Hashanah prayer
recited in all communities today (J. *Rosh Hashanah* 1:3 [57a]); and it
is his personal prayer which was adopted as recently as three
hundred years ago as the special prayer for the Sabbath preceding
Rosh Hodesh.[19] And the Geonim continued this process of in-

stituting new regulations in order to accommodate Jewish law to new circumstances in Jewish life.[20]

The pattern of Jewish self-government in Babylonia conformed to the classical pattern we described in the first chapter of this volume; namely, a dual administration consisting of the political leader, the *reish galutha*, and the religious-judicial leader, the *reish methivta*. How this functioned in the period of the Geonim is described by a modern historian of the period as follows: "In order to institute a *takkanah*, the Geonim of the two Yeshivot would meet together with the exilarch. The exilarch was included not only in order to give political force to the new regulation, but also because the exilarch was a partner with the Geonim in bringing order to the judicial system in the Caliphate of Bagdad. In all communities the judges were appointed either by the gaon of the district or by the exilarch, and they also would have the power to remove a judge from office if the complaints against him warranted it. When all the parties agreed to the new regulation, letters bearing the stamp of the exilarch were despatched to all communities. Within the borders of the caliphate the regulations were enforced by the local admininstration; but they were also accepted by the Jewish courts outside the borders of Babylonia where the Geonim had no political authority, as, for example, in the lands of Christian Europe."[21]

It is true that at times there were clashes between the exilarch and the gaon, but each complemented the other in making possible Jewish autonomy; the exilarch in *assuring* the right to autonomy under a non-Jewish ruler, and the gaon in *exercising* the right according to Jewish law and tradition. Even after the tremendous change in the non-Jewish government took place as the Moslems took over from the Persians in the middle of the seventh century and established the caliphate, the Jewish community retained its autonomy. Caliph Ali officially recognized the Exilarch Bostanai and the Gaon Mar Isaac as the heads of the Jewish people under his jurisdiction, and thus the hegemony in Jewish life of these two offices was extended for another four hundred years.

We must not, however, lose sight of the fact that this autonomy was enjoyed in the *golah* under a condition described by our Sages as *shibud malkhuyot*, subjection to foreign rulers, and thus subject to the good will of the non-Jewish ruler. Of one of the first heads of a Yeshiva in Babylonia, Rabbi Shila, contemporary of Rabbi Judah I, it is related that he, in his capacity as head of the Jewish court of law, administered lashes to a Jew who had had intercourse with an Egyptian woman. The culprit then went to the palace and complained, "There is a Jew who executes judgments without the king's permission." Whereupon an officer was dispatched to summon Rabbi Shila before the Persian authorities. He was asked to explain his action, which he did in a rather oblique manner (exact details will be found in the source). Then he began to recite the verse "Thine O Lord is the greatness and the power" (I Chron. 29:11). They asked him what he was saying. He replied: "This is what I was saying: 'Blessed is the Merciful One who gave us a kingdom here on earth similar to the kingdom in Heaven, and gave you a ruler with merciful laws.'" So they said to him: "The honor of the kingdom is so precious to you, here is the judge's staff and go and judge" (*Berakhot* 58a).

Furthermore, Jewish religious freedom was curbed when the Sassanids overthrew the Parthians and became the rulers over Babylonia (middle of the third century). Jews were compelled to withdraw the Hanukkah lamps into the interior of their homes even though the Halakhah required that they be placed outside at the front entrance, because the new rulers were devotees of Ormuz, the god of fire, who did not permit any profane fire to be kindled on his sacred day (*Shabbat* 21b).[22] Such a restriction is not conceivable in a sovereign Jewish state, as witness today in Medinat Yisrael, where the eight-branched candlelabra burn brightly from the rooftops of every public building during the holiday of Hanukkah. Only in an independent Jewish state can the Jew enjoy absolute religious freedom.

Another significant mitigation of Jewish autonomy under a foreign ruler that has its origin in Babylonia is the ruling laid down by Samuel that "the law of the kingdom is law" (*dina de-malkhutha dina*), binding the Jewish citizens of the state equally with all other citizens. This ruling had particular application as far as taxes, land registration, and the public domain were concerned, and therefore was not necessarily a negative or harmful aspect of Jewish life. Nevertheless, rabbis at all times had to make it clear that it does not apply if it' is discriminatory or interferes with Jewish religious obligations.[23]

The Psalmist says: "I have seen an end to every purpose, but your commandment is exceedingly broad" (Ps. 119:96). The constantly shifting exigencies of history brought the glorious period of Babylonian Jewry to an end, but its heritage to Jewish generations remains strong and vital. Several factors contributed to the decline and eventual disappearance of both the institution of the *reish galutha* and the famous Yeshivot of Sura and Pumbeditha. Just as the fanatic hostility of the Christian Church led to the downfall of the patriarchate in Eretz Yisrael, so did the increasing fanaticism of the Moslems lead to the extinction of Babylonia as the center of Jewish authority for all Israel. Furthermore, the internal dissensions within Jewish life itself, the bitter quarrels among various contenders for the positions of exilarch and gaon, brought about the weakening and ultimately the disappearance of these organs of Jewish self-government. And the most significant factor was the continued movement of Jews to the distant borders of both the Christian and Moslem Empires. As the second millennium of the common era dawned, Jewish settlements could be found in all of Western and Central Europe, including England, and in all of North Africa, known as the Maghreb. Jewish life now consisted of two main centers, each drawing its religious guidance from the same source, the Babylonian Talmud, but each with its distinctive nuances of interpretation and local custom. The Jews in Christian Europe became known as Ashkenazim because their earliest settlements were in the Rhine region bordering Germany, referred to by Jews as *Ashkenaz*. The Jews in Moslem Europe (Moorish Spain) and North Africa became known as Sephardim, for Spain in Jewish literature was called *Sepharad*.[24] In our continuing discussion of Jewish autonomy in Exile, we now have to distinguish between these two main centers and survey briefly how each of them managed to maintain its autonomy amidst a none too favorable environment.

In The Middle Ages

The last gaon who commanded the respect and authority of almost all the Jewish communities of the Dispersion was Hai ben Sherira Gaon.[25] He died in the year 1038, and with his passing away there also passed away from Jewish life a central figurehead to whom questions of Jewish law and custom would stream from all directions. His place was taken by a series of individuals, spiritual heads of local communities or local Yeshivot. The authority of such an individual extended beyond the borders of his locality only as far as his renown extended; that is, as far as his superior erudition and piety were recognized by other rabbis and communities, and they were willing to be guided by his decisions. From now on, "the cornerstone of the entire edifice of Jewish autonomy was the local community."[26]

Halakhic sanction for the authority of the local scholar and community was given by two eminent teachers of the time, one an Ashkenazi and the other a Sephardi. Rabbi Jacob Tam (Rabbenu Tam), the outstanding member of the group of French talmudists known as the Tosafists, averred that the *beit din* of the contemporary scholar of renown is equal in status to the courts of the ancient Tannaim. Rabbi Solomon ibn Aderet of Barcelona (Rashba) asserted in a *teshuvah* that "within its borders each community possesses the authority equal to that of the Geonim."[27] Nevertheless, there was a significant difference between the authority of the gaon and that of the post-geonic scholar, a difference that expressed itself in the degree of boldness with which they respectively addressed themselves to questions of Jewish law. The gaon conceived of himself as the halakhic authority for all Israel and his pronouncements as universally binding; whereas the scholar did not arrogate to himself the right to speak for all Jewry, and he recognized the right of other scholars to dispute his opinion. Typical of the hesitancy of the post-geonic scholar in applying the powers of the rabbinic court is the *teshuvah* of the Rashba in connection with the power of the local court to annul marriages performed in defiance of a local *takkanah*. "Not everywhere may we say, 'The Rabbis have annulled the marriage'; only where they [the Rabbis of the Talmud] have said so is it said; where they did not say it, we do not say it on our own.''[28]

The Sages assure us that the Almighty "does not smite Israel unless He first creates for them a cure" (Megillah 13b). Before the decline of the gaonate something occurred which ultimately enabled the leaders of Diaspora communities to assume the prerogatives vacated by the gaon. What at the time seemed to be a tragedy turned out to be in the long run the salvation of Jewish learning. The event, as recounted by Rabbi Abraham ben David in his Sefer ha-Kabbalah, is briefly as follows: Four distinguished Babylonian scholars embarked at Bari, southern Italy, to attend the wedding of a colleague's daughter in Siponto. While at sea they were captured by a Moslem naval officer out to capture Christian vessels. He sold the scholars as slaves, each in a different city. In each city the captive was redeemed by the local Jewish community, which then took note of his excellence in talmudic lore and appointed him head of the local academy. Rabbi Shemariah was redeemed in Alexandria, whence he made his way to Fostat, the old Jewish neighborhood of Cairo, where later Maimonides settled. Rabbi Hushiel was redeemed by the community of Kairouan, Tunis, which had long depended upon the Babylonian gaonate for religious guidance but now found an authoritative scholar in its midst. And Rabbi Moshe ben Hanokh was redeemed by the thriving and influential community of Cordova in Moorish Spain. His superior understanding of the Talmud was recognized by the local spiritual leader, who yielded his office to Rabbi Moshe. (The teller of this tale says that he does not know the name of the fourth scholar).[29]

The aforementioned scholars settled in communities of Sephardic Jews. Sephardic Jewry's roots were in Babylonia, and they followed the customs and rituals of Babylonian Jewry.[30] They were creative not only in talmudic scholarship; they also produced an immense literature in the fields of biblical studies, philosophy, and poetry. In this they were stimulated by the flourishing Arabic culture of the early Middle Ages. The Jews in Moslem countries continued to enjoy the autonomy in regulating their own affairs which had been enjoyed under both Persian and Islamic rulers for centuries. In addition to the rabbinic leader of the community there was also a lay leader who had the title *nagid* and was held in great esteem by the non-Jewish ruler.

To indicate the extent to which the community exercised its power over its members, we can rely upon the following testimony of Maimonides in his Commentary to the Mishnah (*Hullin* 1:2): "Know that it is a tradition from our fathers . . . that in our times, the time of the *galut*, when Jewish courts are no longer empowered to administer capital punishment, that this is so only with respect to a Jew who transgresses a capital sin; but as for heretics . . . the one who first preached a heresy is to be put to death so that he should not lead Israel astray and corrupt their faith; *and this has actually been done to many persons in the Maghreb.*"[31] Such stringent measures reflected the insecurities of Jewish life among hostile Moslems and Christians, and the scars left by the Karaite schism. However, for the Jew who transgressed ritual law or refused to abide by the decision of the local Jewish court in financial matters, the punishment meted out to him was flogging and being put under the ban of the *herem*, or excommunication. These means of enforcement were employed in both Sephardic and Ashkenazic communities in order to maintain discipline among their members.

Ashkenazic Jewry's roots were in Eretz Yisrael, and therefore their ritual and customs largely followed those of Palestinian Jewry.[32] Even before the destruction of the Second Temple, there was an organized Jewish community in Rome which was able to redeem the many captives brought there from Eretz Yisrael by Titus.[33] From Rome Jews spread in all directions with the expanding Roman Empire, and with them they took their religious heritage. Tradition has it that Charlemagne invited the Makhir family to settle in Narbonne, in the Provence region of France, and the Kalonymus family to settle in Mainz (Mayence, or *Magentza* in Hebrew literature) on the Rhine. By the beginning of the second millennium of the common era, Narbonne and Mainz were prominent centers of Jewish learning with famous Yeshivot headed by renowned scholars. Of two communities in southern Italy it was said: "For the Torah goes forth from Bari, and the word of the Lord from Otranto."[34]

Ashkenazic Jewry, in contradistinction to Sephardic Jewry, had to wage a constant struggle in order to maintain its autonomy. Monarchs, bishops, and feudal lords were all contending for the right to rule over the Jews, who found it necessary to petition for the right to rule over themselves as far as their internal affairs were concerned. We therefore find, for example, that Ashkenazic rabbis were constrained more than their Sephardic colleagues to limit the application of *dina de-malkhuta dina;* i.e., limiting the interference of the non-Jewish overlord in the autonomy of the Jewish community.

In governing the community, the halakhic authorities did not hesitate to exercise the traditional prerogative to institute *takkanot* in order to make Jewish law conform in greater measure to the realities of local custom and point of view. Most well known among these *takkanot* are the bans against polygamy and divorcing a woman against her will, instituted by Rabbenu Gershom Me'or ha-Golah of Mainz. (These bans were not adopted by Sephardic Jewry.) A generation later, Rashi, the great expositor of Bible and Talmud who made these basic texts of Judaism accessible to all levels of the Jewish population, received his basic education in the Yeshivah of Mainz. And Rashi's grandchildren were the founders of the schools of the Tosafists, upon whose commentaries to the Talmud much of subsequent halakhic decision was based. The Tosafists acknowledged that many restrictions (*gezeirot*) enacted by the Rabbis of the Talmud no longer applied to medieval Jewry because of their different social and economic conditions. For example, the restriction against selling animals to non-Jews imposed in talmudic times "was only in their days when many Jews lived together and a Jew could sell to another Jew and not incur a loss; but now what can one do, if he cannot sell [to a non-Jew] he will incur a loss."[35]

Because of the many expulsions suffered by the Jews in the Middle Ages, the trend in rabbinic literature in the fourteenth and fifteenth centuries was less talmudic commentary and more simple codes of Jewish law and practice to guide Jews as they settled in new communities. These codes stressed the local custom, or *minhag,* and as a result the divergence in practice between Ashkenazim and Sephardim became more fixed. By the time the Sephardi Rabbi Joseph Karo published his *Shulhan Arukh*, in the sixteenth century, it could not serve Ashkenazic Jewry without being amended by the many glosses of Rabbi Moses Isserles of Cracow, who set down the practice prevalent among European Jews.

We can sum up this period in the history of Jewish autonomy by saying that the Jews in the many lands of the Diaspora were able to regulate their internal communal affairs because of the insistence of their rabbinic leaders that they conduct themselves in accord with their own religious traditions, which were so antithetic to the religious traditions and moral standards of their non-Jewish neighbors. The latter, in turn, contributed to the phenomenon of Jewish self-government in Exile because of their effort to keep the Jews segregated from the commercial and social activities of the majority.

In Modern Times

The fourteenth and fifteenth centuries were periods of further migration for a wandering people, culminating in the creation of new autonomous communities and centers of Jewish life. The Sephardim, expelled from Spain and Portugal, moved in several directions; some to North Africa, where they were welcomed and easily absorbed by the local co-religionists, and some to Italy and the Balkans and from there to Eretz Yisrael. Others found refuge in Holland and subsequently England, and still others in the New World, the Americas. The last two groups of emigrés established small communities centered around the synagogue, and hence the historic Spanish and Portuguese synagogues, the first Jewish institutions in England and America.[36] The Sephardim of North Africa and other Arab lands remained in their communities, continuing their traditional way of life and regulating, under the leadership of their rabbis, their religious, social, and commercial activities. They did so, however, under the malevolent eyes of their Moslem neighbors, who

treated them as less than second-class citizens.[37] Gone from
Sephardic Jewry in these lands—as gone also from the Arabs—was
the broad cultural spectrum, embracing philosophy and secular
poetry which had characterized their forebears in the Middle Ages.
Now the mystical teachings of the Zohar, the "Bible" of the Kabbalah, joined the Talmud as the major interest of their spiritual
leaders. The Sephardic community established in Safed was distinguished by the number of scholars who devoted themselves to the
study of the Kabbalah, developing it under Isaac Luria (ha-Ari) and
Haim Vital from a purely theoretical theology to a system of practical measures.

The Ashkenazic Jews of France and Germany moved eastward,
after a series of expulsions, to Poland, Lithuania, and Russia.
Casimir the Great of Poland had welcomed the Jews to his country
in 1334, granting them commercial privileges and the right of self-
government. Subsequent Polish kings reaffirmed these privileges,
and the Jews took advantage of the opportunity to establish thriving
communities governed by their own religious traditions, with eminent heads of Yeshivot assuming their traditional role as the main
communal leaders. Before the end of the sixteenth century these
communities established a central organization known as the Vaad
Arba Aratzot, or Council of Four Lands. This council was primarily
responsible for the assessment and collection of taxes imposed by
the Polish government upon the Jews, though it also regulated the
administration of the local communities. For example, it decreed that
the appointment of rabbis must be based solely upon personal
qualifications, and it defined the duties of the lay leaders called parnassim.[38] The Lithuanian communities organized their own council,
calling it Vaad ha-Medinot, or Council of Provinces.

It is interesting to note that the Jews who settled in Poland and
Russia, in contradistinction to all other Jews who settled in new
lands, did not adopt the language of their new country but continued to speak the language they brought with them from Germany. The Yiddish language, of course, is a jargon, with a large admixture of Hebrew and a smaller admixture of local expressions; but
its basic etymology is medieval German. Perhaps the primary cause

of this historic anomaly is the low cultural level of the Polish people, consisting largely of an illiterate peasantry. Furthermore, East European Jewry in the post-medieval period—not unlike the contemporary Sephardim—had little cultural interests beyond the study of talmudic lore. Philosophy and other secular studies were not only deemed unimportant; they were considered a dangerous opening to the winds of heresy.[39] But before we describe how this attitude gave birth at the beginning of the nineteenth century to a serious schism in Jewish life, for the sake of historic continuity we should make mention of several crises which passed over European Jewry in the seventeenth and eighteenth centuries.

Though most of the Polish rulers were inclined to favor their Jewish subjects—after all, Jewish business enterprise helped to swell their coffers—the ignorant and superstitious peasantry was constantly being aroused to hostility against the Jews by the Christian clergy. *Pogrom* is a word of Russian derivation and originally meant "devastation," but now it has come to mean brutal attacks of inflamed mobs against Jews. A wave of pogroms swept over Eastern Europe during the years 1648—55, initiated by the leader of the Ukrainian Cossacks, Chmielnicki; and he found willing partners in the Poles. (Three centuries later the Nazi hordes also found willing partners in Poland.) As in previous persecutions, the unquenchable faith of the Jew in his divinely ordained destiny endowed him with a stubborn courage to maintain his traditional way of life and communal institutions against all odds.

Nevertheless, persecution does exact its toll, and not only in the number of innocent lives mercilessly butchered. The desperate situation of Jewry, living on a volcano which erupted from time to time in pogroms, led thousands upon thousands of Jews to become entranced by the visionary mouthings of two pseudo-Messiahs, first Shabbatai Zvi and then Jacob Frank. Misguided and beguiled Jews were led ultimately to a repudiation of their religious faith and their membership in the Jewish people. Only the firm opposition to such false prophets on the part of the rabbinic leadership, which insisted on the halakhic norms of Jewish practice, preserved the bulk of Jewry from being led astray.

"It is an ill wind that blows no good." Out of the desperation of the Jewish situation arose a movement which calmed Jewish souls and restored to them the gladness and hope enshrined in the Jewish heritage. The movement, known as Hasidism, was born in the towns and villages of southeastern Poland, and despite the opposition to it at first by the established rabbinic leadership, it soon captivated the hearts and minds of thousands of devoted followers. Hasidism transformed the esoteric mysticism of the Kabbalah to a faith both in the benevolence of the Creator whose spirit permeated all of Nature and in the innate goodness of man. In the course of time there developed a convergence between the established rabbinate, which saw the preservation of Israel's traditional way of life in concentrated talmudic studies, and the Hasidic leadership. Today there is little that divides the heads of the Yeshivot and the heads of the Hasidic dynasties in their essential views. Both are agreed that the preservation of Judaism lies in the rigid maintenance of the traditional modes of practice, to the exclusion of any Jewish involvement in the radical changes brought about by the two movements of modern times which now have to be considered in relationship to Jewish autonomy; namely, the Emancipation and the Enlightenment.[40]

Emancipation and Enlightenment

Prior to the nineteenth century Jewish autonomy in Exile was based upon the special legal status accorded Jewish communities by the non-Jewish sovereign. With the spread of the Emancipation initiated by the French Revolution, granting Jewish citizens equal political status with all other citizens, this basis was removed. Now, for example, taxation was imposed upon Jews as individuals and not as members of a separate community, and Jews could participate in the civic affairs of the general community. More significantly, Jews regarded their acquisition of equal rights as an invitation to leave the confines of the ghetto and partake in the cultural activities of their non-Jewish neighbors. As a result, membership in the Jewish community became a voluntary act, and those Jews who wished to sever their affiliation with the community of Jews could now do so with comparative ease. Those Jews who wished to retain their identification with the Jewish community now expressed it in affiliation with a purely religious rather than national entity. But the more or less homogeneous concept of the Jewish religion as a system of divine commandments to be performed according to the prescriptions of the Halakhah was challenged by a growing segment of the community which subscribed to the new doctrines of Reform Judaism. Whereas heretofore, as has been pointed out several times in the course of our discussion, the primary leaders of Jewish self-government were halakhic scholars, now they were no longer able to exercise their authority over dissident individuals. Indeed, Reform Judaism not only repudiated the Halakhah, it also rejected the national aspirations of the Jewish people to return to Zion and reestablish the Jewish State.

A further undermining of the role of religion in Jewish life, thus weakening the structure of Jewish autonomy, was the phenomenon of the Haskalah, or Enlightenment, which began to entice more and more Jews away from the traditional modes of Jewish life. Emancipation and Enlightenment worked hand in hand to wean Jews away from long-established norms and views. The tradition of learning which had been nurtured for generations by the dictum of the Mishnah (Pe'ah 1:1) recited daily in the morning prayers, Talmud Torah ke-neged Kulam, "The study of the Torah is equal to all [deeds of righteousness],"[41] was transferred from the study of Talmud and Codes of Jewish Law to the study of secular subjects. In general, the nineteenth century saw the decline of religious faith and observance in face of the rapid advances in science and technology. There was, of course, a vigorous reaction to the liberalization of Jewish life and thinking by the traditional rabbinate, which pronounced a ban against the study of secular subjects, including the language of the country, in Jewish schools. The negation of secular culture by the more conservative Orthodox rabbis and heads of Yeshivot persists to this day,[42] they being little concerned with how religious Jews schooled only in the intricacies of Talmud and

Codes and lacking in secular knowledge and training, will be able to conduct the affairs of an independent Jewish state in our complex twentieth-century civilization.

The great hopes which Jews had placed in Emancipation, that it would bring relief from discrimination and persecution, were not realized. How could one hope to eradicate by simple governmental edict the accumulation of centuries of preachment and incitation to overt hostility! Furthermore, in Central Europe there was a reaction against the Napoleonic reforms, and these never reached Czarist Russia, where the bulk of European Jewry resided. The situation of the Jews under the czars became more and more oppressive, leading to the development of a movement for "auto-emancipation," the precursor of modern Zionism. Led primarily by "enlightened" Jews—indeed, its most vigorous opponents were the traditional rabbis—this movement's basic ideology maintained that the Jewish people are a nation not by virtue of their allegiance to the teachings of the Torah, a principle which had been enunciated by Saadia Gaon in the tenth century, but by virtue of their long history, which had generated a "national consciousness." Religious faith to these Zionists was a non-essential, though concededly important, ingredient in the growth of this national consciousness, and it could not serve as the basis for creating a revived Jewish nation. Jewish nationhood could be revived, it was argued, only if the Jewish people terminated the situation of Exile; i.e., only if they left the lands of the Diaspora and settled in a land where they would establish an independent, sovereign Jewish state. And historic consciousness dictated that this land be Eretz Yisrael, the only place where the Jewish people had experienced Jewish statehood in the past. It must also be noted that the dominant wing of the Zionist movement was convinced that a revived Jewish state could be built only on the doctrines of political and economic socialism.

In Mandated Palestine

The stubborn resolve of European Jewry for auto-emancipation, combined with the long experience of autonomy in the lands of the Dispersion, encouraged the Yishuv, the growing settlement of Jews in Eretz Yisrael, to create an organ of self-government even before the establishment of the State of Israel.[43] The stimulus for the creation of a political framework to conduct the affairs of the Yishuv, including such matters as economic development, education, foreign relations, and aliyah (the immigration of Jews to Palestine, a burning question at the time), had been provided by the Balfour Declaration in 1917 and its reaffirmation in the Mandate over Palestine conferred upon Great Britain in 1920. It is true that neither the Declaration nor the Mandate mentioned a sovereign Jewish state; they only spoke of "the establishment of a *national home* for the Jewish people." It was only in 1936 that the Peel Commission conceded that "by the words 'establishment of a national home' His Majesty's government recognized that in the course of time a Jewish state was likely to be established." Even though Theodor Herzl far back in 1895 had written *Der Judenstaat* (The Jewish State), Zionists were shy of stating openly that their goal was the creation of a sovereign Jewish state.[44] Only in 1942 did all the Zionist parties, meeting in New York, adopt a resolution which stated that "Palestine be established as a *Jewish Commonwealth* integrated in the structure of the new democratic world." (This was during World War II, when it was hoped that a new democratic world would emerge after the defeat of Hitler.)

Nevertheless, the pioneering settlers in Eretz Yisrael knew that the ultimate goal, even though unexpressed, was a *medinah*, and that the Yishuv constituted a *medinah ba-derekh*, the road to a full-fledged, internationally recognized Jewish state. They therefore proceeded to elect by democratic vote a National Assembly, which in turn elected the Vaad Leumi, the National Council, which was, in effect, the Parliament of the *medinah ba-derekh*. It is interesting to note that the Mizrachi Organization was at first opposed, on religious grounds, to granting women the right to vote, but later yielded to the majority opinion that a Jewish state must be democratic, with equality of the sexes a basic principle.[45] To this day, right-wing Orthodoxy, as represented by Agudat Yisrael, objects to women participating in elections and holding public office.

There was one task of an independent government which autonomous Jewish communities in the past had not assumed, but which the Yishuv did undertake, and with creditable success. This was the task of *haganah*, of self-defense, by means of an organized and properly equipped army. Though the British government had declared that it favored the establishment of a national home for the Jewish people, its representatives in Palestine did everything to discourage it. The Yishuv was subjeced to constant murderous attacks by the Arabs, while the mandatory power did everything to deprive the Jews of the ability to defend itself. As a result, the Haganah, the defense forces of the Yishuv, became an underground army which not only had to protect Jewish settlements against Arab marauders but had to resort to every sort of strategem in order to conceal its efforts from the British army stationed in Palestine for the purpose of maintaining law and order. The hostile British attitude prompted extreme elements among the Jews to launch random attacks against British personnel, but such acts were looked upon with disfavor by the Haganah.

We have now come full cycle round to the very beginning of our discussion, where we stated that every commonwealth has "the primary obligation of protecting the security of its people from any assault by an enemy." With the organization of the Haganah, the Yishuv proved that it was ready for the appropriate moment when it would be called upon to change its status from a *medinah ba-derekh* to a *medinah be-pho'al*, an actually functioning state. That moment came when Britain finally decided that it had to give up the Mandate and hand over the future of Palestine to the United Nations. The Vaad Leumi, which had created the instruments of self-government, had fulfilled its function of preparing the Yishuv for complete political independence. At the final session of the Vaad Leumi, held on February 13, 1949, the chairman, David Remez, spoke these words: "As the river flows into the sea, so Knesset Yisrael [the organized Yishuv] flows into Medinat Yisrael, which will endure forever."

We are convinced that there is a divine plan and purpose to the history of the Jewish people. Therefore, before we consider how the modern State of Israel incorporates the ideals of a Jewish state and strives to build its society in the image of the ancient hopes of the Jewish people, we must inquire into the purposes of Israel's protracted Exile and how Israel expressed its aspirations for Redemption. To that we devote the following two chapters.

9

The Compensations of Exile

The prophet Isaiah, speaking in the name of God, asserts: "Behold, the former things have come to pass and new things do I tell; before they spring forth I announce them to you" (Isa. 42:9). So is it with the broad pattern of Jewish history; it was told long before it began to unfold, announced by God even before we became a people. In the first covenant made by God with Abraham, the *brith bein ha-betharim* (the covenant sealed between the pieces), God said to Abraham: "Know surely that your offspring will be strangers in a land not theirs, and they will be enslaved and oppressed . . . but afterwards they will go free with great wealth" (Gen. 15:13–14). Here in a nutshell is the quintessence of Jewish history, Exile followed by Redemption.

This is a recurring pattern. Twice was it later foretold to the Jewish people, made part of the everlasting covenant between God and Israel: once at Mount Sinai (Lev. 26), and a second time forty years later in the plains of Moab at the edge of the Promised Land (Deut. 28). Nahmanides explains the repetition; the first prediction forecast *Galut Babel*, the Babylonian Exile of the sixth century B.C.E., and the second forecast *Galut Edom*, the Roman Exile of the first century C.E.

Though the ways of the Lord are hidden and we cannot always fathom the rationale of Jewish history, it behooves us to inquire after the meaning and purpose of our checkered history. Indeed, we are commanded to do so if only to vindicate God's working through human history; to be able to say with conviction: "All His ways are just, a faithful God and never false, righteous and proper is He" (Deut. 32:4).

Exile as Punishment

In the two covenants between God and Israel mentioned above, *galut* is postulated as punishment, dire retribution for Israel's failure to hearken to God and observe His commandments. Our Sages readily understood this as far as the First Exile is concerned. Israel in the days of the First Temple had committed the three cardinal sins of idolatry, murder, and sexual immorality. At the time of the Second Exile, however, such abominations could not be ascribed to the Jewish people. "Why was the Second Temple destroyed?" ask the Rabbis, "Did not the Jews then occupy themselves with Torah and mitzvot?" "Because," the Rabbis answer, "there was *sin'at hinnam*, unjustified hatred between Jew and fellow-Jew" (*Yoma* 9b).[1] Not completely satisfied with this explanation, the Rabbis offered another. "Jerusalem was destroyed because its inhabitants based their actions upon strict conformity with the law of the Torah and did not go beyond the requirements of the Law [i.e., in helping those in need]" (*Baba Metzia* 30b).[2]

The Rabbis also had to find an explanation for the inordinate and seemingly endless length of the Second Exile as compared with the brief period of the First (seventy years; Jer. 29:10). (If the Rabbis of the Talmud, who lived two hundred years after the *hurban*, found the Second Exile unduly long; how much more so must we, who live nineteen hundred years after the *hurban*, be sorely pressed to find an explanation for its length.) "The end of the Exile for the earlier Jews was disclosed because their sins were disclosed; the end of the Exile for the later Jews was not disclosed because their sins were not disclosed [i.e., they hid their sins, making a hypocritical pretense of piety]" (*Yoma* 9b).

Jewish Solidarity

Now we may be able to accept the Exiles of Babylonia and Rome as punishment for Israel's sins; but why were Exile and bondage ordained for the Israelites in Egypt, before they had received the Torah and hence before they could be held responsible for transgressing its commandments? We may well ask, as Abraham had asked, "Shall the judge of all the earth not exercise justice?" (Gen. 18:25). No doubt we must conclude that the experience of Exile, being strangers in a land not theirs, and even bondage and oppression under cruel taskmasters, engendered certain positive values which were essential for Israel's development as a godly people. The Torah refers to Egypt as a *kur ha-barzel*, an iron cauldron, saying: "The Lord took you and brought you forth out of the iron furnace, out of Egypt, to be unto Him His very own people" (Deut. 4:20). Egypt was a forge in which the peoplehood of Israel was molded. Common suffering forges the bonds of national solidarity. The Israelites in Egypt suffered, not as individuals, but as members of the people of Israel. When Pharaoh first planned to enslave them, he said: "*Behold*, the people *of the children of Israel*, etc." (Exod. 1:8). This is the lesson we have learned and transmitted to all generations. When a Jew is made to suffer because he is a Jew and for no other reason, then every fellow-Jew feels his pain and is stirred to action to relieve the suffering, even though he himself at the moment is not subjected to any harassment.

Such was the experience of Moses. Moses himself was not enslaved; he grew up as an Egyptian prince, adopted as a son by the daughter of Pharaoh. But when "he went out to his brothers and saw their burdens he saw an Egyptian smiting a Hebrew, one of his brothers . . . he smote the Egyptian" (Exod. 2:11−12). And this has been the experience of Jews ever since. There is no other people on earth throughout all history that can match the Jewish people in the spontaneous and ready assistance that the more fortunate among them have rendered their less fortunate brothers. All Exiles that Israel has suffered have deepened within its members the consciousness that "all Jews are responsible one for the other" (*Sifra* to Lev. 26:37; *Shebuot* 39a). We do not bear the mark of Cain, who said: "Am I my brother's keeper?" (Gen. 4;9). We bear the mark of Esther, who said: "How can I endure to see the evil that is to befall my people; how can I endure to see the destruction of my birthplace?'' (Esther 8:6).

Jewish Social Sensitivity

Furthermore, the experience of bondage and oppression has sensitized every Jew to all bondage and oppression. We appreciate the blessings of freedom all the more precisely because we have endured the hardships and indignities of slavery. Thus the Jew is the first to cry out against injustice and tyranny. He is in the forefront of all movements of social justice, "to loosen the fetters of wickedness, to undo the bands of the yoke, to let the oppressed go free" (Isa. 58:6). We can empathize with the stranger all the more precisely because we ourselves have been strangers, aliens in lands not our own. So does the Torah affirm when it commands us: "Do not oppress a stranger for you know well the feelings of the stranger since you yourselves were strangers in the land of Egypt" (Exod. 23:9). Nay more, "As a native among you shall be the stranger who resides with you; love him as yourself, for you were strangers in the land of Egypt" (Lev. 19:34).[3]

When the Torah admonishes against dealing unjustly with those who are most vulnerable to exploitation and injustice, it includes the stranger with the orphan and the widow. "You shall not wrong nor oppress a stranger, for you were strangers in the land of Egypt. You shall not ill-treat any widow or orphan" (Exod. 22:20—21). When the Torah speaks of the obligation to succor the needy, it includes the stranger with the poor. "When you reap the harvest of your land, you shall not reap all the way to the corner of your field . . . you shall leave it for the poor and the stranger" (Lev. 19:9—10). Maimonides, when recording the mitzvah of rejoicing on the Festival with eating and drinking, adds the following: "When one eats and drinks he is duty-bound to feed the stranger, the fatherless, and the widow with other unfortunate poor; and he who shuts the doors of his abode and eats and drinks with his wife and children but does not give food and drink to the poor and the miserable of spirit, it is not a rejoicing of the mitzvah but a rejoicing of his stomach. . . . Such a rejoicing is shameful."[4] Thus the Jew has been taught to be most ready and generous in philanthropy, "to share his bread with the hungry, and bring the homeless poor into his house; to clothe the naked when he sees him, and not to hide himself from his needy kin" (Isa. 58:7).

Jewish Faith in the Redeemer

The prophet has said: "A righteous man lives by his faith" (Hab. 2:4). The experience of *galut* has taught the people of Israel to live by its faith in God, the Redeemer of Israel. And this faith in God is expressed in crying out to Him in our anguish, as did the children of Israel in Egypt. "And the children of Israel groaned from the toil and cried out, and their plea for help from the toil rose up to God" (Exod. 2:23). Perhaps the command implied in the first of the Ten Commandments, "I am the Lord your God, Who took you out of the land of Egypt, from the house of bondage" (Exod. 20:2) is just this: "Israel, live by your faith in your Redeemer."[5] We have indeed fulfilled this commandment with all intensity of devotion and loyalty, our history affirming the contention of Job (13:15): "Though He slay me, yet will I trust in him." Inextinguishable faith has given us the stamina and resolve to persevere amidst the harshest of circumstances. Had we lost it, God forfend, we could not have survived to this day.

Paradoxical as it may seem, God inflicts suffering upon us so that we should be cognizant of the fact that He is "the sustainer of life in kindness . . . supporter of the falling and healer of the sick"; that to Him we must turn for our daily sustenance as well as for relief from sorrow and distress. The Sages say: "Why were the matriarchs barren; because the Holy One, blessed be He, yearns to hear the prayer of the righteous" (*Bereishit Rabbah* 45:4.) Is there any prayer in all of Scripture—nay, in all of human expression—as stirring in its emotion, as full in its outpouring of thanksgiving, as majestic in its extolling the powers of the Almighty, as the prayer of Hannah, the barren woman who became a mother (I Sam. 2:1—10)!

Jewish Distinctiveness

The experience of living "in a land not their own" at the very beginning of its peoplehood has taught the Jewish people how to retain its particular identity in a world so universally antagonistic to and corrosive of its basic faith and ideals. On the passage "And there he [Jacob][6] became a nation" (Deut. 26:5) our Sages comment: "This teaches us that the Israelites were distinguished there" (i.e., they retained their peculiar way of life and had not assimilated Egyptian manners and customs).[7]

When Balaam surveyed the Israelites encamped in the wilderness shortly after their leaving Egypt, he was struck by a quality which was to characterize them throughout their subsequent history. "Here is a people that dwells alone, not reckoned among the nations" (Num. 23:9). "Dwelling alone" does not mean dwelling completely isolated physically from all other peoples, shut off from the rest of the world by impenetrable ghetto walls. It does mean that Israel dwells alone by preserving its own particular culture, its own beliefs and peculiar customs, rendering its individual members distinguishable as Jews even when mingling with other peoples.[8]

It is a fact of life, however, that no person or people is completely immune to the influence of its cultural environment; and therefore the people of Israel required constant admonition "not to follow the practices of the land of Egypt wherein you dwelt, or the practices of the land of Canaan whither I am bringing you; nor shall you practice their statutes" (Lev. 18:3).[9] Even a cursory reading of the Prophets will disclose the sorry fact that the Israelites in Canaan did not heed this admonition; they practiced all the abominations of the Canaanites against which the Torah had warned. In a chapter reviewing Israel's many backslidings, the Psalmist charges: "They mingled with the nations and learned their practices" (Ps. 106:35). The Sages of the Talmud, interpreting Ezekiel's castigation of the

Jewish people for their sins, charged: "You have done like the worst among the Gentiles, and have not done like the best of them" (*Sanhedrin* 39b).

In the days of Ezra and Nehemiah, "the people of Israel, the priests, and the Levites, did not keep themselves separate from the peoples of the lands, practicing their abominations . . . for they took wives from their daughters for themselves and for their sons, so that the holy seed mingled with the peoples of the lands [Ezra 9:1—2] . . . and their sons, half spoke Ashdodite and do not know how to speak the language of the Judeans" (Neh. 13:24). And we know very well the tremendous influence of Hellenistic culture upon the inhabitants of Judea in the days of the Second Temple. The dangers inherent in these negative influences alerted the Rabbis to institute legislation designed to reduce the contact between Jew and non-Jew. "The bread and oil of Gentiles were banned lest we drink of their wine; their wine was banned lest we marry their daughters; their daughters were banned lest we fall into idolatry" (*Abodah Zarah* 36b).[10]

These halakhic restrictions built up a wall of separation between Jew and non-Jew, enabling the former to "dwell alone" in the many lands of the Diaspora, a part of humanity but apart from it. And as a result of its many Exiles the Jewish people built up an immunity against the overwhelming influence of the non-Jewish environment. It is a moot question as to what extent Jewish law and custom today have been determined by the outlook and customs of non-Jewish neighbors. It would be idle to deny the fact of such influence, though many historians tend to exaggerate it. On the other hand, one cannot truthfully contend that such influence has always been of a negative and harmful character. What can be asserted without fear of contradiction is that the Jewish people has always been aware of its special position among the peoples of the earth; affirming what King David said: "Who is like Your people Israel, one nation in the earth" (II Sam. 7:23).

As the people of Israel gathers once again in the land of its fathers, it must retain this sense of distinctiveness (*yihud*) and special purpose (*yi'ud*). The world today, with its advanced methods of global communication, is fast becoming one world as far as general cultural values are concerned. It is neither possible nor even desirable for the citizens of the new Jewish state to attempt to withdraw themselves into a cultural island and deny themselves free communication with all that is going on in the world. But they must take to heart the lessons learned in the Exile by building their own cultural fortress on the foundation of their past history and traditions, ensuring that their state will be distinguishable as a *Jewish* state, nurturing for its posterity its divinely appointed purpose to be "a kingdom of priests and a holy nation."

Israel a Light to the Nations

Israel's distinctiveness and its awareness of its special destiny is a direct consequence of its faith that it is a Chosen People, chosen by God to be His precious treasure. "For you are a people consecrated to the Lord your God; the Lord your God has chosen you to be His treasured people [*am segulah*] from among all the peoples on the face of the earth" (Deut. 7:6). This is a basic tenet of our faith, oft repeated in our liturgy.[11] Unfortunately, this dogma of traditional Judaism has been grossly misinterpreted, both by Jews and non-Jews. An egregious example of one of the latter is the late renowned historian Arnold Toynbee, who branded Israel's concept of the Chosen People as a conceited claim to racial superiority that has passed over into the Christian dogma that "there is no salvation outside the Church," and that, in turn, has spawned the evil of Western imperialism lording it over the primitive peoples of Asia and Africa. Other detractors of the Jewish people have equated it with the Nazi theory of Aryan superiority, and condemned it as the source of the unbridled nationalism of the nineteenth and twentieth centuries which is at the root of all international warfare and confrontation. Reform Jews, influenced by these malicious interpretations, have eliminated from their prayerbook all expressions of Israel's chosenness.

A look at the sources of Judaism, both biblical and rabbinic, will demonstrate that Israel's chosenness was not conceived for its own national aggrandizement at the expense and to the detriment of other nations. On the contrary, its primary purpose is for the blessing and enhancement of all other peoples. Nay more, being chosen as it were to be the favorite people of God has imposed upon Israel special burdens and responsibilities. "Only you have I known from all the families of the earth, therefore I shall visit upon you all your iniquities" (Amos 3:2). The first divine message communicated to the first Jew, Abraham our Father, concluded: "Through you all the families of the earth will be blessed" (Gen. 12:3). And this blessing will come to pass only as Abraham and his descendants communicate to all nations that come within their ambience their faith in the One God, Creator of heaven and earth, Who demands of His creatures justice and righteousness. Thus Israel is chosen to be "the servant of the Lord," whose task is to banish the darkness and superstition of idolatry by spreading the light of the true faith. "I the Lord have called upon you in righteousness, and have taken hold of your hand, and have fashioned you, and have made you a people of the covenant, a light of the nations. You are My witnesses, says the Lord, and My servant whom I have chosen" (Isa. 42:6, 43:10).

To better accomplish this task, God has ordained Exile for His people. "God has caused Israel to go into Exile only so that converts [gerim] may be added to them," say our Sages (Pesahim 87b). The prophet who lived one century after the First Exile could already say: "From the rising of the sun to its setting My name is great among the nations; everywhere is incense offered to My name" (Mal. 1:11). In the Middle Ages, both Yehudah Halevi and Maimonides acknowledged the spread of faith in One God by Christianity and Islam because of the Judaic teachings which they incorporate.[12] And despite the widespread lack of moral principle exhibited today by political—and even some religious—leaders, one cannot deny that Israel's dispersion among the nations has moved humanity at large to a profounder appreciation of the principles of justice and charity. Thus the particularism of Judaism has a universal purpose; the Jewish longing for the Redemption of Israel is the prologue of its longing for the Redemption of all mankind.

This universalist aspect of Judaism has not been fully understood, especially when it was appropriated by the Church, which conceives one of its major purposes to be the conversion of all peoples to Christianity. When Judaism speaks of the conversion of the Gentiles to the true faith, it does not mean that it seeks the adoption of Judaism in its totality by every non-Jew. On the contrary, any applicant for full conversion to Judaism is discouraged. We say to him: "What do you see in Judaism? Be aware that Judaism imposes many restrictions which do not apply to the righteous non-Jew. Now you are not liable to observe them; the moment you convert, you will be liable. And aren't you aware that Jews today suffer persecution and discrimination, and the moment you adopt Judaism you subject yourself to the ignominious lot of the Jew?" (*Yebamot* 47a). What Judaism seeks of the non-Jew is that he undertake to fulfill "the seven mitzvot of the sons of Noah," which if universally accepted and practiced would set up a society of law and order based upon the sanctity of human life and the equality of all persons.[13] This is the meaning of the prophetic statement that in the end of days "All the peoples will walk each in the name of its God, and we will walk in the name of the Lord our God forever" (Mic. 4:5). That is, each people will continue to worship the true God in its own particular way, while the Jewish people will continue to observe its own religious traditions.

Another misconception of Judaism's universalism was manifested by the leaders of Reform Judaism when they eliminated from their prayerbook all references to Israel's national redemption and return to Zion. Israel's mission and everlasting destiny, they mistakenly argued, was to live permanently in Exile among the *goyim* in order to bring to them the word of God as preached by the Hebrew prophets. They little realized that Israel's mission has two aspects: first, to teach our non-Jewish neighbors the basic universal principles of morality through personal example of moral rectitude, and then to teach the family of *goyim*, i.e., the nations qua nations, the true concept of nationhood. The former would be accomplished as Jews are dispersed amongst the peoples of the earth; the latter when there is restored to the Jewish people its own independent

state, a state that will serve as the example par excellence of the ideal
state.

The Boon of Jewish Dispersion

The final compensation that Israel has derived from its Exiles and
dispersion over the face of the earth is found in the following
talmudic statement: "The Holy One, blessed be He, was charitable
with Israel in scattering them among the nations" (*Pesahim* 87b).
The charity consisted in the phenomenon that all Jews were not exiled to only one country, making them totally vulnerable to the evil
design of a Haman "to destroy, to kill, to exterminate all the Jews,
from young to old, children and women, all in one day" (Esther
3:13). Now if attacked and destroyed in one country, there would
survive in another country a sizable group from which the Jewish
people could regenerate itself. Nay more, the surviving group would
rescue and rehabilitate the living remnant of the attacked group.
This was a tactic learned from our Father Jacob. When he prepared
himself for a confrontation with his brother Esau, "he divided the
people with him into two camps, saying, If Esau will come to one of
the camps and smite it, then the remaining camp may yet escape"
(Gen. 32:8–9). Upon which the Sages comment: "The *smitten
camp* refers to our brothers in the south [i.e., in Judea]; the *remaining camp* refers to our brothers in the Exile" (*Bereishit Rabbah*
76:3). Saving remnants and remnants saved has been a repeated
feature of Jewish history, and never to a greater extent than in our
most recent history. Would the Jewish people ever have been able to
recover from the devastation of the Nazi Holocaust if American
Jewry were not present and ready as an unfailing source of regenera-
tion and continued hope for a vital future?

We have so far made no reference in our discusssion of Israel's
experience of Exile to the cultural wealth which accrued to the
Jewish people during their dwelling in the Diaspora and which has
now become an integral part of our heritage. The Babylonian
Talmud, the biblical commentaries and philosophic works of the

Middle Ages, the varied literature of the modern era of Emancipation, all are products of Jews in Exile who have enriched Jewish life and thought. Verily, God's promise, "And afterwards they will go free with great wealth" (Gen. 15:14), has been fulfilled, a compensation for centuries of suffering and bondage. We therefore dare not forget or ignore or denigrate—as some native Israelis are wont to do—the experience of *galut.* The revived Jewish state is not a continuum of ancient Judea, but a continuation of Jewish history in all its phases. We must conclude with Yehuda Halevi that "there is a hidden wisdom in God's allowing us to remain in Exile, comparable to the wisdom concealed in the kernel of a seed" (*Kuzari* 4:23). As the seed planted in the ground contains within itself, undisclosed to the naked eye, the potential of germination and fruition, so the seed of Exile has germinated and produced a people refined in its character, consolidated in its loyalties, fortified in its faith, enriched in its knowledge, and educated for its universal role.

In the final analysis, however, the ultimate goal of Jewish history is not dispersion, but ingathering; not Exile, but Return; not bondage, but freedom. How the Jewish people in Exile kept their sights upon this ultimate goal and eagerly awaited Redemption is the subject of the next chapter.

10

I Believe with a Perfect Faith in the Coming of the Messiah

Legend has it that the Messiah, whose coming will usher in the Era of Redemption for the people of Israel, was born on Tish'ah B'ab, the day of the destruction of the Holy Temple in Jerusalem.[1] Actually, the anticipation of the advent of a scion of the House of David to rule over a united and independent Kingdom of Israel reached a high pitch a century before the *hurban*. Indeed, it was the charged atmosphere of expectation that made it possible for Jesus the Nazarene to declare himself the King Messiah, and for his followers to accept this declaration as gospel truth.[2] During the second century B.C.E., a spate of apocalyptic literature appeared, predicting the imminent approach of the "End of Days." Almost all of these eschatological writings were rejected by the Tannaim two centuries later as not appropriate for inclusion in the *kitvei ha-kodesh*, the Hagiographa or Sacred Writings, and were consigned to the category of *seforim hitzonim*, or Apocrypha.[3] One book, however, was accepted and sanctified by its inclusion in the canon of Sacred Scripture; namely, the Book of Daniel. Consequently, its eschatological chapters (10–12) became the basis for all subsequent Messianic hope and speculation.

Daniel was by no means the first to speak of *aharit ha-yamim*, the End of Days; though—as we shall see—he added to the concept certain novel elements. The first to speak of the End of Days was our Father Jacob, who summoned his children to his deathbed in order to reveal to them "what will happen to you in the End of Days" (Gen. 49:1).⁴ The phrase *aharit ha-yamim*, coined by Jacob and later employed by the prophets (Isa. 2:2, Mic. 4:1), implies that there is an end-purpose, or ultimate goal, to history.⁵ Thus was implanted in Jewish consciousness the unique idea that history is not an unending concatenation of fortuitous events, but a progression of humanity that will ultimately eventuate in a perfect world. This perfect world will come into being when the people of Israel experience the *Ge'ulah Shelemah*, the Complete Redemption. The concept of Redemption, with its concomitant figure of the Messiah, in itself underwent progression and expansion of formulation in the course of Jewish history.

The Stages of Redemption

In all accounts of the Redemption, there occurs a prior revelation that announces its advent. We have already referred to the first such announcement, made by God to Abraham (see above p. 130). Later, when God told Moses that the divine promise to Abraham was about to be fulfilled, Moses was instructed to announce it to the children of Israel. "Therefore say unto the children of Israel: I am the Lord, and I will bring you out from under the burdens of Egypt, and I will deliver you from their bondage, and I will redeem you with an outstretched arm and with great judgments, and I will take you to Me for a people" (Exod. 6:6−7). The Sages see in these verses four expressions of *ge'ulah*, the basis for the ruling that "even the poorest in Israel shall not drink less than four cups of wine" at the Seder meal on the first night of Passover (Mishnah *Pesahim* 10:1; J.T. ibid.). These four cups of wine are also symbolic of the future Redemption, when the Almighty will give the nations who oppressed Israel during its Exile four bitter cups of retribution to drink, and He will give Israel four sweet cups of consolation to drink (J.T. ibid.). There is also a fifth expression of *ge'ulah* following the first four: "And I will bring you in unto the land concerning which I lifted up My hand to give it to Abraham, to Isaac, and to Jacob: and I will give it to you for a heritage: I am the Lord" (v. 8). This expression is represented at the Seder table by a fifth cup of wine, "the cup of Elijah," the one who is destined to announce the coming of the Messiah.[6] The use of more than one expression for the Redemption indicates that it will not come to pass in one instantaneous moment, but in stages, in a series of events leading to and culminating in the *Ge'ulah Shelemah*, the Complete Redemption.

Moses made another announcement of Redemption, on the last day of his life as the children of Israel were poised to cross the Jordan into the Promised Land. After warning them of the dire sufferings they were bound to undergo in the future Exile, he assured them that they would eventually be redeemed. In this announcement, Moses implied that the future Redemption will take place in three stages:

1. The people of Israel will repent of the idolatry which brought about the Exile, and will return to the exclusive worship of God and the observance of His commandments. "And it shall be when all these things will come upon you . . . you will reflect in your heart among all the nations whither the Lord your God has driven you, and you will return unto the Lord your God and hearken to His voice according to all that I command you this day, you and your children, with all your heart and with all your soul" (Deut. 30:1–2). This stage will come to pass while the people are still dispersed in Exile.

2. The people will then be gathered from the dispersion and be returned to the land of their fathers. "Then the Lord your God will return your captivity and have compassion upon you, and will return and gather you from all the peoples whither the Lord your God has scattered you" (v. 3). The Tannaim are divided as to whether the "Ten Lost Tribes" who were carried away into captivity by Sennacherib of Assyria are to be included in this process of ingathering. Rabbi Akiba maintains that they are not destined to return, whereas Rabbi Eliezer maintains that they will see the light of Redemption (Mishnah *Sanhedrin* 10:3). Present-day history vindicates the opinion of Rabbi Eliezer. Jews from Kurdistan, Afghanistan, and India,

some of whom are undoubtedly descendants of the Ten Lost Tribes, have now been ingathered and returned to Eretz Yisrael.[7] (Incidentally, the term employed by the Torah for the people in Exile is *shevut*, and the first law passed by the Knesset after the establishment of the State of Israel is *hok ha-shevut*, the law guaranteeing the right of every Jew to return to Eretz Yisrael and settle therein.)

3. The people, returned to their homeland, will settle therein permanently and enjoy blessings greater than those enjoyed by their forefathers. "And the Lord your God will bring you into the land which your fathers possessed and you will possess it; and He will do you good and increase you more than your fathers" (v. 5).[8]

Repentance: The Forerunner of Redemption

Two Tannaim who lived in the generation of the *hurban* disputed a fundamental question concerning the Redemption as outlined above. Rabbi Eliezer maintained that stage 2, i.e., return to the land, cannot begin unless and until stage 1, i.e., return to God, comes to pass. He said: "If Israel repents, they will be redeemed; if they do not repent, they will not be redeemed." Rabbi Yehoshua, on the other hand, maintained that the Exile cannot endure forever; there has to be a limit to Israel's suffering in the Diaspora. Each Tanna adduces a number of scriptural passages to verify his opinion. Finally, Rabbi Yehoshua quotes a verse from Daniel (12:7), after which Rabbi Eliezer remains silent, apparently conceding to Rabbi Yehoshua (*Sanhedrin* 97b–98a). The argument, however, persisted among the Rabbis, as we find the two great Amoraim several generations later similarly divided. Rav maintained the opinion of Rabbi Eliezer that repentance is a sine qua non of Redemption; whereas Samuel argued like Rabbi Yehoshua that just as every period of mourning comes to an end, so must the period of Israel's exile come to an end, whether or not they repent (ibid.).

A closer examination of the biblical chapter cited above will reveal that these two opinions can be reconciled. The Bible actually speaks of more than three stages in the progress toward Redemption. Following the three stages already forecast, the Torah once again predicts: "And you will return and hearken to the voice of the Lord, and you will do all His commandments which I command you this day." And then, "the Lord your God will make you overabundant in all the work of your hand, in the fruit of your body and in the fruit of your cattle and in the fruit of your land, for good" (v. 8—9). The repetition of the phrase "and you will return and hearken to the voice of God" leads us to conclude that there are two stages to Israel's repentance, one before the return to the land and the other after the return. In fact, the Talmud speaks of two different categories of repentance, one induced by suffering, and the other by the love of God (Yoma 86a). The first manifestation of Israel's repentance will come as a result of Israel's intense suffering in the Diaspora. This will arouse God's compassion for His people, for Israel's Exile will have reached its climax and the time for the ingathering of the dispersed will have arrived.[9] Indeed, Rabbi Yehoshua avers that when the time for the ingathering comes and Israel is not yet repentant of its sins and worthy of Redemption, "The Holy One, blessed be He, will raise up over Israel a king whose evil designs are as severe as Haman's, whereupon Israel will repent" (Sanhedrin 97b). (Now we may well ponder if this sequence of events parallels that of our own times, the climactic suffering heaped upon our people by Hitler, followed by the kibbutz galuyot we are now witnessing.)

Once the process of ingathering proceeds—and its duration may well depend upon human as well as Divine initiative—Israel will possess the land of its fathers by establishing therein an independent and sovereign commonwealth. Thus established, the people, out of a sense of gratitude and love for God for having saved them from utter annihilation, will return to God and observe His commandments with all their hearts and with all their souls, and thus create a society of justice and righteousness. In this ideal society prosperity and peace will reign and all will be secure with nothing to fear. Then God's covenant with His chosen people will be fully and eternally confirmed. This is the aharit ha-yamim, the End of Days, which marks the culmination of the Messianic era.[10]

The Prophetic Concept of the End of Days

The covenant, as revealed by God (Lev. 26:3–9) and by Moses (Deut. 28:1–14), gives us but the barest outline of the future ideal society. It remained for Israel's prophets to fill in and elaborate upon the glorious promise and hope given to God's chosen people, and through them—as we shall see—to all humankind. After the division of the Jewish kingdom into two—the Kingdom of Judah in the south and the Kingdom of Israel in the north—in the days of Rehoboam son of Solomon, and with the increasing threats to both kingdoms by the growing power of the Assyrian Empire, the people began to look back with nostalgia upon the reigns of David and Solomon. It could not be forgotten that King David had initiated, and his son Solomon had brought to majestic fruition, the two greatest achievements in Jewish history, the one temporal and the other spiritual: the expansion and consolidation of Jewish hegemony over a vast area, and the building of the splendid House of the Lord, the Beit ha-Mikdash dedicated to the worship of the Lord God of Israel. The times of David and Solomon were pictured in the most idyllic terms. The wealth and power and universally recognized wisdom of King Solomon were described in elaborate detail (I Kings, chaps. 5 and 10). Typical are the following statements: "Judah and Israel dwelt securely, every man under his vine and under his fig tree, from Dan to Beer-sheba, all the days of Solomon" (5:5); "Silver was thought of as nothing in the days of Solomon" (10:21); "All the earth sought the presence of Solomon to hear his wisdom" (10:24).

Thus it came about that visions of the ideal future were seen as a restoration of the Davidic dynasty in all its glory and power. Outstanding among all these visions were those of Isaiah. In a rhapsodic chapter (11), he predicts that the future king of Israel "shall come forth as a shoot out of the stock of Jesse [the father of David], upon whom shall rest the spirit of the Lord, the spirit of wisdom and understanding, the spirit of counsel and might, the spirit of knowledge and the fear of the Lord." He will rule with justice, protecting the weak and slaying the wicked. Nay more, Nature itself will be transformed from a jungle of the strong devouring the weak into a paradise of peace and harmony. "The wolf shall dwell with the lamb, and the leopard shall lie down with the kid . . . and a little child shall lead them.[11] . . . They shall not hurt nor destroy in all My holy mountain, for the earth shall be full of the knowledge of the Lord as the waters cover the sea. In that day shall the root of Jesse that stands as a banner of the peoples, unto him shall the nations seek."

In a previous chapter (2), Isaiah had portrayed *aharit ha-yamim* as an era of universal peace, when "nations will beat their swords into ploughshares and their spears into pruning-hooks; nation shall not lift up sword against nation, neither shall they learn war any more." And the source of all wisdom and guidance will be God's word, spoken from "the mountain of the Lord, the House of the God of Jacob; for out of Zion shall go forth the Torah, and the word of the Lord from Jerusalem."[12]

All the prophets understood that such idyllic peace could not be achieved without a prior demonstration of the transitory nature and ultimate futility of wickedness and the lust for power. Therefore, the oppressors of the weak and the poor, who seized power through ruthless injustice, will be cut down, when the "Day of the Lord" comes to pass. On that great and awesome day of retribution—and a day here can only mean an epochal period of time—"the loftiness of man shall be brought low, and the haughtiness of men shall be humbled, and the Lord alone shall be exalted in that day" (Isa. 2:11). Not only will the haughty and the wicked individuals in Israel meet their just deserts; all the mighty nations that had oppressed Israel were included in the scathing previews of the prophets, all of them doomed to be bereft of their dominion and their peoples exiled.

The mighty, of course, do not easily surrender their dominion. Great battles will ensue, as the wicked attempt to hold on to their power. But to no avail, the outcome of the battle is foreordained. Good will triumph over evil, for the Lord has spoken; and the just will live on to enjoy the long-awaited vindication of their righteousness. But the battle will be a fierce one; the whole world will become a battlefield as a cataclysmic disaster befalls the earth on the Day of the Lord. The final battle will be waged in the Holy Land, on the mountains of Eretz Yisrael. The prophet Ezekiel, referring to his predecessors who had spoken of the End of Days when Israel will be dwelling securely in their homeland, predicts that even then a mighty nation, Gog, will wage a tremendous battle on the land of Israel.[13] God's anger will then be aroused, "and on that day there will be a great upheaval. The fish of the sea and the birds of heaven and the beasts of the field . . . and all men that are upon the face of the earth will tremble in My presence. The mountains will be destroyed, and the steep places and every wall will fall to the earth . . . . And I will judge him with pestilence and with blood, and I will rain down upon him and upon the many nations that are with him a torrential rain and stones of hail, fire and brimstone" (Ezek. 38).

Such and similar prophecies introduced into the Messianic concept an awesome and terrifying period which will encompass Israel at the time of Redemption. Daniel predicts that then "there will be a time of trouble such as never was since there had ever been a nation" (Dan. 12:1). The hardships that will transpire at the time of "the footsteps of the Messiah," spelled out in all their horrifying detail by the Sages (Mishnah *Sotah* 9:15), were so vivid in the minds of the Rabbis that some of them exclaimed: "Let him come, but I do not want [to live] to see him" (*Sanhedrin* 98a). These are the *hevlei mashiach*, the birth pangs of the Messiah, which became an integral part of the Messianic faith.

Elijah: The Bearer of Good Tidings

We said that the coming of the Messiah is to be heralded by someone with a message from on High, a bearer of good tidings. Isaiah describes him as follows: "How beautiful upon the mountains are the feet of the messenger of good tidings; he announces peace, he is the harbinger of good tidings who announces salvation" (Isa. 52:7). The last of the prophets, Malachi, reveals the name of this hitherto anonymous messenger. "Behold I send to you Elijah the prophet before the coming of the great and awful Day of the Lord" (3:24). Most probably, Elijah was chosen for this pleasant task because of his ascension to heaven in a whirlwind while yet alive (II Kings 2), and presumably kept alive for this very purpose. At any rate, Elijah has become in Jewish tradition an ever-present intermediary between Heaven and earth. He is called "the angel of the covenant," present at the circumcision of every Jewish male child, where a special chair *(kissei shel eliyahu)* is reserved for him. We have already mentioned the cup of wine reserved for him at the Seder, and indeed we open the door of our homes on Seder night in order to welcome him, hoping that he brings the coveted tidings concerning the Messiah. Eliyahu ha-Navi is also reported to have visited and conversed with certain Rabbis of the Talmud (e.g., *Baba Metzia* 85b). The Talmud relates that Rabbi Yehoshua ben Levi (Palestinian Amora, first half of the third century) found Elijah at the entrance to Rabbi Simeon ben Yohai's grave and asked him: "When is the Messiah coming?" Elijah answered: "Go and ask him yourself." "Where can I find him?" "He is at the entrance to the City of Rome." Whereupon Rabbi Yehoshua went there and greeted the Messiah, who was binding up the wounds of the sick. "When are you coming?" Rabbi Yehoshua asked. "Today," was the ready response. Rabbi Yehoshua then returned and reported this to Elijah, accusing the Messiah of telling a falsehood since he did not come on that day. Whereupon Elijah explained, "Messiah meant the *today* of the verse, 'Today if you will hearken to His voice' [Psalms 95:7]."

The expectation of Elijah's arrival was so real to the Rabbis that it affected their halakhic decisions. Thus it was ruled that consecrated food, unfit for consumption because of a doubt concerning its ritual cleanness, should not be burned—"perhaps Elijah will come and declare it clean" (*Pesahim* 15a,34a).[14] Furthermore, "Israel was assured that Elijah will not come on the eve of a Sabbath or Festival, lest he disturb their preparations for the holiday" (*Erubin* 43b). His arrival was most expected on a Saturday night, after the outgoing of the Sabbath rest. Thus the hymns composed for and sung on Saturday nights are all dedicated to Eliyahu ha-Navi, and express the hope that "may he speedily come unto us with Messiah the son of David." The Messiah himself, however, may come on a Friday, for as soon as he comes non-Jewish servants will attend to the necessary preparations for the Sabbath while the Jews go out to welcome their redeemer (*Erubin* 43b).

Expectations and Calculations

It was natural to assume that the glorious period of the End of Days, so optimistically portrayed by the prophets, would be realized after the Return to Zion from the Babylonian Exile and the building of the Second Temple.[15] If at the beginning of this period Israel did not enjoy complete sovereignty in its homeland—an integral condition of the Complete Redemption—then at least with the establishment of the Hasmonean dynasty it was natural to assume that the Redemption was nigh. However, the unmessianic realities of the Hasmonean period posed a dilemma. On the one hand, the dawn of the Messianic period was said to be a time of cataclysmic events and great disasters, and in the toppling of mighty empires in the wars of the Greeks and Romans one could see exactly what had been predicted. On the other hand, the amazingly sweeping conquests of these peoples from the north did not seem to bring any closer that utopian age of the ultimate triumph of righteousness over evil. So the puzzling question arose, Where do we stand in relationship to the coming of the End of Days? When can we really expect the coming of the Messiah?

Answers to these questions were given in the apocalyptic literature mentioned above. But the answers were framed in veiled terms, and revealed only to a select person or group by some mysterious messenger from on high. Daniel received several of these mystical revelations, but was told: "Conceal the vision, for it is for many days [in the future]" (Dan. 8:26, 12:4, 8). One revelation was conveyed to him by the angel Gabriel (Dan. 9:21; incidentally, the first time an angel is mentioned by name in the Bible). Another, by "a man clothed in linen . . . whose body was like beryl, his face as the appearance of lightning and his eyes as torches of fire, his arms

and feet like the color of burnished brass, and the voice of his words
like the voice of a multitude" (Dan. 10:5—6). He said to Daniel: "I
have come to make you understand what will befall your people in
the End of Days" (Dan. 10:14), but Daniel could not fully comprehend the allusions to various periods of time. Nevertheless, he
was assured, "Happy is he that waits in hope. . . . you will rest and
you will rise to your fate in the End of Days" (Dan. 12:12—13).[16]
Here Daniel was assured that he would be among "the many that
sleep in the dust of the earth who shall awake, some to everlasting
life" (Dan. 12:12); namely, the righteous who will be resurrected in
the End of Days in order to receive the merited reward of being alive
in an era of universal peace and prosperity.

Daniel's apocalypses set into motion a train of ideas—
speculations would be a better word—concerning the End of Days.
First of all, the rabbinic designation for this future ideal period was
the term used by Daniel, the *ketz*, or end, rather than the term used
by the prophets, *aharit ha-yamim*. Perhaps this was due to the
emphasis that had been put upon the unprecedented troubles that
would mark the dawn of the new era, and people were more wishful
for the *end* to the troubles than for the blessings of utopia. The term
mashiah, or anointed, had been used by the prophets to denote kings
in the present unredeemed world; in post-biblical literature,
however, *mashiah* referred specifically to the scion of David who
would restore Israel's political independence. Thus another favorite
designation by the Rabbis of the future king of Israel was *ben
David*, son of David.

Mashiah was conceived as a person, though very little is said by
the Rabbis concerning his personality and activities. Of greater interest was the state of affairs that would prevail in the world in
yemot ha-mashiah, the days of the Messiah. Here fantasy had free
rein. "The period of gestation will be one day" (*Shabbat* 30b);
"non-fruit-bearing trees will bear fruit; bread and clothing will
grow ready-made on trees" (*Kethubot* 111b). The resurrection of the
dead, *tehiyat ha-meithim*, was declared to be an incontrovertible
dogma of Judaism, already alluded to in many biblical verses

(Mishnah *Sanhedrin* 11:1), and the resurrected dead will rise from their graves fully clothed (*Kethubot* 111b). Furthermore, they will be wined and dined; the wine stored for the occasion from the Six Days of Genesis, the fish from the prehistoric Leviathan, and the meat from an ancient wild ox.[17] According to a popular folk song, at this Messianic feast Moses will teach Torah, Aaron the high priest will bless the assembled guests, and King David will entertain with music.

The most intriguing legacy of Daniel, taken up by scholars and mystics in all succeeding generations down to this very day, was his statement, "I, Daniel, meditated in the books over the number of years whereof the word of the Lord came to Jeremiah the prophet that He would restore the ruins of Jerusalem" (Dan. 9:2). Our sacred literature was fine-combed to find clues to the time of the End. Numerical values (*gimatriyaot*) and acrostics, combinations and permutations, were employed in order to ferret out veiled references to the Messiah. All signs signaling the approach of the Redemption were examined in the light of the existing situation, and it was not difficult to discern parallels. Some went beyond mere calculation; they attempted to hasten Messiah's coming through their intense devotions and supplications, or by means of esoteric behavior.[18] One sober-minded talmudic sage demurred and imprecated: "May the bones of those who calculate the Ends be blown away; for they say, 'Since the predicted time has arrived and it did not come, it will never come'" (*Sanhedrin* 97b). His advice, accepted by the bulk of Jewry in the extended period of the Exile, was: "Wait patiently for it, as it is said, 'Though it tarry, wait for it, for it will surely come, it will not be late' [Hab. 2:3]."

Messianic speculation, however, did not cease. It received tremendous impetus in the sixteenth century with the spread of the teachings of the Kabbalah and the upheavals in Jewish life due to the Expulsion from Spain.[19] And the contemporary upheavals in Jewish life, the Holocaust and the founding of Medinat Yisrael, have also supplied grist for the mills of present-day *mehashvei kitzin*, calculators of the End.

Would-be Messiahs

Messianic speculation not only was a result of the upheavals in our
history; it also was a cause of them. Signs and omens of the imminent coming of the Messiah engendered the emergence of men who
claimed to be the divinely chosen instruments of Israel's Redemption. David Alroiy came out of the East (Kurdistan) in the twelfth
century, and Shlomo Molkho came out of the West (Portugal) in the
sixteenth century, each of them arousing the hopes of the Jewish
masses with their messianic claims. The greatest upheaval in Jewish
life was brought about by Shabbatai Zvi in the seventeenth century.
His claim to be the Messiah captured the imagination and fervor of
Jews in both Europe and Asia, and generated a movement whose
repercussions lasted for over a century. The last such upheaval,
sweeping in its wake thousands of beguiled followers in Eastern
Europe, was created by the claims of a depraved individual by the
name of Jacob Frank.[20] All the aforementioned and many other
would-be Messiahs failed in their attempts to lead the dispersed of
Israel back to Eretz Yisrael and restore therein Jewish sovereignty.
They also led many to abandon their religious faith. Hence, the more
realistic among the spiritual leaders of Judaism, who saw in these
abortive movements a danger to the traditional way of Jewish life as
defined by the Halakhah, strove to persuade their communities to
ignore these Messianic claims while maintaining their patient and
passive waiting and longing for the miracle of Redemption.

The Christian and Moslem Challenge

The length of the *galut* and the lowly position of the Jewish people
in the Diaspora made such persuasion all the more necessary. Not
only did these distressing facts of life try the patience of the Jewish
masses; they also provided Christian and Moslem polemicists with
testimony to their argument that the Jews had long since lost their
claim to be God's Chosen People, destined to be redeemed from their
Exile. The three great Jewish theologians of the Middle Ages, each

from his particular point of view, refuted the anti-Jewish challenge by minimizing the immediate significance of *yemot ha-mashiah;* and comforted their people by stressing the rewards to be obtained by observing the mitzvot in Exile. The original title of Yehudah Halevi's *Kuzari* is "The Book of Argument in Defense of the Despised Faith." In it, he argues that Israel's long suffering is in itself part of the historical process that will ultimately bring about Israel's deliverance, when the nations of the world will finally recognize the superiority of Judaism. Maimonides stresses his belief that "in *yemot ha-mashiah* there will occur no cataclysmic change in Nature; on the contrary, the world will continue in its accustomed course. . . . In any event, the order and details of the happenings in those days are not a principle of religion. A person should therefore not occupy himself a great deal with the legends dealing with these things, since they lead neither to the fear nor to the love of God. Rather, one should wait and have faith in the matter in general." Nahmanides, in his public disputation with the Christian clergy, affirmed that "our Torah is not dependent upon a Messiah, since he is but a king of flesh and blood" (i.e., not divine like the Christian Messiah). In his Book of Redemption *(Sefer ha-Ge'ulah),* he again asserts that the coming of the Messiah is not a sustaining element of his faith; the essential thing is the observance of the laws of the Torah.[21]

The contrasting effects of the mystic calculators and the rationalist soothsayers can be explained as follows: "There is a hope that acts as an explosive, and a hope that disciplines and infuses patience. The difference is between the immediate hope and the distant hope."[22]

The Attitude of the Rabbis

The belief in the coming of the Messiah was expressed in prayer and in principle of faith right after the destruction of the Temple by the Romans, and continued to be expressed in an increasing number of liturgical poems *(piyyutim)* as the number of years of the Exile increased. Nevertheless, for the most part this faith did not lead to any practical program for the resettlement of Jews in Eretz Yisrael and the establishment therein of an independent Jewish commonwealth. Furthermore, though the main goal of Redemption as expressed in prayer was the rebuilding of the Beit ha-Mikdash on its ancient site, no actual program to build the Temple was initiated. In fact, in the year 362 C.E. the emperor Julian addressed a letter to all Jewish communities of the Roman Empire in which he promised that after the war against the Persians he would visit Jerusalem and have it rebuilt at his own expense. He even appointed a special overseer who was charged to proceed with the building of the Temple. And yet there was no enthusiastic response on the part of the Jews. Why was this so?

In the first place, Jews could not conceive of the rebuilding of the Temple without the coming of *Mashiah ben David*, a scion of the House of David. Indeed, his chief task was to be just that. Furthermore, the belief had already become ingrained that the Temple would not be rebuilt by human hands, but miraculously overnight by God Himself. In the prayer recited on Tish'ah B'ab the Jew affirmed: "You, God, burned it [the Temple] by fire, and with fire You will surely rebuild it." No need, therefore, to engage architects and builders and proceed with any actual building.[23]

The matter runs a little more deeply. The attitude of the Rabbis toward the fact of *galut* was ambivalent, as many were reconciled to it and did not consider it an unmitigated disaster.[24] The first attempt to restore an independent Jewish commonwealth after the *hurban* was that of Bar Kochba, and most of the Rabbis did not support his rebellion against Rome. When Rabbi Akiba pointed to Bar Kochba and said, "This one is the King Messiah," his colleague Rabbi Yohanan ben Torta derided him and said, "Grass will grow on your cheeks, Akiba, and the son of David will not yet have arrived" (J. *Taanit* 4:5 [68d]).[25]

Later, in the third century, we again find a sharp disagreement among the Rabbis concerning the return to Eretz Yisrael. Rabbi Zeira wanted to leave Babylonia in order to settle in Eretz Yisrael despite the disapproval of Rabbi Yehudah, who said: "Anyone who leaves Babylonia for Eretz Yisrael transgresses a positive commandment; for it is said, 'They shall be brought to Babylon and there they shall be until the day that I remember them, says the Lord' [Jer. 27:22]."[26]

Based on the verse "I adjure you, O daughters of Jerusalem, not to awaken or stir up love until it pleases" (Song of Songs 2:7), the Rabbis aver that God made Israel swear that they would not go back to Eretz Yisrael by force, or rebel against the Gentiles (*Kethubot* 111a). And yet, counterbalancing this statement we have in the same section of the Talmud the assertion that "He who dwells in Eretz Yisrael is as if he has a God; whereas he who dwells outside Eretz Yisrael is as if he had no God."

We have already descirbed how the Sages who lived at the time of the *hurban* comforted the people and assured them that Jewish life could continue unimpaired even though bereft of Temple and state (see above, p. 90). Yet there is no doubt that they and the later Rabbis who cautioned against a mass movement back to Eretz Yisrael yearned sincerely for a speedy Redemption. They were, however, wary lest an ill-planned and precipitate movement to restore Israel's independence would meet with failure and thus crush all hopes for a future restoration of Jewish glory in its ancient homeland. Nor were the Rabbis willing to abandon in one fell swoop the institutions in Jewish life which had been built up over the years in the Diaspora. To reinforce loyalty to these institutions, they predicted that "the synagogues and houses of learning in Babylonia are destined to be transfixed [together with the people] in Eretz Yisrael" (*Megillah* 29a).

Aliyah Movements in Pre-Modern Times

In the Middle Ages, certain Rabbis went so far as to assert that in their day the mitzvah of aliyah, referred to in halakhic terms as the mitzvah of *yishuv Eretz Yisrael*, (i.e., settling in Eretz Yisrael), no longer obtained "because of the danger of the journey." Another Rabbi based this ruling on the grounds that "there are many mitzvot obligatory only in Eretz Yisrael . . . and we are unable to perform them properly."[27]

Nevertheless, the deep yearning for Eretz Yisrael, nurtured in prayer and in commemorating customs, did generate several movements by individuals and small groups to go up to Eretz Yisrael, leaving behind homes and families in the Diaspora. Foremost among those who awakened and stirred up an intense love for the Holy Land was Yehudah Halevi. With him, love for Zion was a grand passion, expressed in moving lyrics which to this day are recited on Tish'ah B'ab. In the year 1141 he began the difficult and dangerous journey from Spain to Eretz Yisrael. He reached Jerusalem, but could not remain there because of the hostility of the Crusaders, who at that time had seized the Holy City from the Moslems. We do not know exactly where and when it happened, but he died of a broken heart as well as a broken body. His literary legacy, however, is immortal, an inspiration to all lovers of Zion.

A half-century after Yehudah Halevi's aliyah, and no doubt inspired by his example, a group of three hundred rabbis from France and England left for Eretz Yisrael under the leadership of Rabbi Yonathan Hakohen of Lunel, a disciple of the great Maimonides. Again, conditions in the Holy Land proved too difficult for the establishment of an ongoing productive community able to absorb additional settlers. Maimonides himself had visited Eretz Yisrael with his father when they had to flee from Spain in order to escape the persecutions of the fanatic Moslems (the Almohades). He relates that he visited the site of "the Great and Holy House" (the Beit ha-Mikdash) and prayed there.[28] Again, the small and impoverished Jewish community could not sustain this universally revered scholar, and he left Eretz Yisrael to settle in Egypt. After he passed away, his remains were transferred to Tiberias, where his grave has become a shrine, visited mostly by Oriental Jews on the anniversary of his death.

Another half-century later, in the year 1267, another great Jewish scholar and leader made his way to Eretz Yisrael. Nahmanides, who had included in the *Sefer ha-Mitzvot* the mitzvah of settling in Eretz Yisrael, fulfilled this religious imperative by undertaking the journey to the Holy Land. Upon arriving in Jerusalem and viewing the ruins of the holy places, he made the memorable statement: "The more holy the place, the greater its ruin; Jerusalem is more desolate than Judea, and Judea is more desolate than the Galil." To Jewish pilgrims who had come from Syria, Nahmanides suggested that they build a synagogue, and he gathered about himself a number of disciples. Here he wrote his great Commentary to the Torah, a brilliant exposition combining both rational and mystical interpretations, studied intently for its inspiring and enlightening clarification of Scripture's eternal truths. Once again, however, the difficult conditions made permanent Jewish settlement impossible.

We have already made mention (above p. 122) of the settlement in Safed in the sixteenth century of refugees from the Spanish Expulsion. The intensification there of the study of the practical Kabbalah gave rise to the feeling that the days of the Messiah were rapidly approaching. This sentiment was most beautifully, albeit succinctly, expressed in the liturgical poem *Lekhah Dodi*, "Come, my beloved," sung before the Sabbath Eve service. In it, the verses of Isaiah forecasting the restoration of Israel's glory under the kingdom of God are couched in rhyming stanzas calling upon the Jewish people to "rise up from the dust of the vale of tears; arouse yourself, for your light has come; by the hand of the son of Jesse the Bethlehemite the Redemption has come nigh." Such Messianic premonitions also gave rise to the abortive attempt to reconstitute the ancient body of authority and leadership, the Sanhedrin (see above p. 110). But they did not give rise to any political or economic program which could conceivably lead to an overthrow of the harsh and corrupt Ottoman rule, which kept the few Jewish settlements in Eretz Yisrael in a static and dependent condition.

Hasidim and Kollelim

The rise of Hasidism in eighteenth-century Europe brought with it a reawakening of the traditional concept of the Messiah, interlaced with legend and suffused with longing.[29] With its avowed purpose of lifting up the spirits of the downtrodden masses who were disillusioned by the Sabbatian and Frankist movements, Hasidism spread more and more tales about the true Messiah, whose personal sufferings was a reflection of the sufferings of the Jewish people languishing in Exile. The prayers of the *tzaddikim*, the Righteous Ones who were the spiritual leaders of the Hasidim, concentrated upon the release of the Messiah from his own captivity in order to be free to carry out his divine mission of bringing the Redemption.

European Jewry had for centuries employed for its regular prayers the Ashkenazi version *(nusah Ashkenaz)*. In a bold move, the Hasidim abandoned this traditional version for the Sephardi one *(nusah Sepharad)*, which was prevalent in Eretz Yisrael.[30] They did this as a consequence of their having incorporated into their religious ideology the fundamental teachings of the Kabbalah, whose expounders were mostly Jews of Sephardi origin. They also added to their prayers selections from the Zohar, the sacred text of the Kabbalah, and hymns composed by Rabbi Isaac Luria (known by the acronym *ha-Ari*), the outstanding kabbalist of sixteenth-century Safed.

This affinity with the Kabbalah and with the prayers recited in Eretz Yisrael led to a small but significant aliyah to Eretz Yisrael by a few hardy Hasidim, headed by Rabbi Gershon of Kuty, brother-in-law of the founder of Hasidism, Rabbi Israel Baal Shem Tov. They sought the privilege of being present in the Holy Land to greet the Messiah leading the procession of the ingathering tribes of Israel. These new settlers were, generally speaking, not men of commercial—let alone, agricultural—enterprise. Their life's purpose was simply to dwell in the Holy Land, an avocation in itself, reciting the Psalms or delving into the mysteries of the Zohar. Their sustenance came from their less-privileged co-religionists living in the Diaspora. In every European country, the Jewish communities established *kollelim*, funds for the support of Jews living in Eretz Yisrael. We still see signs today in the older sections of Jerusalem advertising that this particular residential quarter was built by a particular *kollel*.[31]

The support rendered by Diaspora Jews for their brothers in Eretz Yisrael was no new phenomenon in Jewish life. We have seen (above p. 41) how already in the days of the first Return to Zion, the Jews who remained in *hutz la-aretz* gave generously of their means to help the new settlers establish themselves. In talmudic times, most eminent rabbis would undertake a journey to foreign lands in order to solicit support for the scholars in the Holy Land.[32] In the pre-modern period, special emissaries known as *shedarim* (an acronym for "messengers of the rabbis") would travel about Europe and Asia—in the late nineteenth century they even visited the United States[33]—collecting contributions for the indigent Jews living in Eretz Yisrael. Since it was a mitzvah to dwell in the Holy Land, the Jew in the Diaspora could fulfill this religious duty vicariously by making it possible for others to dwell therein.[34] The funds thus collected would be distributed by local committees, and the subsidy each resident received was known as *halukah*, or "distribution."

Followers of Hasidism were not the only settlers who went up to the Holy Land to be sustained by the contributions of their fellow-Jews in the Diaspora. A group of *mithnagdim*, i.e., "opposers," so called by the Hasidim because of their opposition to Hasidism, also established themselves in eighteenth-century Jerusalem. They were disciples of the famed Gaon of Vilna, Rabbenu Eliyahu of blessed memory, who brought with them their particular customs, and they founded synagogues of their own in order to pray according to their traditional Ashkenazi version of the liturgy.

A Historic Conclusion

Our review so far of the oft-expressed belief in the coming of the Messiah demonstrates that fervent faith is not ipso facto translated into practical program. On the one hand, enshrouding the faith in a nimbus of supernatural events leads one into an all-too-literal interpretation of the Psalmist's doctrine, "If the Lord does not build a house, they who build it toil in vain" (Ps. 127:1). Supernatural events can come to pass only through superhuman—i.e., Divine—

effort; therefore human hands need not toil. On the other hand, human efforts can be blessed with success only if a *possible* situation exists. No human effort, no matter how zealous and sincere, can overcome an existentially impossible set of circumstances. The failure of all Messianic endeavor in the long Exile that followed the *hurban* was thus due to a combination of the two factors involved: an acceptance of and resignation to the situation of Exile because of a mystic conception of Redemption; and the absence of objective conditions which could have made it possible for rational striving to be crowned with success.

We believe that the above-quoted doctrine of the Psalmist means that God Almighty builds the House of Israel by giving His blessing to Israel's toil for Redemption. He it is Who in His divine wisdom knows "the time of the End," and when that time comes He creates conditions in the world which make it possible for human effort to succeed. Our next chapter will outline briefly the thoughts and activities of the few, albeit elite, figures in modern Orthodox Judaism who conceived of the Redemption in the light of the aforementioned concept.

11

From Religious Faith to Practical Program

The first half of the nineteenth century was a period of ferment and gestation in Jewish life. New ideas gave birth to new movements, and new movements led to the abandonment of old ways (see above, pp 124f). Jews who clung to traditional concepts and time-honored ways—they whom we now call "Orthodox"—could not fail to react by voicing their vigorous condemnation of new-fangled ideas and the slightest deviation from practices consecrated by their inclusion in the halakhic codes. Their slogan was: *hadash assur min ha-Torah*, "anything new is forbidden by the Torah."[1]

There was one movement, however, to which Orthodox Jews were divided in their reaction; namely, the Zionist movement. The bulk of Orthodoxy was uncompromising in its opposition to Zionism, and on two grounds. First of all, the leaders of the Zionist movement were secular Jews who not only did not observe the mitzvot of the Torah; they argued that religion in general, and the Jewish religion in particular, could only be a hindrance to the reestablishment of the Jewish nation in its ancient homeland.[2] Many of these secular Zionists adopted socialism as their substitute for Judaism, convinced as they were that a Jewish state could come about only if it was Socialist.[3] With such *posh'im*, or transgressors, argued the Orthodox, it was forbidden to join in any endeavor; and they found confirmation in the statement of Nittai of Arbel: "Keep far from an evil neighbor, and do not join yourself to a wicked person" (*Abot* 1:7).

Furthermore, the Orthodox clung to the belief that Israel's Redemption will come about only when the Almighty Himself acts as the Redeemer. It is not only presumptuous, it is blasphemous, for

163

Jews to initiate a movement whose purpose is to bring Divine prophecy to realization; namely, the ingathering of the scattered tribes of Israel and the establishment of an independent Jewish commonwealth in the Land of the Fathers. Here again, traditional sources—particularly the Talmud—were produced as evidence that it is forbidden "to awaken or to stir up the love until it please" the Almighty (see above, p. 2).

The first traditional Jew to voice a contrary opinion and to translate Messianic hope into a practical program was a Sephardi rabbi by the name of Yehudah Alkalai, whose period of activity on behalf of the modern Return to Zion began in 1840 and spanned more than three decades. He argued that the Redemption must be inaugurated with action by the Jewish people themselves; they must organize and unite, choose leaders, leave the lands of the dispersion, and redeem Eretz Yisrael from Turkish rule through purchase and development. He traveled extensively in the capitals of Europe to propagandize his ideas, and he organized a committee called Hevrat Yishuv Eretz Yisrael, "The Company for the Settlement of Eretz Yisrael."

The first Ashkenazi rabbi to campaign for these ideas was Zvi Hirsch Kalischer, the rabbi of Thorn in Eastern Germany. He endeavored to found a society of rich Jews which would finance the pioneers who would settle in agricultural colonies in the Holy Land. He proposed the establishment of an agricultural school to train these pioneers in working the land, and he pointed out the need to organize a *mishmar*, a guard of young people who would protect the new settlements from hostile Arab neighbors. As a result of his efforts, and with the cooperation of other rabbis in Germany, the Paris-based Alliance Israélite set up, in 1870, an agricultural school called Mikveh Yisrael, or "Hope of Israel," a name taken from the Bible (Jer. 17:13). Incidentally, one of the first religious kibbutzim, Tirat Zvi in the Beit She'an (Beisan) Valley, is named after Rabbi Kalischer.

There gradually formed a small circle of Orthodox rabbis, each one a recognized talmudic scholar, who followed the initiative of Kalischer and raised their voices on behalf of the participation of religious Jews in the growing Zionist movement, which at that time was concentrated chiefly in Eastern Europe in the Hovevei Zion ("Lovers of Zion") organization. Their program was directed mainly toward the productive settlement of Jews on the soil of Eretz Yisrael, which had so long lain desolate; in contrast to the program later initiated by Theodor Herzl, which concentrated on political agitation for the recognition of the Jewish national aspiration by the political powers in Europe. Foremost among the followers of Kalischer was Rabbi Shmuel Mohilever of Radom and Bialystok, Poland. He preached that the Zionist movement was based upon the traditional faith in the coming of the Messiah, and therefore it was not only permissible but even mandatory to join forces with all Jews, even the non-religious, for the realization of the Messianic hopes. Practicing what he preached, he participated in the conference of the Hovevei Zion held in Kattowicz in 1855. Among the other prominent rabbis who tried to persuade Orthodox Jewry of the legitimacy and urgency of Zionism were Eliyahu Guttmacher and the eminent Naftali Zvi Yehudah Berlin, head of the famous Yeshiva in Volozhin and known by the acronym *ha-Netziv*.

The Mizrachi Movement

A most forceful disciple of Mohilever was Rabbi Isaac Jacob Reines. He demonstrated his independent thinking by founding a Yeshivah in Lida, Poland, in which secular subjects were included in the curriculum, something frowned upon by the traditionalists. With the formation of the World Zionist Organization by Theodor Herzl at the close of the century, Mohilever and Reines founded its religious component in 1902. They named this wing of Zionism Mizrachi, a combination of the words *mercaz ruchani*, or "spiritual center." For it was the contention of these religious Zionists that the renaissance of Jewish life in the ancient Homeland was not only for the purpose of saving a harassed people from the physical onslaughts of anti-Semites, but also for the salvation of its spirit by the revitalization of Torah learning and practice, which could develop normally only when the center of Jewish life is in the Holy Land. The motto of the Mizrachi was *Eretz Yisrael l'am Yisrael al-pi Torat Yisrael*, "The Land of Israel for the people of Israel in accord with the Torah of Israel." The movement assigned Rabbi Yehudah Leib Fishman (later, Rabbi Maimon, the first minister of religions in the newly established State of Israel) to supervise its institutions in Eretz Yisrael, and Rabbi Meir Berlin (later, Rabbi Bar-Ilan), son of the *Netziv*, to organize branches of the movement in the Diaspora.

It must be remembered that these religious Zionists had to wage a war of ideas on three fronts. First of all, like all religious Jews, they had to fight against the inroads of Reform Judaism, which not only rejected the authority of the Halakhah but also strongly opposed the Zionist movement. The reformists maintained that Zionism was treason to the countries in which Jews lived and—theoretically at least—enjoyed all civil rights; and they expurgated from their prayer books all references for the hoped-for Return to Zion.[4] Secondly, Mizrachi leaders had to contend with the opposition of the unswerving traditionalists, who published manifestos condemning the Mizrachi for its having joined the Zionist movement, which, they claimed, jeopardized the future of Torah-true Judaism. Thirdly, religious Zionists were engaged in a continuous battle with the secular Zionists, who strove to divorce Jewish nationhood from its religious origins and character.

Rabbi Abraham Isaac Hakohen Kook

The outstanding ideologue of the Mizrachi concept of Zionism—though he personally did not join the movement formally—was the late Rabbi Abraham Isaac Hakohen Kook, who helped found the *Rabbanut ha-Rashit*, the Chief Rabbinate in Eretz Yisrael, and became its first Ashkenazi chief rabbi. Rabbi Kook may be described as the twentieth-century "transmigration of soul" (*gilgul*) of Yehudah Halevi. Like the medieval singer of Zion, Rabbi Kook was a harmonious combination of poet and philosopher, animated by a passionate love for Eretz Yisrael and the Jewish people.

Rabbi Kook's rabbinate flourished in the first four decades of this century, a time when the twofold program of Zionism, the resettlement of Jews in the Holy Land, and the recognition by the world powers of the Jewish people's national aspirations, was beginning to advance toward its goal. His major thesis, as propounded in numerous writings as well as in personal activity, may be summarized as follows: Modern secular Zionism is an integral part of the religious ideal of *teshuvah*, the return of Israel to its sacred destiny, and therefore any Zionist activity is ipso facto sacred. This aspect of Jewish nationalism, its *kedushah*, or holiness, distinguishes it from the nationalism of all other peoples. Practical Zionism, redeeming the sacred soil of Eretz Yisrael from its desolation, and transforming it by dint of the sacrificial labor of the halutzim (pioneers) into the fertile "garden of the Lord," is the outer garment of Israel's spiritual aspirations. It is the body of Israel's soul, both of which are essential for the restoration of Israel's divine image. This image will not only enhance Israel's prestige among the *goyim*, it will also enhance the spiritual life of all the nations. Therefore, argued Rabbi Kook, it is wrong to oppose secular Zionism. On the contrary, we must encourage it and direct it toward its proper goals. Rabbi Kook was fully and painfully aware that modern Zionism had forgotten the roots from which it sprung, and he did not cease to bemoan this fact. But this made it all the more necessary for religious Jews to participate in the Zionist effort, so that the secularists would come to realize the true nature and objective of Jewish nationalism.

Rabbi Kook illustrated his attitude toward the non-religious halutzim by comparing them to the laborers who built the Beit ha-Mikdash in the days of Solomon. These builders may have been simple masons far removed from the lofty principles symbolized by the House of God, but their work resulted in a glorious edifice dedicated to the worship of the Almighty, God of Righteousness and Peace. So would the efforts of the modern builders of Zion result in a homeland that will be "a light unto the nations," reflecting the teachings of the Torah for all mankind.

To demonstrate his appreciation of the work of the halutzim,

Rabbi Kook would visit the non-religious kibbutzim, where his saintly character and affectionate words made for a better understanding of religious Jewry on the part of the halutzim. Though he was grieved by the total lack of religious observance in the kibbutzim, he was optimistic that eventually their members would return to the ways of traditional Judaism. Rabbi Kook was impelled by the mystical faith expressed in the Kabbalah and Hasidism that every Jew contains within himself a spark of loyalty to Torah which in the course of time, and with proper nurturing, would be fanned into a flame of spiritual enlightenment and devotion.

This positive—one might almost say "reverential"—attitude toward the work of redeeming the land through agricultural activity is reflected in Rabbi Kook's decision concerning Shemittah, the Sabbatical year, when sowing and reaping in the field is forbidden by the Torah (Lev. 25:1—5). In 1910 he ruled that the land may be tilled during Shemittah provided it is sold to a non-Jew for that year.[5] He emphasized that this was an emergency measure "due to overriding necessity." To apply the rule of Shemittah in all its stringency, argued Rabbi Kook, would spell economic ruin for the kibbutzim, which would in turn affect the future of Klal Yisrael, the entire Community of Israel.

For this decision, and for his general attitude toward Zionism, Rabbi Kook was severely attacked by the rabbis of the *Yishuv ha-Yashan*, the Old Settlement of pious Jews which antedated the modern Zionist settlement. The Old Settlement stubbornly continued to look with disfavor and contempt upon the activities of the *posh'im*, the transgressors, and they refused to acknowledge that any positive results would accrue to the Jewish people as a whole from the Zionist endeavors. Rabbi Kook attributed a great measure of the blame for the secular basis of Zionism on the refusal of the Orthodox element to understand the changes taking place in the world which affected both the Jewish people and the attitude of the non-Jewish peoples to their Jewish neighbors. He saw in what was happening, in the settlement of Jews on the soil and in the Balfour Declaration, which officially recognized Palestine as the Jewish Homeland, an *athaltha dige'ulah*, a beginning of Israel's Redemption, and the realization of its Messianic hopes. To counter the epigram of the traditionalists that "everything new is forbidden by the Torah," Rabbi Kook asserted: *Hayashan tithadesh vehahadash tithkadesh*, "The old will be renewed and the new will be sanctified."

Rabbi Kook's recognition of this new era in Jewish history led him to the founding of two important institutions in Eretz Yisrael, both of which proved to have great significance in the life of the Yishuv as it advanced from a *medinah ba-derekh* to a *medinah be-pho'al* (see above, p. 128). For a long time he had been thinking of opening a new type of Yeshivah, an institution pervaded by the spirit of Israel's rebirth. Whereas the old-type Yeshivah restricted itself to the study of Talmud and Codes, the new one would broaden the intellectual horizons of the students with an analysis of the philosophy of Judaism, with identification with the new trends in Jewish life, especially as manifested in the Zionist movement, and with an appreciation of the values inhering in modern secular culture. Rabbi Kook hoped that the new institution, which he called "the Central Yeshivah," now known as Yeshivah Mercaz Harav, would attract students from all over the world, and that these students would, upon the completion of their studies, return to the Diaspora to spread the teachings of their master. Rabbi Kook was also not averse to having Yeshivah students take courses at a university. He was one of the main speakers at the opening of the Hebrew University on Mount Scopus in 1925. In his speech, he emphasized that a university sponsored by the Jewish people and situated in the Holy City of Jerusalem should preserve the traditional Jewish attitude toward learning, namely for the sake of the improvement of humanity, and not merely a school of preparation for a career.

The Chief Rabbinate of Israel

One of the prophecies which constituted an integral part of Messianic fulfillment was "I shall restore your judges as at the first, and your counselors as at the beginning" (Isa. 1:26). The "judges as at the first" are the ordained scholars of old, whose judgments were delivered and sanctioned by the Sanhedrin, whose authority extended over all Israel. The rabbis of today, though not possessing the full competence and authority of the erstwhile members of the Sanhedrin, are nevertheless charged with the same responsibility of interpreting the laws of the Torah as they are to be applied in the contemporary situation. But rabbis today have no universal jurisdiction; their decisions commit only those individuals who accept them. To be able to judge for Klal Yisrael, the rabbis would have to assemble and create the equivalent of the ancient Sanhedrin, a Supreme Court of Jewish Law. To prepare for the eventual achievement of such a corpus, Rabbi Kook proposed the establishment of a Chief Rabbinate that would be composed of rabbis "great in their knowledge of the Torah, in their integrity and wisdom, and in their recognition of the ways of the world." In a message prepared for the rabbis assembled to establish this new institution, Rabbi Kook said: "It is inconceivable in this period of national renaissance that the rabbinate should not revitalize itself. The rabbis must raise themselves to the greatest heights and work with the community in all aspects of the national rebuilding and creativity. The rabbis must understand that there is no segment in the nation which has no need of the influence of the rabbinate." As was to be expected, the only religious group which formally accepted the authority of the Chief Rabbinate was the Mizrachi. The right-wing Orthodox, organized in the Agudat Yisrael, maintained that there is no need for a new authority since the so-called *Gedolei Torah*, the heads of the traditional Yeshivot and of the Hasidic groups, remain the competent authorities in any question of religious law or procedure.

The Chief Rabbinate was organized in 1921, with two chief rabbis, an Ashkenazi and a Sephardi, and an elected Council of Rabbis. In 1949, when the State of Israel was established, the Chief Rabbinate became an official organ of the state. It was vested with the power of supervising the rabbinic courts, certifying its judges (*dayyanim*) and officially recognized rabbis of communities. Since all marriage and divorce were placed in the exclusive jurisdiction of the rabbinic courts, one can see the vital role that the Chief Rabbinate can play in Israeli society.

Rabbi Kook's teachings continue to guide and inspire the religious Zionists of today, and his disciples play an increasing role in shaping the life and thought of many Israelis. One of his disciples, Rabbi Moshe Zvi Neriah, founded the first Bnai Akiba Yeshivah in Kfar Haroeh (*Haroeh* is the acronym of Rabbi Kook), and is regarded today as the spiritual leader of all Bnei Akiba Yeshivot. (Later we shall discuss these Yeshivot in more detail.) Rabbi Kook's son, Rabbi Zvi Yehudah, who succeeded his father as the head of Yeshivah Mercaz Harav, is the spiritual mentor of Gush Emunim ("Faithful Bloc"), a movement determined to establish Jewish settlements in Judea and Samaria, that portion of Eretz Yisrael which the Arabs and the United Nations regard as "occupied territories," but which the Gush regards as "liberated territories." A disciple of one of Rabbi Kook's most noteworthy disciples[6] is the present Ashkenazi chief rabbi, Shlomo Goren, whose many years of service as chief chaplain of the Israel Defense Forces is well known. Spiritual leaders of Israeli communities are being culled more and more from the ranks of graduates of Yeshiva Mercaz Harav. In general, there is now, forty years after Rabbi Kook's demise, a growing interest in his writings, and a search for solutions to contemporary problems in the light of his teachings.

Religious Settlements

The participation of religious Jews in the Zionist movement meant participation not only in its political organ, the World Zionist Organization, but also in actual settlement on the land. Of course, such settlements would by their nature have to abide by the requirements of the Halakhah, and consequently had to be separate from the non-religious settlements. This was no simple matter. The laws of the Torah which involve agriculture and its products apply only to Eretz Yisrael (Mishnah *Kiddushin* 1:9). For centuries these laws had not been practiced by the overwhelming majority of the Jewish people, since they lived in *hutz la-aretz*. Those Jews who lived in the small Jewish communities which existed in Eretz Yisrael before modern times did not engage in agricultural work. The products they consumed were produced by non-Jews, and therefore were exempt from the aforementioned laws. This long-standing situation is reflected in the fact that the Babylonian Talmud, which has been and still is the principal text for talmudic studies, does not contain any Gemara on *Seder Zeraim* (Order of Seeds), the division of the Mishnah which deals with the laws of agricultural activity and its products (with the exception of the first Tractate, *Berakhot*, which deals with the prayers and benedictions which apply universally).[7]

One of the first problems with which the religious settlers were confronted is the prohibition the Torah imposes on work on the field once in seven years, the Sabbatical year of Shemittah. We have seen above (p. 168) how Rabbi Kook helped solve this problem. Another law which posed great difficulties for religious settlers engaged in dairy farming was the prohibition against milking on the Sabbath (*Shabbat* 95a). At first, this problem was solved by milking into pails, which rendered the milk unfit for human consumption, since the Torah prohibits only such milking as results in a potable liquid. This, of course, represented an economic loss. With the advance in agricultural technology, milking machines which are pre-set to operate automatically on the Sabbath were introduced and are widely used today in religious settlements. The milk produced in such fashion may be consumed and is economically viable.[8]

Despite these difficulties, which compounded the sheer physical difficulties faced by all Zionist settlers, groups of young religious men, some of them former Yeshivah students, were determined to establish colonies in Eretz Yisrael which would demonstrate that it is possible for religious Jews to return to the soil without sacrificing or compromising their Judaism. Nay more, this youth wanted to demonstrate that religious Jewry could set up settlements that would exemplify the noblest ethical and moral teachings of the Torah. The Torah is a *Torat Hayyim*, applicable to Jews engaged in all sorts of economic activity without having to depend upon the services of non-Jews.

Religious settlements on the Land, following the general pattern, are of two kinds. There are the moshavim, settlements where each family lives in its private quarters and has its own parcel of land, but the agricultural products are marketed cooperatively. Then there are the kibbutzim, established by groups of young European Jews who organized themselves into communal societies such as prevailed in the general non-religious kibbutzim. Most of the religious moshavim were established in the twenties and thirties of this century; most of the religious kibbutzim in the late thirties and forties. A rather unique religious settlement was established in 1924 by a group of Hasidim under the leadership of the Rebbi of Kozhnitz, and is called Kfar Hasidim.[9] Many Oriental Jews who came on aliyah in the early fifties from Yemen and North Africa were settled in religious moshavim. Special mention should be made of the cluster of religious kibbutzim established in the hills of Hebron called Gush Etzion. They were destroyed by the Arabs in the War of Israeli Independence, but reestablished by sons of the former settlers after the Six-Day War.

The organizational support given the religious settlements came primarily from Hapoel Hamizrachi, the labor wing of the Mizrachi movement, organized as an independent group in 1922. It conducted its activity on behalf of the religious working class under the banner of *Torah Va-Avodah*, "Torah and Labor." This slogan captured the imagination of young religious Jews in all parts of the globe, and branches of Hapoel Hamizrachi were established in *hutz la-aretz* in order to support the movement in *Aretz.* Their program was twofold: to promote the economic and social interests of religious laborers, and to enhance their religious and cultural life through pursuit of traditional Jewish studies. Religious kibbutzim were a prime factor in stimulating a profounder study of the religious aspects of a Jewish state, a study which unfortunately had been neglected for centuries.[10] Rabbis who heretofore had been engaged almost exclusively in theoretical study as far as mitzvot obtaining only in Eretz Yisrael are concerned, were now pressed to make decisions *halakhah le-ma'aseh*, practical decisions for immediate application. Herein is a concrete example of how the modern Return to Zion and its soil is revitalizing the study of Torah.

The National Religious Party

For quite some time, Mizrachi and Hapoel Hamizrachi were separate organizations even though they subscribed to the same general ideology of religious Zionism. The leaders of Mizrachi were mainly rabbis and businessmen, some of whom looked askance at the "Socialist" tendencies of Hapoel Hamizrachi. The latter, on the other hand, felt that the older organization did not appreciate sufficiently their *halutziyut*, their pioneering activity, which represented to their minds the most constructive element in religious Jewry. It was only after the establishment of Medinat Yisrael, when the need for the religious elements in the Yishuv to present a united front in the kaleidoscope of Israeli politics became urgent, that the two branches of religious Zionism merged into the *Miflagah datit le'umit* (Mafdal for short), i.e., the National Religious Party. Attempts to include in a united religious front the non-Zionist elements in Orthodoxy; namely, the Agudat Yisrael, ended in failure. The gap between the religious Zionists, who see in Medinat Yisrael a sign of "the beginning of the sprouting of our Redemption," and the religious non-Zionists who do not see any religious significance in the State of Israel because of its non-acceptance of the Halakhah in its entirety as the law of the Land, is too wide to be coalesced in one political party. Despite its reservations concerning the religious significance of Medinat Yisrael, let alone its Messianic significance, Agudat Yisrael constitutes an Israeli political party with elected representatives in the Knesset. The mere fact that so many traditionalist Orthodox, with their multifarious educational and philanthropic institutions, are part of the Israeli scene, contributes significantly to the religious character of the state. It is only to be regretted that they fail to be moved from their stubborn "neutrality" towards the State by the dramatic events which have punctuated the Jewish history of our times.

Religious Education

Education—and for traditional Jewry this means primarily Torah education—is a pursuit to be followed from the cradle to the grave. The Sages say: "As soon as a child knows how to talk, his father teaches him Torah" (*Succah* 42a). For the other terminus of the life-span, Maimonides rules: "Till when is a person duty-bound to study Torah, till the day of his death."[11] Though the Torah has placed the responsibility for educating the young upon the parent (Deut. 6:7), very early in Jewish life the need for community-sponsored schools became apparent (*Baba Bathra* 21a).[12] At all times, and under all circumstances, Jews did not neglect this basic obligation of Talmud Torah, the teaching and learning of Torah.

One of the basic conditions under which Mizrachi joined the Zionist movement was the right to conduct separate schools in which religious subjects and values would be the core of the curriculum and would be taught by religious teachers. Even before the establishment of Medinat Yisrael, the several Zionist parties were conducting separate school systems, in addition to many privately sponsored schools, each with its particular educational philosophy. With the establishment of the state, state-conducted schools were divided into two streams, *mamlakhti* (literally, "of the realm"), or general, and *mamlakhti-dati*, or national religious. In addition, the state supports but does not conduct the schools of *hinukh atzma'i*, the independent educational system conducted by Agudat Yisrael.

Education by the parent begins in the home; education by the community begins in the nursery or day-care center. The distaff wing of the Mizrachi, the T'nuah Ishah Datit Le'umit (Movement of the National Religious Woman), has accepted the responsibility of sponsoring religious nurseries, as well as religious vocational high schools for girls. Kindergartens are already part of the compulsory state-school system, and so we have *mamlakhti-dati* schools from kindergarten through high school. On the high school level, there is a special Mizrachi-oriented network of Yeshivah high schools called Bnai Akiba Yeshivot Tikhoniyot. The first of these schools was founded in 1940 (see above, p. 171), and the network now embraces seventeen schools distributed over the length and breadth of the country. These Yeshivot are the laboratories in which is produced the dedicated religious youth which distinguishes itself by its combination of love of Torah and devotion to Medinat Yisrael. Each school has a dormitory, so that its students live in a religious atmosphere twenty-four hours a day, including Sabbaths and High Holy Days. In addition to the study of Talmud and Codes, these schools teach secular subjects which enable its graduates to earn a te'udat bagrut, a matriculation certificate for higher education. Bnai Akiba students can be recognized by their kippot serugot, the knitted skull caps which now have become the hallmark of religious Israelis.

In recent years, the Bnai Akiba school system has added a number of religious high schools for girls which they call ulpanot, i.e., study centers. Other schools for girls which contribute to the religious character of Israeli society are the Beit Yaakov schools, the female branch of hinukh atzma'i. There is another religious high school for boys, Yeshivat Hadarom in Rehovot, which has a program and philosophy similar to those of the Bnai Akiba schools, but is sponsored by the Rabbinical Council of America. Attached to Yeshivat Hadarom is the first religious teachers seminary for men in Israel, which is also the first to have made a hesder (see below, p. 177) with the army. The Rabbinical Council also sponsors a vocational high school for boys in Moshav Gan Yavneh near Ashdod, the bulk of the students coming from underprivileged families of Oriental Jews. Several other vocational schools which combine religious with technical training are known as Torah U'Melakhah (Torah and Work) institutions.

Higher Education

Graduates of religious high schools who want to join the mainstream of Israeli society and at the same time maintain their religious way of life have several options before them. If they want to continue their Torah education in the spirit of religious Zionism—and thus are unwilling to enter one of the traditional Yeshivot—they can enter one of the several Yeshivot in Israel which are conducted in the ideology of the Mizrachi. The first such Yeshivah was established by the Mizrachi in the historic town of Yavneh, the site of the Sanhedrin after the destruction of the Second Temple. It is called Kerem B'Yavneh after the first convocation of the Sages following the defeat of Bar Kochba and the Hadrianic persecutions (*Berakhot* 63b). Whereas students of the traditional Yeshivot are exempt from service in the Israeli Defense Forces (*Zahal*), an arrangement (*hesder*) has been made between the Army and Mizrachi-oriented Yeshivot whereby the students alternate between periods of study in the Yeshivah and periods of service in the army. (The first such *hesder* was made at the initiative of the late Rabbi Yehudah Zvi Meltzer with the Teachers Seminary of Yeshivat Hadarom.) The students of these Yeshivot Hesder distinguished themselves in the Six-Day and Yom Kippur Wars (1967 and 1973) by their heroism, and reflected great honor upon religious Zionism. What particularly impressed their non-religious comrades-in-arms was their scrupulous observance of religious rituals under most difficult conditions during combat. Their devotion to Torah study is so great that even in army camps they continue their study of the Talmud. Indeed, a temporary Yeshiva was organized in a field tent in Goshen, Egypt, when it was occupied by the Israeli forces, and a *rosh yeshivah* was transported by the Army to deliver a lecture in Talmud.

A religious young man or woman who wishes to continue his or her education on the university level has several choices. The Mizrachi movement sponsored the creation of a religious coeducational university, Bar-Ilan University, named after the late Rabbi Meir (Berlin) Bar-Ilan. Its first president, who conceived and organized its original program, was the late Dr. Pinhas Churgin, erstwhile head of the Teachers Institute of Yeshiva University and a leader of American Mizrachi. Bar-Ilan does not differ greatly from other Israeli universities in its academic program, but it provides an opportunity for religious students to pursue an academic career in a congenial atmosphere. (This is not to imply that a student in another Israeli university is compelled in any way to compromise his religious convictions or observances.) Recently, Bar-Ilan opened a Yeshivah department, where former Yeshivah students are enabled to continue their talmudic studies in a Yeshivah atmosphere and on an intensive level in the forenoon, and pursue their academic studies in the afternoon. It remains to be seen whether this synthesis of Torah and Mada (secular knowledge), which is the hallmark of Yeshiva University in New York, will take hold in Israel, where it has been strongly opposed by the traditional Yeshivot.

For religious young men who want to continue their Torah studies and at the same time prepare for some branch of engineering, there is the Jerusalem Institute of Technology, founded and headed by an eminent religious physicist, Professor Ze'ev Lev of the Hebrew University. This institute, in addition to preparing religious engineers, serves the religious community in Israel in a very practical way. It researches methods of automation for industry so as to avoid *hillul Shabbat* (desecration of the Sabbath) in factories which must continue to operate seven days a week.

For religious young women who are shy about attending a coeducational school and yet are desirous of continuing their academic studies beyond high school, there is the Jerusalem College for Women (*Mikhlalah le-Banot*), where the emphasis is upon religious rather than purely scientific studies. There are, in addition, religious teachers seminaries for young women who are seeking a career in teaching. Religious girls can also opt for a nursing career by enrolling in the School of Nursing of Shaare Zedek Hospital in Jerusalem, which renders medical treatment with maximum adherence to all requirements of the Halakhah. This hospital, as well as the Center for Torah Studies of Yad Harav Herzog, maintains special departments for research into the compatibility of modern medical practice with the Halakhah.

The Israeli Army

Some graduates of religious high schools choose to enter the Israeli Army (*Zahal*, Israeli Defense Forces) right after graduation in order to discharge the compulsory three-year service required of almost all Israeli youth. Others prefer to enter the special branch of the army known as Nahal, the acrostic of *no'ar halutzi lohem*, or "fighting pioneering youth," in which a young man (or, for that matter, a young woman, for this program is open to women also) joins a paramilitary agricultural settlement situated in some border area. Service in Israel's army does not mean that a religious youngster has to sacrifice his religious observances or compromise his religious convictions, for Zahal provides for the special needs of the religious soldier.

At the insistence of the Mizrachi that all public institutions of the State of Israel be conducted in conformity with the Halakhah, the Israeli army observes many religious requirements. Its kitchens are kosher, and the Sabbath is observed as far as the exigencies of army life permit, especially an army which has to be constantly on the alert against attacks from the surrounding enemy.[13] Army camps conduct *Sedorim* on the first night of Passover, and celebrations of the other Jewish Festivals are held. A chaplain corps is maintained to see to it that soldiers who wish to participate in prayer services have the means to do so. A special division of the chaplain corps is charged with the sad and harrowing task of identifying the bodies of soldiers who are killed in combat and bringing them to proper Jewish burial. Identification of bodies is essential in the case of married soldiers, so that their wives may be permitted to remarry.

A great deal of the credit for organizing the religious life in Zahal belongs to its first chief chaplain, Rabbi Shlomo Goren. An outstanding talmudic scholar, with the courage of his convictions, and inspired by the Messianic character of the State of Israel as he sees it and expresses it, he has interpreted the Halakhah in such a way as to make it viable in a modern army. One of his more notable halakhic decisions was the one he made after the disappearance of the Israeli submarine *Dakar*. After substantiating his analysis with citations from many halakhic sources, he ruled that the wives of the men lost in the *Dakar* may remarry, even though the bodies had not been found, since the assumption that they have died is incontrovertible.

One of the issues which has divided religious Jewry in connection with the army is the question of compulsory service for women (*giyus banot*). The traditional Orthodox are uncompromisingly opposed to any sort of national draft for women, even for noncombatant roles.[14] The Mizrachi, though also opposed to the drafting of women into the regular army, favors the voluntary recruitment of women for at least one year of national service (*sheirut le'umi*) in a non-military environment, such as social service in a disadvantaged community. At present, any young woman who can demonstrate that she comes from a religious home is exempt from the military draft.

We cannot leave this discussion of religious life in the Israeli Defense Forces without noting the moral values which guide Zahal in war and in peace. No army has treated its prisoners of war with as much humaneness and care as has the Israeli army, especially when contrasted with the barbaric treatment Israeli prisoners received at the hands of their Arab captors. No occupying army has been as patient with and helpful to its defeated enemies as the Israeli army is with the Arabs of the West Bank. This is evidenced by the "open-bridges" policy which permits West Bank Arabs to have free communication with fellow Arabs who are constantly proclaiming that they are "in a state of war" with Israel. The recent "good-will gate" at Israel's border with Lebanon, inviting sick Lebanese to receive medical treatment in Israeli hospitals at a time when the rest of the world is indifferent to the fate of the Lebanese people, is further evidence of the "religious" character of the state and its defense forces.

Bnai Akiba

No pioneering movement can continue to flourish unless it captures the fancy of the young, who possess that happy combination of idealism and physical strength. Every branch of Zionism, from the extreme left to the right, has its youth organization, and religious Zionism is no exception. Its youth movement is called Bnai Akiba, named after the famous Tanna who stood out from amongst his colleagues both in his system of scriptural interpretation[15] and in his support of Bar Kochba as the Messiah (see above, p. 156). Organized in 1929, Bnai Akiba receives most of its recruits from pupils of religious schools. Its major objective is to persuade its members to live in a religious kibbutz. But before the physical preparation for such a life by assignment to a kibbutz or a special *hakhsharah* (preparation) camp, comes the ideological preparation through a youngster's participation in the programs conducted by the various Bnai Akiba centers. Combining physical activities—sports, and especially the favorite Israeli sport of *tiyulim*, or field trips—with lectures and study groups, Bnai Akiba youth develop an intense love of Eretz Yisrael and complete identification with Medinat Yisrael. The many Bnai Akiba chapters which have been organized in the Diaspora are a major source of religious young people who decide to build their future in Eretz Yisrael. The Bnai Akiba movement is a reservoir which refreshes the Yeshivot Hesder and the religious kibbutzim with a flow of new members, maintaining the full participation of religious Zionists in the continued growth and security of the State of Israel.

Summary

We have described how the translation of Messianic faith into a practical program for Israel's Redemption led to the organization of religious Zionism in the Mizrachi movement, and to the establishment of settlements and institutions which give the State of Israel much of its religious character. The basic ideas which animated religious Zionism from its very inception, and which continues to be its raison d'etre today with the State of Israel an established reality, are two-fold. First, as far as Jewish peoplehood is concerned—and in this it is unique and not to be compared with other peoplehoods—religion (i.e., Torah as interpreted by the Halakhah) and nation are one and indivisible. Though religious Zionists concede that in this day and age religion is a private matter as far as the individual is concerned, and that a Jewish state cannot compel all its citizens to observe the mitzvot of the Torah, they unequivocally maintain that where the Jewish state as an entity is concerned—for example, in all its public institutions—the prescriptions of the Halakhah must be lived up to. This, of course, implies that the Halakhah is cognizant of the novel situation in the history of the people brought about by the existence of an independent Jewish state in the twentieth-century world.

Secondly, the Jewish people is one and indivisible, embracing all Jews, religious and non-religious alike. Consequently, religious Zionism has not lost its purpose with the establishment of the state. Its continuing major concern is the shaping of the religious character of Israeli society, guarding against the insidious influence of those Jews who, because of either ignorance or distortion of Judaism, eat away at the basic character of the Jewish people, and lead to defec-. tion from its ranks (assimilation) and a loss of identification with one's true heritage. In contradistinction to other groups in Orthodox Judaism,religious Zionism insists that religious Jews should not confine all their educational efforts and associations to their "in-group," thus creating a religious ghetto, but must accept responsibility for the religious enlightenment of all segments in Jewish life.

It remains for us to assess to what extent religious Zionism has succeeded in its efforts to make the State of Israel a Jewish state *al-pi Torat Yisrael*. Nay more, it behooves us to assess in what way Medinat Yisrael represents in actuality *Ge'ulat Yisrael*, Israel's Redemption as conceived by the prophets and sages of Israel. To this we devote our next, and final, chapter.

12

The Jewish State
and the State of Israel

The State of Israel was born out of the union of two disparate historical factors: (1) the traditional aspiration of the Jewish people for *ge'ulah*, Redemption from Exile; and (2) in an era of general national emancipation, the awakening of an oppressed Jewry to emancipate itself from the ubiquitous and incessant plague of anti-Semitism. We may call the first factor "religious," for it stems from a faith in a Divine promise. The second we may call "political," for it was stimulated by the new political movements of the nineteenth century. The hope of those motivated by the first factor was the emergence of a "messianic" state, guided by the laws of the Torah. The hope of those motivated by the second factor was the creation of a "normal" state, with the separation of church and state which characterizes most modern national entities.

As a result of these two divergent aspirations, the State of Israel today lives, in many respects, a divided life; and presents to different segments of the Jewish people a different physiognomy. As far as religious Jews are concerned, some see in Medinat Yisrael at least a partial realization of the age-old hopes for Redemption; whereas others see in it no more than one more country in which Jews are able to live out their lives in their traditional accustomed way, patiently praying and waiting for the coming of *Mashiah ben David*. As for the non-religious, some see the State of Israel as the state of the entire Jewish people with no basic differentiation, outside of civic allegiance, between Jews who reside in the state and those who reside in the Diaspora; whereas others see it as a state of

Israelis with an evolving culture distinct and different from the traditional culture of dispersed Jewry, destined to end eventually in two separate peoples, Israeli and Jewish. It is this multifocal image which makes the assessment of Israel's religious significance—which is the basic purpose of our analysis—so difficult.

Anti-Semitism and the State of Israel

It must, however, be made clear that the dichotomy outlined above is not as clear-cut and sharp as appears on the surface. The "political" Zionists who strove for a normal state did not conceive their goal to be merely "a state like all other states." The early non-Orthodox Zionists, men like Moses Hess and Leon Pinsker and Theodor Herzl, even though their point of departure was anti-Semitism, pictured the future Jewish state as a "model" state, one which would not only solve the problem of anti-Semitism but in which would be incorporated the ideals of social justice preached by the ancient Hebrew prophets.[1] Such a picture was inspired by the Messianic tradition deeply imbedded in the consciousness of these secular Jews. It was this connection between what appeared on the surface to be completely secular nationalism and the religious heritage of the Jewish people which impelled secular Zionists to reject any territory other than Eretz Yisrael (e.g., Uganda, offered by the British) as a solution to the Jewish problem. And it was only because socialism claimed to be a "messianic" movement that would solve all of humanity's problems, including that of anti-Semitism, that secular Zionists married their socialism to their Zionism, maintaining that the latter would succeed only if it incorporated the former in its national framework.

It is more difficult to explain the marriage of Marxism to Zionism, when the avowed ideology of the former is *ipse dixit* inimical to the existence of a Jewish state.[2] Nevertheless, paradoxical as it may seem, the Knesset includes several Marxist members who by their statements would in any other country be considered traitors. An example, indeed, that the Jewish state is unique and unparalleled!

As for religious Zionists, the elimination of anti-Semitism also was both stimulus and hope; they also were impelled by the wretched condition of the Jews in *galut*, and inspired by the apocalyptic picture of the homage and tribute that would be rendered the redeemed people of Israel by the *umot ha-olam*, the nations of the world. Did not Isaiah predict that "all who were incensed against you shall be ashamed and confounded; they who strove against you shall be as nothing and perish" (Isa. 40:11)? Nay more, God had promised: "Behold I will lift up My hand to the nations, and set up My ensign to the peoples. . . They shall bow down to you with their faces to the earth and lick the dust of your feet" (Isa. 49:22−23).[3] The Rabbis of the Midrash made this observation: "Israel was compared to the dust of the earth [Gen. 13:16] and to the stars of heaven [Gen. 15:5]. In this world they are like the dust of the earth, treaded upon by all; but in the future they will be like the stars above, shining upon all."[4] For prophet and sage alike, the future glory of Israel, with complete freedom from slander and persecution, was an integral part of *yemot ha-moshiah*.

Thus Maimonides concludes his forecast of the Messianic era: "Then there will be no persecutor hindering Jews from the tranquility essential for their concentration upon the study of the Torah."[5]

Though the elimination of anti-Semitism was the common hope of all Zionists, events following upon the establishment of the State of Israel prove that this hope was too sanguine and unrealistic, at least for the founding generation and their children. It should, perhaps, have been understood by the early Zionists that the creation of an independent Jewish state could not by itself and in short order eliminate such a deep-rooted prejudice as anti-Semitism, which has existed in one form or another, and for one reason or another, or for no rational reason at all, ever since the Jewish people became recognized as a separate people. It started in Egypt, long before we established an independent state, its perpetrators imputing to us disloyalty to the host country (Exod. 1:10).[6] It received great reinforcement when our forefathers were still wandering in the wilderness and were accused that they are out "to lick clean all our [Midian's and Moab's] surroundings as an ox licks clean the grass of the field" (Num. 22:4). When we first became dispersed in Exile, we aroused the animosity of that arch anti-Semite Haman, who authored the classic anti-Semitic charge that we are "a certain people scattered abroad and dispersed among the peoples. . . their laws are diverse from those of every people, nor do they keep the king's laws; therefore it is not worth for the king to leave them be" (Esther 3:8). We had an independent state during the days of the Second Temple, but it did not prevent the Stoics from becoming "the first professional Jew-haters," slandering the Jewish people with the most execrable and fantastic fabrications.[7]

Christianity and the State of Israel

The anti-Semitism preached and indoctrinated by Christianity over and over again through the centuries is too well known for us to have to describe it; and it is too deeply rooted in the canons of the church for us to expect its vanishing with the establishment of a Jewish state. Curiously enough, Zionism and the State of Israel have been both condemned and encouraged by Christian spokesmen. There were Christians, who, out of their profound hatred of the Jews, were anxious to get rid of them, but were not ready to adopt Hitler's "final solution" by means of mass extermination. They looked favorably upon the Zionist movement if only it would create a place to which Jews could be expelled. Yet when the State of Israel was established, they were faced with a dilemma. For Christian theology teaches that the Jewish people have been rejected by God, never to be redeemed as a nation, because of their rejection of Jesus. The return of Jews to the Promised Land, however, and their establishing therein an independent Jewish commonwealth, is an apparent refutation of this theology, and therefore has to be discredited. The present Pope's overt condemnation of any action taken by Medinat Yisrael to defend itself against terrorists is undoubtedly based upon such reactionary theology.

On the other hand, fundamentalist Christians who believe that the Jews of today are the children of Israel to whom the Promised Land was promised, support the return of the Jewish people to Zion and the establishment therein of a Jewish state because they see in these events a fulfillment of biblical prophecy. An example of such support, which happened to prove crucial in the short history of the State of Israel, was President Truman's immediate recognition of the state against the advice of his State Department. Harry Truman was a Southern Baptist, and undoubtedly was influenced in his decision by his religious background. The fact remains, however, that most Christian clergymen remain indifferent when Medinat Yisrael is faced with a challenge to its very existence.

Though anti-Semitism has been muted, albeit not eradicated, in most Christian circles, it has been taken over, lock, stock, and barrel, by the Arabs and their sympathizers. True heirs of Hitler's racist doctrines, which they supported with unabashed vigor during World War II, the Arabs and their Soviet backers are today the major source of anti-Semitic propaganda in all its ugly manifestations. Despite the protestations of anti-Zionists that their venom is directed only against the State of Israel and not against Jews in general, they do not hesitate to employ the crudest arguments of classic anti-Semitism in their supposedly purely political views.

Though the existence of the State of Israel has not eliminated the scourge of anti-Semitism, it has brought many non-Jews to view the Jewish people in a more sympathetic light. Many observers contend that this is due to a guilt feeling induced by Christian indifference to the fate of Jewry during the Hitler period; but there is no doubt that the very fact that Jews were able to resurrect their national independence from the ashes of the Holocaust, and reaffirm in a concrete way their indomitable will to survive, raised the prestige and admiration of both the individual Jew and the Jewish people as a whole in the eyes of a vast number of non-Jews. Even before the establishment of the Jewish state, the heroic efforts of the Zionists against all odds to bring Jews back to Zion created a great deal of

Gentile sympathy for the cause. Many were deeply impressed by the idealism of the halutzim, the social and economic structure of the kibbutzim, and the success in fructifying a land which had lain desolate for so many centuries.

Respect for Jews was greatly enhanced throughout the world by the brilliant military successes of the Israel Defense Forces. What emotionally detached observer could fail to be impressed by and admire the rout of forces overwhelmingly superior in numbers by the Israeli army in war after war! The image of Israel was that of a young David defeating a brute Goliath. This image, however, has been dimmed considerably because of the expansion of Israeli territory, by the artificially prolonged plight of the Palestinian refugees, and by the growing economic power of the Arabs, which threatens to strangle the economies of the Western countries if they persist in their sympathetic attitude toward Medinat Yisrael. A glaring example of such a reversal of attitude was demonstrated by the late General DeGaulle, who could not swallow the "impudence" of the Israelis in winning the Six-Day War without his prior consent.

The Family of Nations and the State of Israel

The Jewish people does not abandon its hope that the day will come when all the nations of the world will give full recognition to Israel's right to survive and to pursue its independent course in the territory it now occupies. Nay more, they will accord full appreciation to Israel's excellence as a peace-loving and peace-pursuing nation. The day will undoubtedly dawn—though we cannot predict how soon—when the State of Israel, instead of suffering a contemptible position in the United Nations, will enjoy a position of leadership and eminence in a Council of Nations cleansed of its cacophonous acrimonies and living up to its noble charter. I dare say that when this comes to pass, the headquarters of such an all-embracing council will be transferred to Jerusalem, even to the Temple Mount, in fulfillment of biblical prophecy.

If I interpret Maimonides correctly, the recognition by world powers of Israel's right to live unchallenged and unmolested in Eretz Yisrael has vital halakhic significance. In discussing the *kedushah* (sanctity) of Eretz Yisrael as it pertains to the observance of those mitzvot dependent upon the Land (see above, p. 45), Maimonides distinguishes between the *kedushah* with which Eretz Yisrael was endowed by Joshua's conquest of the Land, and that with which it was endowed by the return to Zion in the days of Ezra.The first *kedushah*, Maimonides rules, became null and void when Israel was exiled by Nebuchadnezzar; whereas the second *kedushah* remains valid forever. He goes on to explain his ruling as follows: "The obligations arising out of the Land as far as the Sabbatical year and the tithes are concerned had derived from the conquest of the Land by the people [of Israel], and as soon as the Land was wrested from them the conquest was nullified. Consequently, the Land was exempted by the Law from tithes and from [the restrictions of] the Sabbatical year, for it was no longer deemed the Land of Israel. When Ezra, however, came up and hallowed [the Land], he hallowed it not by conquest but merely by the act of taking possession. Therefore, every place that was possessed by those who had come up from Babylonia and hallowed by the second sanctification of Ezra is holy today, even though the land was later wrested from them."[8]

Rambam's commentators find difficulty in understanding the legal distinction between "conquest" (*kibbush*) and "taking possession" (*hazakah*), since the conquerer also takes possession. If one bears in mind, however, the political circumstances at the times of Joshua and Ezra, we can comprehend Maimonides' distinction. At the time of Joshua, no political power recognized Israel's right to possess the Land; but at the time of Ezra it was Cyrus of Persia, whose dominion extended over the entire Middle East, who granted Israel the right to return to Judea, and thus gave official recognition to Israel's act of possession. An act of possession based upon such recognition, Maimonides avers, cannot be invalidated.

When, as we fervently hope, *all* the nations will recognize Israel's right to possess *all* of Eretz Yisrael, the *kedushah* of the Land will extend over the entire territory included within the borders of the State of Israel. The hallowing by Ezra, which has remained valid to this day, extended only over a very small portion of Eretz Yisrael. In the full flowering of Israel's Redemption, the Land's holiness will extend, by virtue of Israel's internationally recognized act of possession, over all the territory envisaged and outlined by the Torah (see above, p. 43).

Diaspora Jewry and the State of Israel

One of the striking phenomena in Jewish life which accompanied the renaissance of Jewish statehood in Eretz Yisrael, and which must be considered in our assessment of the religious significance of the State of Israel, is the effect it has had on a multitude of Jews in the Diaspora who were on the fringe of Jewish life or on the brink of complete assimilation. Many Jews attempted to conceal their Jewish origin; for them, as for Heinrich Heine, Judaism was an *ungluck* (misfortune) which only served to hinder them in the achievement of their social or economic ambitions. Other Jews were afflicted with the disease of *selbst-hass*, hating themselves because of their Jewish origin, and projecting their hatred on anything that smacked of Jewishness. Agnostics and atheists, who prided themselves on their emancipation from the superstitions of religion—and of the Jewish religion in particular—could find nothing to justify a continued attachment to Jews who strove to maintain their religious heritage. Jews who grew up in Communist countries and were spoon-fed anti-Zionist doctrine; Jews who grew up in democratic countries and received no Jewish upbringing or education whatsoever, and consequently knew nothing of the Jewish past or of Jewish hopes for the future; for all these there was nothing special about Judaism or being Jewish, and any emotional or intellectual concern about the fate of Jewry which they may have seen in their parents or grandparents had no meaning for them.

All the aforementioned Jews were, in some mysterious way, profoundly affected by the phenomenon of a Jewish state fighting for its life. They who had attempted to conceal their Jewishness now openly acknowledged it; they who had been ashamed of their Jewishness were now proud of it; they who had abandoned their religious faith now sought to reestablish contact with it. The State of Israel was a catalytic agent, joining together that which had been sundered, fanning the dying embers of Jewish consciousness. For Jews who had been drained of their Jewishness, and whose only means of expressing it was a shoddy and vulgar caricaturing of Jewish mannerisms, Medinat Yisrael supplied a positive and meaningful content. It gave a purpose to those who had lost all purpose—*a concern for the fate of Israel, the people and the state alike, for the fate of one was linked with the other.*⁹

These Jews have been redeemed, redeemed from the abyss of total assimilation. If not for the State of Israel they would be—to quote the woman from Tekoa—"as water spilt on the ground, which cannot be gathered up again" (II Sam. 14:14). And, as she continued, "God has devised means that he who is banished be not banished from Him forever." True, these Jews as yet have little else as the content of their Jewishness other than support of Israel; but *mitzvah goreret mitzvah*, this one mitzvah will eventually draw in its train many more mitzvot, enriching both their concept and practice of Judaism. This sole link to the Jewish people as represented by the State of Israel will lead to the forging of other, stronger, links binding them to all aspects of Jewish life. And if they themselves do not advance further in their return to Judaism, there exists the hope that their children will. The Torah relates that before Moses slew the Egyptian who smote an Israelite, "he turned this way and that, and saw that there is no man" (Exod. 2:11); which the Midrash interprets as follows: "He saw that no righteous descendents would arise from him unto the end of all generations."¹⁰ No non-Jew, let alone any Jew, is completely banished from Jewish life if we can foresee his children, or children's children, becoming loyal and observant Jews.

The State of Israel is contributing to the enrichment of Jewish life everywhere. As in past periods of our history, Jewish youth from all parts of the Diaspora come to Israel for a period of study. The Yeshivot of Eastern Europe destroyed by the Holocaust have been reincarnated in Eretz Yisrael. Students of American Yeshivot spend one or more years continuing their talmudic studies in the Holy Land. A further token that Medinat Yisrael is a focal point, not only for the Return to Zion but for a Return to Judaism as well, is the cropping up in Eretz Yisrael of a number of educational institutions specially designed to teach Judaism to a youth, including "hippies" and leftists of various sorts, that was completely estranged from Jewish life and possessed not even a modicum of Jewish knowledge. Furthermore, Jewish schools in the Diaspora rely more and more upon teachers from Eretz Yisrael to staff their faculties.

Some early Zionists, Ahad Ha'am in particular, saw the goal of Zionism as the creation of a state whose chief function would be, not the absorption of persecuted Jews from the Diaspora, but to serve as a spiritual center from which a revitalized Jewish culture would radiate to the communities in *hutz la-aretz.* Ahad Ha'am understood that "a society is such only by reason of its consciousness and its will to survive," and he envisaged a revived Jewish state in Eretz Yisrael as the source of this national consciousness for world Jewry. A concrete example of the state's performance of such a function is its fixing the twenty-sixth day of Nisan as *Yom Ha-Sho'ah,* Memorial Day for the six million victims of the Holocaust. Medinat Yisrael has, in effect, revived the centrality of Eretz Yisrael in Jewish life.

For religious Jewry, whose ties with Jewish life are based upon religious tradition, Medinat Yisrael does not assume the same crucial role as it does for their non-religious brethren. After all, Judaism has survived for so many centuries without a Jewish state, and without the community in Eretz Yisrael playing a central role in Jewish life. The crucial factor in the survival of the Jewish people in all its vicissitudes has been its adherence to Torah, and therefore many Orthodox, Torah-true Jews do not view the creation of Medinat Yisrael as a factor in Israel's Redemption. However, they fail to take into account two basic considerations. First, *Malkhut Yisrael,* a commonwealth of Jews in the Holy Land, regardless of the degree of Torah-observance of its leaders and/or its inhabitants, is in and by itself a religious value. See what the Bible says concerning Jeroboam, son of Joash, king of Israel in Shomron (Samaria). "He did what was evil in the sight of the Lord . . . He restored the borders of Israel . . . For the Lord saw the affliction of Israel that it was very bitter . . . And the Lord did not say [i.e., wish] to blot out the name of Israel from under the heaven, and He saved them by the hand of Jeroboam son of Joash" (II Kings 14:24–27). We can say no less, and indeed much more, concerning the kingdom of Israel today as represented by the State of Israel.

Secondly, the conditions in the Diaspora today are different from those which prevailed in previous centuries. Jews today live in open societies, exposed to the allurements of their non-Jewish surroundings, easy prey to the ravages of assimilation. And in pluralistic democratic societies, the powers of excommunication (*herem*), once exercised to restrain deviations from accepted Jewish norms, are no longer existent. A State of Israel that stems the tide of assimilation is the divine means of saving Jews for Judaism. All logic and sentiment leads us to the conclusion that Medinat Yisrael is an unmistakable sign that we are living in the era of *athalta di-ge'ulah*, the beginning of Israel's Redemption.

The Ingathering and the State of Israel

"Behold, these shall come from afar. . . . Lift up your eyes round about and behold, all these gather themselves together and come to you. . . . Then you will say in your heart, Who has begotten me these . . . and these, Who brought them up?" (Isa. 49:12, 18, 21).

A sure sign of Israel's Redemption, "written in the Torah, and repeated in the Prophets, and reiterated in the Writings," is *kibbutz galuyot*, the Ingathering of the Exiles. If we but lift our eyes and see, whence came these immigrants who have come to settle in Eretz Yisrael since the establishment of Medinat Yisrael and with its active assistance, we can only express our amazement. They have come, as the prophets predicted, from the North and the South, from the East and the West; from lands of persecution and lands of plenty; from dictatorships and from democracies; from primitive societies and from cultured societies; from traditional communities and from emancipated communities; from religious homes and from non-religious homes; "all, all have gathered themselves together and come to you."

Concerning some of these immigrants we have asked ourselves, "who has begotten me these?" When the Benei Yisrael came from India, rabbis questioned their lineage. Are they really of Jewish descent? May we welcome them into *kahal ha-Shem*, God's community, and permit them to marry into our faith?[11] Concerning other immigrants, those who came from Soviet Russia, we have asked, "who has brought these up?" What has inspired them to want to leave the land of their birth and upbringing, a land where the word *Zion* was anathema, where the Hebrew language and the study of Torah were banned, where application to go to Israel meant loss of job and status, and was met with derision and ostracism? Should we not conclude with the prophet, "And all flesh shall know that I the Lord am your Saviour; and your Redeemer is the Mighty One of Jacob" (Isa. 49:26).

True, this aspect of Redemption is not without *hevlei mashiah*, the pangs of the Messianic era, which are the inevitable concomitant of a people emerging from Exile and dispersion to national renaissance. Settling *olim* from so many different climes and cultures is not achieved without a host of serious problems, many of them a result of the yet unredeemed character of Israeli leadership and society. We cannot forget the shameful chapter of *yaldei Teiman*, when the children rescued from Yemen were forcibly robbed by agents of the Israeli government of their traditional piety and folkways. Shorn of their *peyot* (earlocks), thrust into the anti-religious environment of left-wing kibbutzim, these innocent youngsters were beguiled into a repudiation of all that they had been taught was sacred. This was not the Redemption for which their parents had prayed; nor did it bring any of the social blessings to which the secularist Zionist aspires. Non-religious Israelis failed to distinguish between the positive values of strong family traditions, which enable an immigrant to adjust to his new environment without too sharp a break in his life-style, and the negative features of unprogressive attitudes, which have to be altered in order to take a constructive place in a developing twentieth-century state. The process of Redemption has been immeasurably slowed down by the anti-religious prejudices of many who are responsible for the *klitah*, or absorption, of those who are being ingathered.

Medinat Yisrael has also not been spared the psychological harm suffered by many *olim* because of their sudden transition from an Oriental to a Western society. The social, economic, and educational gap which divides Israeli society into two camps, the advantaged and the disadvantaged, is a source of frustration which hinders the development of a "redeemed" society. If, as we believe, the process of Redemption is one which can be hastened through our human will and endeavor, a major effort must be made by Medinat Yisrael to reduce and eventually eliminate this gap. Though the division between Sephardi and Ashkenazi Jewry is the result of centuries-long historical circumstances and cannot be eliminated in one generation, it must be borne in mind that one of the purposes of the Ingathering is to bring together the dispersed tribes of Israel so that they coalesce into *goy ehad ba-aretz*, a unified people in its ancestral Land.

In a beautiful symbolic chapter, we read how the prophet Ezekiel was commanded by God to take two pieces of wood representing the two kingdoms of Judah and Ephraim (Judea and Samaria) and bring them nigh to each other so that they become one in his hand. The symbolism is clearly explained: "Thus says the Lord God: Behold I will take the children of Israel from among the nations whither they are gone, and I will gather them on every side and bring them into their own land; and I will make them one nation in the land, upon the mountains of Israel, and one king shall be king to them all; and they shall be two nations no more, neither shall they be divided into two kingdoms any more at all" (Ezek. 37:21−22).[12] At present, the Chief Rabbinate of Israel has two chief rabbis, a circumstance which has enhanced neither the prestige nor the efficacy of the rabbinate. As we look forward to the elimination of the social and cultural division between the Sephardi and Ashkenazi components of Israeli society, so must we look forward to the day in the not too distant future when the two rabbinates become one, "and one chief rabbi shall be rabbi to them all."

During the long course of the process of Redemption there will remain one division dividing the Jewish people, a division depending solely upon place of residence. As far as we can see, and as far as we can hope, many many Jews will remain in *hutz la-aretz*. Nevertheless, all Jews will be united in their love for Eretz Yisrael and their loyalty to Medinat Yisrael. Commenting on the verse in Psalms (87:5), "And of Zion it shall be said, This man and that was born in her," the Talmud says: "Both the man born in her and the man who looks forward to seeing her" (*Kethubot* 75a). A basic goal of Medinat Yisrael, again a token of its redemptive role, is to encourage every single Jew in the Diaspora "to look forward to seeing it"; if not to settle in it, at least to make a pilgrimage to it. But the major effort must be devoted to encouraging Jews to make Eretz Yisrael their permanent home. The results so far of the program to increase aliyah have not been very encouraging. Many *olim* who have made the attempt to settle in Eretz Yisrael have been disappointed and have returned to the *galut*. And many more who have entertained serious thoughts of coming on aliyah have hesitated and postponed their decision to take this fateful step in their lives. Even more disappointing is the distressing phenomenon of many Israelis leaving Eretz Yisrael to seek their happiness and good fortune in *hutz la-aretz*. A bit of earnest soul-searching will reveal the basic cause of this turning back of the clock of Redemption. Diaspora Jews heed the call to Return to Zion because they seek personal redemption; redemption from the emptiness and vain materialism of the *galut*. Furthermore, they are motivated by the desire to participate personally in this great historic process of Israel's Redemption now taking place in Eretz Yisrael. In Israel they hope to find idealism and spirituality; a sense on the part of Israelis that they have been chosen by Divine destiny to fashion an ideal society in the land of the prophets. Such a sense would not have allowed the development in contemporary Israeli society of the self-seeking materialism which has prompted such a large *yeridah* (going down from Eretz Yisrael) to *hutz la-aretz*, nor the growing incidence of crime, the lack of ethical and moral integrity, the absence of identification with the goals of Zionism and with the Jewish people as a whole.

The Ingathering of the Exiles will proceed at a rapid pace, and thus hasten the process of Redemption, when Israelis realize its ultimate purpose as defined by the prophet: "He [God] gives a soul to the people upon it [the Land], and spirit to them that walk therein" (Isa. 42:5).

The Halakhah and the State of Israel

Israel's Redemption is all-embracing; it includes not only the People of Israel and the Land of Israel, but the Torah of Israel as well. When the people were exiled, the Torah was exiled with them; and just as exile is an abnormal situation for the people hindering their normal development, so exile is an abnormal situation for the Torah, limiting its normal development. The Sages make the following comment on the verse in Lamentations (3:6): "'He has made me dwell in dark places, as those who have been long dead'; this refers to the Talmud of Babylonia" (Sanhedrin 24a). They also said: "As soon as Israel was exiled from its proper place, there is no greater neglect of the Torah than this" (Hagigah 5b). With the restoration of the People of Israel to the Land of Israel, we should be looking forward to the restoration of the Torah to its pristine function and glory.

To understand what we mean when we speak of the "normal development" of the Torah, we must first briefly examine its nature. The Torah, which is the basis of the religious faith of the Jewish people, has produced a unique religion, namely Judaism, for a unique people. Its uniqueness lies in the fact that it is a constitution for a concrete national entity, and not merely a manual of worship or a catechism of certain theological dogmas. Hence it encompasses all aspects of human activity, political and social as well as ritual. True, Judaism is based upon Divine revelation, but it is also true that the meaning of revelation unfolds in the course of historical time. Thus our Sages have equated *halikhot*, "ways of life," with *halakhot*, "the laws of the Torah" (*Megillah* 28b). They also have asserted that once the basic Law was revealed at Sinai, its interpretation and the halakhic decisions based upon it are no longer to be revealed from Heaven but are given over to the human masters of the Law (*Baba Metzia* 59b).[13] The master of the Law proceeds on the assumption that for every contingency he can find some phrase or word, or even letter, in the revealed text that can serve as the basis for a decision. Furthermore, a decision reached by a court composed of the masters of the Law by inference from the text does not possess the eternal incontrovertibility of the text itself; it is subject to revision by a later court. Thus Maimonides rules: "A high court which expounded the Law by one of the rules of inference according to its understanding and rendered a decision on that basis, and then a later court finds a reason to reverse the previous decision, it may do so and judge according to its own understanding."[14] This is the method of Halakhah as it was practiced in talmudic times and which made possible the normal development of Jewish Law.

It is not clear exactly what the redactor of the Talmud meant when he said that "Rav Ashi and Rabina are the end of *hora'ah* [instruction or halakhic decision]" (*Baba Metzia* 86a), but it no doubt put a brake on continued *midrash halakhah*, i.e., halakhic deductions from the text of Scripture.[15] Maimonides, in his review of the history of the Torah's development, writes: "Rabina and Rav Ashi and their colleagues are the end of the great sages of Israel who transmitted the Torah *she-be'al-peh* [the Oral Law]. . . . All Israel are duty-bound to follow everything in the Babylonian Talmud . . . since all of these things were accepted by all Israel. All the scholars who arose after the composition of the Talmud studied it, bringing to light its obscurities and explaining its subject matter." Maimonides attributes this break in the continuity of halakhic development to the far-flung dispersion of Israel and the consequent paucity of students of the Law.[16]

Furthermore, the Halakhah has built within itself several self-limiting features which have limited its normal development. It has adopted the principle that once a *beit din* instituted a certain restriction (*gezeirah*), that restriction remains in force even though the circumstances which prompted its adoption no longer exists, unless and until a subsequent *beit din* formally adopts a resolution nullifying it (*Betzah* 5a).[17] At the same time, the principle was accepted that "one *beit din* cannot nullify the decision of a previous *beit din* unless it is greater in wisdom and numbers" (*Eduyot* 1:5); and it is also assumed that "the generations are getting lesser and lesser [in wisdom]."[18]

Despite the aforementioned limitations, the Halakhah did continue to develop and remain vital during the long period of the Exile. It responded, and continues to respond, to changes in circumstances, to advances in technology and the discovery of new methods of communication, demonstrating its inherent viability and contemporaneity. But these responses during the Exile were given to the religious questing of an individual, or a group of individuals, such as a community. The Halakhah before the present era was not called upon to respond to the special requirements of a national entity; it did not develop a *hilkhot medinah*, laws concerning a state. Thus the Halakhah has been confronted with a formidable challenge with the creation of Medinat Yisrael.

The difficulty of formulating a *hilkhot medinah* for Medinat Yisrael does not lie primarily in the lack of precedent or methods of halakhic development. In the first place, the present-day halakhic authorities are faced with the fact that Medinat Yisrael is in one sense a Jewish state, but in another sense it is a state like all other states, where there is "a wall of separation between church and state." Secondly, there is the difficulty experienced by halakhic masters in making a psychological adjustment to such a radical change in Jewish life. Halakhah, by its very nature, is traditional and conservative, instinctively resistant to the introduction of new norms. Furthermore, *hilkhot medinah* implies that a ruling applies to the Jewish people as a whole; and for such we need a halakhic body which assumes and enjoys a universal authority, something egregiously absent today.

One aspect of the Halakhah for which there should have been no insuperable difficulty in making adaptations to the needs of the modern State of Israel is the area of civil law.[19] The Halakhah has dealt since its inception with matters between a man and his neighbors, even as Moses charged the judges of his day: "Hear out your fellow men, and decide justly between any man and a fellow Israelite or a stranger" (Deut. 1:16). A study of the *Hoshen Mishpat*, the section of the *Shulhan Arukh* (Code of Jewish Law) that deals with the whole system of civil jurisprudence, will easily substantiate another dictum of Moses; "what great nation has statutes and judgments so righteous as all this Torah which I set before you this day" (Deut. 4:8). For these righteous statutes to serve as the codex for Israeli courts, they first have to be adapted to modern commercial practices, and the archaic terms of the *Hoshen Mishpat* have to be translated into modern legal terminology. Indeed, in 1948 the late Chief Rabbi Isaac Halevi Herzog founded an institute for precisely this purpose, the Harry Fishel Institute for Research in the Jurisprudence of the Torah. This institute has an allied major purpose, to prepare talmudic scholars to serve as judges in the Israeli rabbinic courts.

The dualistic character of the State of Israel, its Jewishness and its secularity, has led in this area as in others to the establishment of two separate divisions in the judicial system, state courts and rabbinic courts (the judges in the former are known as *shoftim*; in the latter as *dayyanim*). The wide gap between the two, with the judges in the one ignorant of the basic codex of the other, and with the lawyers appearing before the one receiving a different training from those appearing before the other, is further testimony of the yet unredeemed character of Medinat Yisrael. It is particularly distressing that the state law has ignored the rich treasure of our religious law, and is content to continue with a melange of Ottoman and British law. How well do the accusing words of Jeremiah (2:13) apply: "For My people have committed two evils: they have forsaken Me, the fountain of living waters; and have hewn for themselves broken cisterns that can hold no water." The process of Redemption will be hastened in proportion to the increasing rapprochement between the state law and the law of the *Shulhan Arukh*.

The movement toward rapprochement must come from both ends. Not only must the political leaders in Israel, the great majority of whom are secularists, recognize more and more the religious foundations of the state, but the halakhic masters must recognize more and more the Messianic harbingers in recent events and act accordingly. First of all, the Chief Rabbinate has to be expanded in its numbers, in the quality of its members, and in its powers. It should comprise not only rabbis who received their training in the traditional European-oriented Yeshivot, but also "sabra" rabbis who are the products of the *Yeshivot hesder* and of spiritual leaders who led Jewish communities in the Diaspora, particularly in the West. Many of these rabbis will have had secular academic training in addition to rabbinics, with even a few coming from the Conservative movement, provided that they subscribe fully to the authority of the Halakhah and that their personal conduct is consistent with such commitment.

Secondly, this expanded group of halakhic masters has to be organized like a parliamentary body, with permanent and ad hoc committees to examine various proposals submitted by individual members which would then be debated and voted upon in the plenum. (A similar system was in vogue in the days of the Sanhedrin.) Thirdly, after due procedure it should adopt and promulgate various *takkanot* to bring religious practice in line with present realities, as, for example, the phraseology of our prayers.[20] Fourthly, it should review the many *takkanot* and *gezeirot* instituted in the past, even those instituted by the Sages of the Talmud, and declare as no longer binding those inconsistent with present-day circumstances.[21] Such activities would eventually culminate in the further development of that Halakhah which is based on the talmudic interpretation of Scripture.[22] How far we are today from the *Ge'ulah Shelemah* of the Torah can be seen from how little we have advanced in the direction outlined above!

Let it be understood: a fully functioning Chief Rabbinate will be exercising a *religious* authority and not a *political* one, which is the proper function of the Knesset. Even when we speak of an *Eretz*

Yisrael al-pi Torat Yisrael, we do not envision a theocracy, a rule of the state by the religious establishment. As we have pointed out in earlier chapters, the kings of Israel were the political arm of the Jewish people operating within the framework of their jurisdiction, and not the religious functionaries of ancient Israel. A Jewish state based upon the Torah does not mean that ecclesiastics are the officials of government, nor the legislators and administrators of the law of the Land. However, the Chief Rabbinate, once properly constituted and functioning, should be incorporated within the overall structure of the Jewish state's parliamentary system. In addition to being the highest instance for Jews who seek religious guidance and halakhic instruction, it should serve the general populace, the non-religious included, in a capacity corresponding somewhat to the House of Lords in the British Parliament. It would not initiate legislation, but would have the power to veto any law passed in the Knesset which in its judgment is contrary to the basic law of the Torah or to the essential spirit of Judaism.[23] It would also be the body which advises the Knesset concerning legislation which impinges upon the values and insights of Judaism.

We cannot hope for such an integration of the Halakhah in the government of Medinat Yisrael without a change in the attitude of most Israelis toward the Halakhah, a change from negative to positive. Israelis must come to recognize that the Halakhah is the concrete embodiment of Judaism, that Judaism is the soul of a Jewish state, and that Medinat Yisrael must become the Jewish state. We who have faith in the coming of the *ge'ulah* must have faith in the coming of such a change of attitude. This is the meaning of the biblical *teshuvah*, the return of the people to both the Land and the Torah. We who believe that Israel's Redemption can come to pass only when there is a simultaneous movement of God's will and human endeavor, must assume the burden of persuasion and enlightenment, of inspiration and instruction. We must adapt the slogan of Herzl regarding the state: "If you will, it is no legend." With the good will and sincere dedication on the part of the faithful, the Return to Torah—like the Return to Zion—is no mere legend.

The Ideal State and the State of Israel

The Jewish state, like the Jewish people, is *sui generis*, unlike all other states which have arisen in the course of human history, unique both in its conception and in its fulfillment. All other states developed out of the needs and concerns of a group of individuals—a people or a nation—living in a certain geographical area, who banded together in a political framework in order to protect their right to the land which they inhabited. The sole original purpose of creating these states was to safeguard the particular interests of their citizens. Not so the Jewish state, both in its first form in the days of Joshua, and in its last form in our days as Medinat Yisrael. In both manifestations, the Jewish state was conceived before the Jewish people inhabited the land upon which it established its government, its purpose defined prior to 'its actual functioning. And its purpose, its raison d'etre, was not solely the protection of its own citizens, but primarily the preservation of a theology to which all mankind was invited to subscribe.[24] In the Jewish people and state we have the classic example—so often misunderstood—of the particular existing for the sake of the universal; of "the solitary people" serving the spiritual needs of the family of peoples.

How was the Jewish state of our times, Medinat Yisrael, conceived? Let us quote the statements of two outstanding conceivers of this century, one a religious Zionist and the other a secular Zionist, the one a spiritual leader and the other a political leader. Though Rabbi Kook and David Ben-Gurion differed in their concept and practice of Judaism, they agreed in their basic conception of the Jewish state. Rabbi Kook wrote: "The state is not the supreme good of man. However, this is true only of ordinary states, but not of a state whose foundation is idealistic, which is our state, *Medinat Yisrael*, whose only desire is that 'God be One, and His name One.'"[25] This desire is expressed in the basic declaration of Jewish faith, the *Shema*. When we recite, "Hear O Israel, the Lord is our God, the Lord is One" (Deut. 6:4), we mean, "The Lord who now is our God, and not the God of the idolaters, will in the future be the

One and Only God, as it is said, 'For then will I turn to the peoples a clear language, that they may all call on the name of the Lord'" (Zeph. 3:9).[26] David Ben-Gurion wrote: "The State of Israel will be tested, not by its wealth, nor by its army or technology, but by its ethical image and humane values. . . . the establishment of Israel was not and will not be confined to the setting up of national and sovereign instruments for the Hebrew nation. Rather, it will find its complete and supreme restoration in the fulfillment of its historic destiny in the redemption of mankind."[27]

The idealistic goals of the State of Israel lie on two levels, the particular and the universal. The particular is the molding of the moral character of its citizens so that they create an ideal society; and the universal is the moral influence it will bring to bear upon the nations of the world. Let us deal with the second one first.

The dilemma of the modern world lies in its inability to reconcile national sovereignty with international cooperation for the good of all. All attempts so far to set up a world-wide association of governments, which on the one hand will guarantee world peace and human rights, and on the other hand will foster full expression of the legitimate national aspirations of the many peoples inhabiting the face of the earth, have met with failure. This failure, as is evidenced in the League of Nations and the United Nations, is due to the fact that these organizations were created out of the chaos of world wars and the clashing interests of the victorious powers, and not out of a deeper understanding of man as a metaphysical creature whose life is endowed with Divine sanctity. The United Nations may improve man's physical conditions—provided, of course, that it is not waylaid by the shortsightedness of the very nations that most need such improvement—but it will not alter the foundations upon which international cooperation must be built in order to achieve its professed goals until member states change their basic principles. Ideally, it is the Jewish state, conducting its foreign affairs not for selfish privilege or for base political considerations but for the sake of righteousness and humaneness, which should provide the example that will guide mankind out of its present darkness to the light of morality and justice. The Jewish state's ability to perform its spiritual role among the family of nations will come from its constant awareness of its inherent and indissoluble relationship with its own spiritual origins.

That the State of Israel is today remote from such a pivotal position in world affairs is a fact apparent to all. For Medinat Yisrael to serve as an example to the nations of the world, it first has to be admired and looked up to; today it is reviled and condemned. It has consistently been denied a seat in the Security Council; its spokesmen in the General Assembly face a chamber emptied of the representatives of half the member nations. In a sense, this manifestation of hatred and unwillingness to listen is a tribute to Medinat Yisrael and a token of the world's guilty conscience. It has been argued, and with justification, that Christian anti-Semitism is the reaction of a world reluctant to accept the moral teachings of Judaism as preached to it by Jesus, and that the inquisitorial church is the true Antichrist.[28] Similarly, Israel's present ostracism in the United Nations is an expression of the continued rejection by the Moslem and Communist nations of the international decency which Medinat Yisrael represents. We can only conclude that mankind is fighting against its own redemption. Nevertheless, Israel will not and must not abandon its destiny to fight for mankind's redemption.

Now back to the first purpose, the creation of an ideal society in Medinat Yisrael. What is an ideal society? It has two main features: the absence of crime, and the equality of all its citizens. Twice the prophet, when describing the Messianic age, says: "They shall do no evil nor act corruptly in all My holy mountain" (Isa. 11:9, 65:25). We cannot agree less with the late poet Hayyim Nahman Bialik, who, when he heard that a thief had been caught in Tel Aviv, is reported to have said: "Thank God we are a normal people, we have thieves in our midst." The people of Israel was not chosen, nor is it destined, to be a "normal" people with the percentage of criminals accepted as natural by other peoples. In the past Jews were "abnormal" in their very low rate of crimes of violence, and the goal of a sovereign Jewish state must be to reduce this rate to the absolute minimum. And crime includes not only crimes of violence, such as murder and rape and armed robbery, but "social" crimes like dishonesty in business, corruption in public office, and economic exploitation. Whatever the causes of the crime which is rampant in Israel today—and there are extenuating circumstances both internal and external—we cannot advance toward the Redemption of our people until we regard crime as sin, for which man is accountable and from which he has the capability of freeing himself. As much as the state, in its striving toward the ideal, reduces the ugly environmental factors which are the breeding grounds of crime, it must all the more inculcate, through proper upbringing and education, those moral values which stress respect for one's neighbor and enable man to overcome his base passions. The goal should be, "All Thy people shall be righteous"—and then—"they shall inherit the Land forever" (Isa. 60:21).

In an ideal society all citizens are equal. Despite the assertion of the American Declaration of Independence that "all men are created equal," it is a fact that all men are not *born* equal, with the same physical and intellectual potentialities and with the same economic resources. The ideal society strives to reduce as much as is humanly possible the disadvantages which accrue as a result of congenital inequalities. The powers that be in an ideal society will, in this respect as in others, "cling to the ways of God"[29] (*imitatio Dei*) as described by Job's comforter, "He regardeth not the rich man more than the poor man, for they are all the work of His hands" (Job 34:19).

In the first place, poverty should set no limitations on educational opportunity. Schooling on all levels should be available to all without cost, its level and type dependent on one factor alone, the individual's capacity to absorb his studies and advance in them. Medinat Yisrael has set before itself the goal of free universal education, but economic necessity and the cultural lag in the homes of Oriental Jews have slowed the pace of achieving equality in education. What is more serious, however, is the great deprivation in education existing today in the State of Israel due, not to economic poverty, but to ideological barrenness. As a result, most Israeli children are deprived of the knowledge and understanding to which they are entitled. It is exactly as the prophet described: "Behold the

days come, says the Lord God, that I will send a famine in the land;
not a famine of bread nor a thirst for water, but of hearing the words
of the Lord" (Amos 8:11). The general state schools teach almost
everything except the religious tradition which is the cherished
heritage of the Jewish people. The Bible is taught, but as literature
which has no more sanctity than a Shakespearean drama. If not for
the public celebration of the Jewish Festivals, the majority of the
children who graduate Israeli schools would have absolutely no
knowledge of the religious tradition of their own people, and little or
no respect for those who do. Without an education which teaches
both the values and customs of Judaism, Medinat Yisrael will not
achieve an ideal society. The goal here should be, "All thy children
shall be taught of the Lord"—and then—"great shall be the peace of
thy children" (Isa. 54:13).

As far as living standards are concerned, equality, even in an
ideal society, does not mean that everyone's living quarters will be
identical in size and furnishings, and that everyone will enjoy exactly the same material comforts and luxuries. True, in the Messianic
age we are promised universal prosperity and abundance; but following our concept of that ideal period that there will occur no
suspension of the laws of Nature, fortuitous circumstance and personal lack of enterprise will inevitably lead to inequalities in income.
Thus the Torah predicts, "For there will never cease to be needy
ones in your land" (Deut. 15:11).[30] The whole thrust of the Torah is
to place upon both the individual Jew and corporate society the
responsibility to see to it that no person who is unable to provide for
himself a decent and honorable existence, no matter what the cause,
should remain in want. Therefore it enjoins, "There shall be no
needy among you" (Deut. 15:4).[31]

If you wish, an ideal society is a welfare society, but one that
preserves the dignity of the welfare recipient without at the same
time denying the provident and the industrious the enjoyment of the
more abundant fruits of their labor. Above all, an ideal society
recognizes that the highest form of welfare is that which provides
the opportunity for everyone to sustain himself through his own
enterprise. Thus Maimonides reminds us that of the eight degrees of

charity, the highest is "to uphold one's fellow Israelite who has
fallen, and give him a gift or a loan, or enter into a partnership with
him, or provide him with work, in order to uphold him economically
so that he no longer will find it necessary to seek charity. Concerning this it is said, 'Take hold of him, stranger and inhabitant alike,
and he shall live with you' [Lev. 25:35]."[32]

Take note of the verse quoted by Maimonides. It says, "stranger
and inhabitant [ger ve-toshav],"[33] underscoring the insistence of the
Torah that equality in the Jewish state embrace the non-Jewish as
well as the Jewish citizen. This means that there shall be no discrimination between Jew and non-Jew, or between believer and non-
believer, not only before the court of law, but in educational and
economic opportunity as well. Thus our Sages ruled: "Non-Jewish
needy are supported together with Jewish needy; non-Jewish sick
are visited with Jewish sick; non-Jewish dead are buried with Jewish
dead, to ensure peaceful interfaith relations" (Gittin 61a).[34]

Of course, citizens of Medinat Yisrael have to be classified as to
their religion or nationality, since certain matters like marriage and
divorce are under the jurisdiction of ecclesiastical authorities.
Furthermore, the very fact that the State of Israel is a Jewish state—a
state for Jews but not exclusively so—involves an item of discrimination against the non-Jewish citizen. In accord with the biblical injunction concerning the king of Israel, "From amongst your
brothers you shall put over you a king; you may not put over you an
alien person who is not your brother" (Deut. 17:15), the head of
state—the president or nasi—is necessarily a Jew. A Jewish state also
implies that the majority of its citizens are Jewish, and thus the majority of the representatives in the Knesset will be Jews. But non-
Jewish citizens have the right to vote and to hold public office, with
the exception just noted.

In the ideal Jewish state, the quality of life in all its aspects will
be ideal. To paraphrase Maimonides, "Contentment will replace
want; there will be peace instead of war; Israel's sovereignty instead
of humiliating subjugation; settlement of the Land in place of Exile;
successful enterprise in place of financial loss."[35] People will be happy and healthy, and live to an advanced old age. Thus did Isaiah

promise in the name of the Lord: "The voice of weeping shall be no more heard in her, nor the voice of crying. . . . The youngest shall die a hundred years old" (Isa. 65:19—20). Above all, people will have a profounder understanding of the Divine, "And the earth will be filled with the knowledge of the Lord, as the waters cover the seas" (Isa. 11:9). To know the Lord means to know "What is good and what the Lord requires of us; to do justice and love mercy and walk humbly with your God" (Mic. 6:8).

The ideal is an elusive but ever-beckoning goal; not to be fully realized in historical time, but to serve as a compass pointing out to man the direction in which to proceed on his way to a better life. Though present-day society in Israel is yet far from the ideal, it must set its sights toward such a culmination of history if only to justify its existence in the eyes of God and man. But Israel will advance on the road toward Redemption only if its people are constantly aware that they are the "chosen people." A famous ethnopsychologist of the late nineteenth century, Heymann Steinthal, explained its meaning as follows: "We call ourselves the chosen people, not in order to indicate the height on which we stand or ever stood, not in order to appear superior to our fellow man, but in order constantly to visualize the chasm separating our reality from the ideal tasks of our morality, the chasm between our shortcomings and the model life sketched for us by the Prophets. The ugliness of each act of vulgarity and coarseness shall seem to us more repulsive when we have to admit to its being found in 'a Kingdom of priests'; and even the virtues which we might feel entitled to claim shall fall short of the demands of 'a holy nation.'"[36]

Summary and Conclusion

The purpose of this study has been to survey the Jewish state from two aspects, the ideal and the real. It reviews the blueprint for the first Jewish state as handed down by Moses from Sinai; the establishment of the Kingdom of Israel; the role of priest and prophet. It describes how the Jewish people expressed their hopes for a restored Jewish commonwealth in Eretz Yisrael, and how they were able to preserve these hopes despite the long Exile, dispersion, and persecution. It relates how these hopes led to the establishment of Medinat Yisrael, the modern State of Israel, and to what extent this modern state reflects the ancient aspirations. It expresses the hope that the people of Israel living in this state will develop a society that will be the image of the future Messianic age.

We have recorded the prophecy that Elijah the prophet will appear to announce the coming of the Messiah. I venture to say that before he can fulfill that mission he will have to repeat to the Israel of today what he said to the Israel of biblical times: "How long do you halt between two opinions? If the Lord be God, follow Him; but if Baal, follow him" (I Kings 18:21). How long can Israel today halt between two opinions, between Socialism and Judaism? If its faith is in the former, it will be a state like all other states, built upon human folly and vanity. But if its faith is in the latter, it will fulfill its destiny as "a Kingdom of priests and a holy nation" under the guidance and protection of the Almighty.

This is the challenge facing Israel today. May it have the wisdom and determination to choose the path which can only lead to the long-cherished and repeatedly prayed for *Ge'ulah Shelemah*, the Complete Redemption for Israel in its Holy Land and for mankind all over the globe.

Notes

INTRODUCTION

1. Talmud *Kethubot* 111a, quoting the verse in the Song of Songs (2:7), "I adjure you, O daughters of Israel, etc.," says: "This is an oath that Israel shall not go up [to Eretz Yisrael] like a wall" (i.e., by an organized movement of the people as a whole).

CHAPTER 1

1. For the interrelationship between these two terms, see chap. 3, n. 1.
2. See, however, Rashi and Ibn Ezra, who interpret *his* as referring to Eleazar.
3. Mishnah *Sanhedrin* 2:4; Jerusalem Talmud ad loc.
4. Introduction to chap. 2 of *Sanhedrin*.
5. The judges appointed by Moses were organized as officers of war (Exod. 18:21; Deut. 1:15). Apparently, they served in a double capacity, as judges in litigation between a man and his neighbor, and as leaders of battalions. Hence Moses selected *anshei hayyil*, men of the host. See also below, p. 212, n. 18.
6. Note also the fact that in Lev. 4, where the Torah singles out the various leaders of the people as distinguished from the *am ha-aretz*, or common folk, it mentions the *kohen ha-mashia* (the anointed priest, i.e., the high priest), the *ziknei ha-edah* (the elders of the community), and the *nasi* (the chief), but does not mention *melekh* (king). Accepting the identity of *nasi* with *melekh* (*Horayot* 3:3), if the above leaders are singled out in descending order of importance (cf. *Horayot* 3:6), then it would appear to confirm my argument that according to the Torah the king is subordinate to the *kohen gadol*.
7. *Sanhedrin* 20b; Rambam, *Hilkhot Melakhim* 1:1. It is interesting to note that Rambam, even though he decides according to R. Yehudah, employs the expression of R. Nehorai, "because they asked out of grievances."
8. *Sanhedrin* 2:6 (20d).
9. For explanation of *kuthi*, see *Arukh Hashalem* or Jastrow, s.v.
10. The R. Hizkiah mentioned here is not the well-known son of R. Hiyya, but the Amora who lived in Caesarea (Kissarin), teacher of R. Mana and mentioned frequently in the Jerusalem Talmud. See M. Margaliot, *Encyclopedia of Sages of the Talmud*, 4th ed., vol. 1, p. 285.
11. See Num. 31:6 that the trumpets were used in going out to battle.
12. *Shebuot* 14b–15a; *Sanhedrin* 16b.

13. Cf. Deut. 1:13−15 and Sifre ad loc. Also, Rambam, *Hilkhot Sanhedrin*, chap. 2.

14. Cf. Mishnah *Sanhedrin* 1:6, *Yalkut Shimoni* to Num. 11:16. See also *Sinai* 76 (5735): 126−27, for the symbolism of the number seventy.

15. See *Sifre* to Deut. 17:9, "*To the priests, the Levites:* It is required that the Court include priests and Levites. Should I then assume that if not, the Court is invalid? No, for it says *and the judge*, teaching that even if it does not include priests and Levites it is a valid court."

16. The Mishnah (*Sotah* 9:1) ascribes "your elders, your judges" to the Great Court in Jerusalem, whose members would come to the place where the corpse was found in order to measure to which city it was nearest; whereas the priests would recite the prayer "Forgive Thy people Israel." This reflects the situation which prevailed during the period of the Second Temple, when the authority of the priests was confined to matters pertaining to the Temple Service, and the members of the Sanhedrin—who were not necessarily priests—constituted the general leadership of the people and the supreme authority in interpreting and enforcing the laws of the Torah.

17. It is interesting to note the rabbinic comment on this verse: "Not in the manner other commanders do, who send their soldiers [to the front] and they arrive only at the end" (*Sifre* ad loc.). It is in accordance with this tradition that the commanders of the Israeli Defense Forces (Zahal) say to their soldiers, *Aharai* ("After me").

18. However, as long as Eleazar was living and heading the service in the Sanctuary, his son Phinehas was sent out to battle with the host (Num. 31:6). In the section dealing with the preparation for battle (Deut. 20), the Torah assigned a specific function to "the priest," denoted in the Halakhah as the *mashuah milhamah*, the priest anointed for battle. He was to encourage the men before going out to battle; cf. Mishnah *Sotah* 8:1, and Rambam, *Hilkhot Melakhim* 7:1−3. See also *Yoma* 72b−73a and J. *Megillah* 1:10 (72a−b).

19. The statement in the Talmud (*Sotah* 42a) that the king is superior to the high priest reflects the actual situation which prevailed in the post-Mosaic period— as we see in the course of our discussion—but not the ideal situation prescribed by the Torah. Incidentally, our Sages comment that we do not find that Joshua needed to inquire any judgment of Eleazar, because the latter instructed the men of the army concerning a law of the Torah (Num. 31:21) while his master, Moses, was still alive, contrary to the law which states that a disciple may not render a ruling in the presence of his master (*Erubin* 63a).

20. *Sanhedrin* 16a, *Yoma* 73b.

21. Cf. Rambam, *Hilkhot Yesodei ha-Torah* 7:6, and his Commentary to the Mishnah, introduction to *Sanhedrin*, chap. 10, principle no. 7.

22. *Sifra* to Lev. 27:34. Cf. also *Megillah* 2b−3a, *Temurah* 16a, J. *Megillah* 1:5 (70d).

23. Cf. Mishnah *Yoma* 7:5 and Rambam, *Hilkhot K'lei ha-Mikdash* 10:12, the

persons and matters for which it was permitted to inquire of the Urim and Thummim.

24. *Sotah* 48b, *Yoma* 9b, Tosefta *Sotah* 13:2. See also below p. 226, n. 8.

25. The "judgeship" of Deborah was an exception, stemming from her being a prophetess (Judg. 4:4). See the comment of A. S. Hartum ad loc.

26. According to the Sages in *Seder Olam*, followed by many commentators both medieval and modern, the events of *pilegesh b'give'ah* (Judg. 18–20) occurred at the beginning of the period of the Judges.

27. One of the primary functions of the king was to unite the people into one nation. Cf. the statement of Rambam in *Sefer ha-Mitzvot*, mitzvah 173: "The king of Israel will gather our entire nation and lead us." See also the variant reading in R. Haim Heller's edition (Jerusalem, 5705): "He will raise up our faith, etc." This corresponds to the task of the Messianic king; see Rambam, *Hilkhot Melakhim* 11:4: "He will compel all Israel to walk in the [ways of the] Torah."

28. The Midrash (*Yalkut Shimoni*, ad loc.) attributes to Elkanah, the father of Samuel, the revival of the custom to make the annual pilgrimage to Shiloh: "He would make the pilgrimage with his entire family. [On their way] they would lodge in the square of the city and say to its inhabitants, 'Why don't you come with us to the House of the Lord in Shiloh, for out of there go forth Torah and Mitzvot?' The following year five families would join; a year later ten families; until all of the people would make the pilgrimage."

29. Thus Rashi comments: "That day he sat on a great seat, for he was appointed *judge* over Israel."

CHAPTER 2

1. Cf. the commentaries to Gen. 36:31: "Before there reigned any king over the children of Israel." *Midrash Rabbah Vayikra*, chap. 26, end of sec. 7, refers to Saul as "the first king" in Israel. This seems to contradict the many statements of the Sages cited in chap. 1 above that both Moses and Joshua were kings. Moreover, the same *Midrash Rabbah*, several chapters later (chap. 31, sec. 4, and chap. 32, sec. 2), repeats "*melekh* refers to Moses." This seeming contradiction is reconciled as follows: There was a fundamental difference between the kingships of Moses and Joshua and that of Saul. The latter was the first king who became king as a result of the people's demand; whereas the former two received their positions as kings by direct divine appointment. Thus Saul was anointed at a coronation ceremony, whereas Moses and Joshua required no anointing ceremony.

2. *Sifre* to Deut. 17:15.

3. Cf. Rambam, *Hilkhot Melakhim* 1:3: "A king is originally appointed only by a court of seventy elders [i.e., Sanhedrin] and a prophet."

4. Commentary to Deut. 17:15.

5. Cf. statement of Rambam, Commentary to Mishnah, *Kerithot* 1: "That if

there occurred a conflict . . . which man to appoint [as king] . . . , and then later all agreed upon one of them, or the majority followed him . . . or the kingdom was achieved by one of them in any manner whatsoever, then that one is anointed, etc."

6. *Sotah* 7:8.

7. See *Arukh Hashalem*, s.v. *Ben Zion*, for the lineage of Agriphas. See also S. Lieberman, *Tosefta Kipshuta*, vol. 8, p. 683, discussion as to which Agriphas, the first or the second, is the subject of this incident.

8. *Sanhedrin* 20b. Rambam, *Hilkhot Melakhim* 4, rules that a king may exercise all these rights. However, he softens its harshness by saying: "The king should not act too coarsely with the people. . . . he should be gracious and merciful to both young and old . . . and be mindful of the dignity of even the most insignificant person; as it is said: 'If today you will be a servant to this people . . . and you will speak to them good words, etc. [I kings,12:7]." It is somewhat difficult to reconcile the king's right "to confiscate for his servants fields and vineyards and olive groves" with the ruling that the king is prohibited from "confiscating property, and if he does it constitutes robbery [*gezel*]" (Rambam, ibid. 3:8). See also *Hilkhot Gezelah va-Avedah* 5:11–14, where Rambam concludes: "The general rule is as follows: Every law which the king legislates for everybody and does not affect only one individual is not considered *gezel;* but when he confiscates what belongs to a particular person not in accordance with the accepted ruling but as an unlawful act, it constitutes *gezel.*" No doubt this summation is an adumbration of the story of Ahab and Naboth's vineyard (I Kings 21).

Incidentally, this general rule was also applied to the prerogatives of a non-Jewish king whose laws were recognized by the Halakhah as binding upon his Jewish subjects *(dina d'malkhuta dina, Baba Kamma* 113a and corresponding talmudic sources). See S. Shiloh, *Dina* etc., (Jerusalem, 5735), p. 109, n. 153 (he forgot to include Tosafot *Baba Kamma* 58a, s.v. *iy nami*). See ibid; p. 77, for the relationship between Jewish and non-Jewish kings.

9. Cf. Josh. 1:18: "Any man who will rebel against you . . . will be put to death."

10. This power of the king was codified in Rambam, *Hilkhot Melakhim* 3:8, as follows: "The king has a right to kill anyone who shames him."

11. Cf. the comment of Kimhi to II Kings 13:12 that Joash king of Israel enthroned his son Jeroboam during his lifetime "perhaps because he sensed that his other sons might dispute the kingdom, and therefore he enthroned him before he died." See also *Kerithot* 5b: "A king who is the son of a king [who ascends the throne as a matter of inheritance] is not anointed. Why, then, did they anoint Solomon? Because Adonijah had disputed him. Also, Joash [was anointed] because of Athaliah; and Jehoahaz because of his brother Jehoiakim, who was his senior by two years."

12. *Hilkhot Melakhim* 2:5. Cf. *Sefer ha-Mitzvot*, mitzvah 173: "That we were commanded to appoint over us a king . . . so that his status among us is higher than that of the prophet . . . as our Sages expressly stated that a king precedes a prophet." See *Horayot* 13a: "A king precedes a high priest . . . a high priest

precedes a prophet''; whence we infer that a king most certainly precedes a prophet. See also *Menahot* 98a, where R. Yohanan infers that one must always revere a king from the verse ''And he [Elijah] girded up his loins and ran before Ahab to the entrance of Jezreel'' (I Kings 18:46).

13. *Berakhot* 10a,

14. p. 11 and chap. 1, n. 19.

15. *Hilkhot Melakhim* 2:5. See, however, the qualification of this ruling, as Rambam continues: ''Nevertheless, it is a mitzvah for the high priest to honor the king and to seat him and to stand in his presence when he comes to see him.'' Cf. *Horayot* 13a: ''A king precedes a high priest, as it is said: 'Take with you the servants of your lord' [I Kings 1:35].''

16. Thus Kimhi comments: ''He says *before My anointed* because the priest presents himself before the king . . . and the king would not present himself before the high priest except when he had to inquire of the Urim and Thummim.''

17. Cf. Tosafot, *Yoma* 12b, s.v. *kohen gadol*. Also, Rashi, *Berakhot* 4a, s.v. *ve-Evyathar*, who quotes *Seder Olam* to the effect that Abiathar was replaced by Zadok when the Urim and Thummim failed to respond to the former, but did respond to the latter.

18. The Sages explained the use of the term *kohanim* in such a context in that they were scholars, and therefore were entitled to take the first portion (*Nedarim* 62a). Cf. *Sanhedrin* 16b, where it is stated that Benaiah son of Jehoiada represented the Sanhedrin.

19. It is not clear in what capacity Samuel, who was a Levite (I Chron. 6:19), ''ministered before the Lord.'' Kimhi says: ''What was his service? He would occupy himself with the study of the Torah, to know the Lord, and to learn the levitical service of chanting and playing a musical instrument. All this is 'service of the Lord.''' In a previous verse, Scripture says: ''And the youth was ministering unto the Lord before Eli the priest'' (I Sam. 2:11), implying that he served Eli in some special way, and not in an ordinary levitical service.

20. It is clear that the ''linen ephod'' was not the same as the vestment of that name worn by the high priest, which contained the oracle of the Urim and Thummim. It was to this latter ephod that David referred to when, inquiring of the Lord, he said to Abiathar the priest: ''Bring hither the ephod'' (I Sam. 23:9). Thus Rambam writes in *Hilkhot K'lei ha-Mikdash* 10:13: ''That which you find in the Prophets that the priests would gird a linen ephod, they were not high priests, since the ephod of the high priest was not of linen. Even Levites would gird a linen one, as in the case of Samuel the prophet, who was a Levite and concerning him it is said, 'A youth girded with a linen ephod.' This ephod was also worn by the young [aspiring] prophets and by one who was worthy that the Divine Spirit should rest upon him; to make known that he has reached the exalted degree of the high priest, who speaks through the ephod and the breastplate with the Divine Spirit.''In this connection, one recollects what is related by Josephus in his *Antiquities* (vol. 3, bk. 20): ''Some of the Levites who were singers persuaded the King [Agrippa II] to convene a Sanhedrin which would authorize them to wear linen garments similar to

those of the priests. Though this was against the laws of the Torah, their request was granted."

21. That is, after the Lord gave him rest from all his enemies round about (II Sam. 7:1), in conformity with the passage in Deut. (12:10−11): "and He will give you rest from all your enemies . . . then the place that the Lord your God will choose . . . there shall you bring your burnt-offerings, etc." The Talmud (Sanhedrin 20b) confirms this as a halakhic ruling.

22. The RALBAG comments on the passage there, "and he [David] offered burnt-offerings and peace-offerings," as follows: "Now [bringing offerings on] the high-altars [bamot] was not prohibited until the Beit ha-Mikdash was built, and therefore David, even though he was not a priest, was able to offer up the of-ferings" (See I Kings 3:2). Though it is true that according to the Halakhah a non-priest could minister at a bamah (Mishnah Zebahim 14:10), there is no need to in-terpret the passage that David himself performed the service. Shall we also interpret what is said concerning Solomon, "a thousand burnt-offerings did Solomon offer on that altar" (I Kings 3:4), or "for he offered there the burnt-offerings and the meal-offering and the fat parts of the peace-offering" (I Kings 8:64), that Solomon himself performed the service? Nay more, when Solomon brought the Ark from the city of David to within the Temple, it was carried only by priests (I Kings 3,6). See also the statement of R. Abba b. Kahana (J. Megillah 1:14 [72c] and Vayikra Rab-bah 22:6) that one of the infringements of the law permitted to Gideon (Judg. 6:26) and Samuel (I Sam. 7:9) when they themselves offered sacrifices on specially built altars (i.e., bamot) was the fact that they were non-priests.

23. Hilkhot Beth ha-Behirah 1:3.

24. The Sages ruled: "What is vowed or freely offered [as a sacrifice in the Temple] is accepted from non-Jews, but what is not vowed or freely offered [i.e., a sacrifice obligatory upon Jews, such as a sin-offering] is not accepted from them; and so is it explicitly affirmed by [the Book of] Ezra [4:3], as it is said: 'You have nothing to do with us to build a house unto our God'" (Mishnah Shekalim 1:5). However, non-Jews were not permitted to enter the Temple precincts beyond the Rampart (Mishnah Kelim 1:8); and there was an inscription in Greek and Latin at its entrance warning non-Jews not to enter under penalty of death.

25. Berakhot 30a. There has been a curious development of this ruling. The Holy of Holies was at the western end of the Temple; thus those who prayed within the Temple precincts faced and bowed down toward the west. This orientation, no doubt, was designed to counter the sun-worshippers, who faced the east (Ezek. 8:16). Cf. also Mishnah Succah 5:4: "When the people [at the ceremony of drawing the water for the Succot libation] reached the Temple gate going eastward, they would turn their faces to the west and say, 'Our fathers who were in this place, their backs were toward the temple of the Lord and their faces toward the east, and they worshipped the sun toward the east; but we, our eyes are towards the Lord.'"

Babylonian Jewry, which lived east of Eretz Yisrael, faced the west in prayer. (For an explanation of the statement of R. Haninah in Baba Bathra 25b that Babylonia is north of Eretz Yisrael and therefore Jews there should face the south when praying, see *Teshuvot Hatham Sofer, Orah Hayyim* no. 19. See also Tosafot *Baba Bathra* 25a s.v. *lekhol*). When the bulk of Jewry settled in North Africa and Western Europe, Jews oriented themselves in prayer toward the east, i.e., toward Jerusalem. In the course of time, orientation toward the east *(mizrach)* became such a fixed custom that even when Jews migrated to Eastern Europe, which is more north than west of Eretz Yisrael, they continued to face the east instead of facing south in the direction of Jerusalem. In fact, *mizrach* assumed a special sanctity; many hung on an eastern wall of their home a plaque with the inscription "Mizrach," and "Mizrach" was considered the most honorable section in the synagogue. RAMO (R. Moses Isserles of Poland) seems to have been unaware of this geographical change, for he simply quotes the TUR (R. Jacob b. Asher, who lived in Spain): "We face the east because we dwell west of Eretz Yisrael" (*Shulhan Arukh, Orah Hayyim* 94:2). Later authorities (especially R. Mordecai Yaphe, author of the *Levushim* and a pupil of the RAMO) did take notice of this fact and suggested that East European Jews should face southeast. Most Jews in Jerusalem today, especially those praying at the Western Wall, face east since they are west of the Temple Mount. For those living in the new settlements in the northern sector of Jerusalem (Ramat Eshkol, French Hill—Givat Shapira, and Neveh Yaakov), orientation in prayer should be towards the south.

26. Cf. Rambam, *Hilkhot Melakhim* 3:4: "It is a mitzvah to increase all gold and silver in the Temple's treasury, that it be available for the needs of the community and their wars." See also Mishnah *Shekalim* 4:1—2 and *Kethubot* 106a for the community needs which were paid for from Temple funds.

27. *Horayot* 11a.

CHAPTER 3

1. Here it was where Jeremiah laid the foundation for the unstinting loyalty of the dispersed Jews to the countries of the Diaspora in which they were permitted to dwell. He said: "And seek the peace of the city whither I have caused you to be carried away captive, and pray unto the Lord for it; for in its peace you shall have peace."

2. Cf. *Sanhedrin* 98b: "The Holy One, blessed be He, will appoint for them *another David*." Kimhi to Ezek. 37:24, "And My servant David shall be king over them," comments: "The Messiah King will be called David because he will be a descendant of David, or this is an allusion to the resurrection of the dead." In the above verse Ezekiel refers to the future David as *melekh* (king), whereas in the next verse (25) he refers to him as *nasi* (chief). In a later chapter (44) he calls the high priest *nasi*. We may see here a reflection of the different situations which prevailed during the period of the Second Temple, about which Ezekiel prophesied. At first Judea was under the hegemony of Persian, Ptolemaic, and Seleucid kings, who appointed governors over Judea. These governors were referred to as *nasi*. Thus Sheshbazzar is called "the *nasi* for Judah" in Ezra 1:8, and *pehah* (governor) in Ezra

5:4. In the course of time the high priest was recognized by the imperial authorities as the political as well as the religious leader of Judea, and hence he was the *nasi*. Later, after the Hasmoneans achieved political independence for Judea, Simon, brother of Judah the Maccabee, served in this dual capacity and was officially recognized as such by the Roman Senate (142 B.C.E.). A generation later his son Johanan Hyrcanus assumed the title of "king," even though he was not of the House of David, while continuing to serve as high priest (see *Kiddushin* 66a, where it is related that he was told: "It is enough for you the crown of royalty; put aside the high priesthood"; also the reaction of Nahmanides [Ramban to Gen. 49:10] to this non-Davidic dynasty). The Talmud (*Sanhedrin* 98b) reconciles the two designations by Ezekiel of Israel's future leader as referring to two persons, one the king, and the other "half a king"; the latter most probably meaning the governor. See however *Arukh Hashalem* s.v. *kesar*, and Rashi, ad loc., who take it to mean the *mishneh la-melekh*, or viceroy, a term which corresponds more to the office of prime minister (viz. Esther 10:3).

Once the Hasmoneans proclaimed themselves kings, the high priest lost his political authority, and the title *nasi* was transferred to the head of the Sanhedrin, whose pronouncements were primarily of a religious rather than political nature. However, after the destruction of the Second Temple and the end of Hasmonean rule, the *nasi* of the Sanhedrin was regarded as the political head of the Jewish people. Thus the Sages of the Mishnah saw in the *nasi* of their time the heir of the kings, and therefore interpreted the *nasi* of Scripture (Lev. 4:22) as referring to the king, and not to a chief of one of the tribes (*Sifra* ad loc. and Mishnah, *Horayot* 3:3). Consequently, Rabbi Judah ha-Nasi wondered whether his position conferred upon him the status of the *nasi* of Scripture. When Rabban Gamaliel the Elder died, we are told, Onkelos the proselyte burned his personal effects, as was customary with the effects of a deceased king (see, for example, Jer. 34:5). When questioned about this (burning usable goods is a violation of the biblical command "Do not destroy") [Deut. 20:19], he replied: "Is not Rabban Gamaliel worth more than a hundred useless kings?" (*Semahot* 8:6). His action is confirmed in the ruling: "Just as the effects of kings are burned [at their funeral], so are the effects of *nesi'im* burned" (Tosefta, *Shabbat* 7[8]:18; *Abodah Zarah* 11a).

3. The Targum translates the phrase, "The fathers have sinned and the children are punished."

4. Here we see the great moral responsibility which has been placed upon every Jew as a member of the Chosen People; any immoral act which a Jew commits reflects disdain upon all Jews and their religious faith, thus constituting *hillul ha-shem* (desecration of God's Name). The more honorable a position a Jew holds in the community, the greater his responsibility. Cf. *Yoma* 86a: "What constitutes *hillul ha-shem*, etc." Also, Mishnah *Abot* 4:4: "In profaning the Name, it is all one whether it be done unwittingly or wantonly."

5. Rambam, *Hilkhot Beit ha-Behirah* 1:4: "The building to be erected in the future, even though it is discussed in the Book of Ezekiel, is not fully described and defined therein. Therefore, those who built the Second Temple in the days of Ezra

followed the pattern of Solomon's Temple and adapted some of the particulars described in Ezekiel." See also Mishnah *Middot* 2:5, 3:1, 4:1–2.

6. See Rashi to 44:3. Kimhi maintains that the *nasi* here is the Messiah King, as in 37:26.

7. See above, p. 9. For the talmudic reaction to the inconsistencies between the Pentateuchal legislation concerning the priests and that of Ezekiel; see *Menahot* 45a and *Kiddushin* 78 a–b.

8. See above, pp. 42f for a detailed discussion of the boundaries of Eretz Yisrael. It is interesting to note that Ezekiel talks of twelve tribes returning to Israel, thus including the ten tribes of the northern kingdom, which were exiled by Assyria more than a century before the southern kingdom. In chap. 37, Ezekiel prophesied the uniting of the northern tribes—"Ephraim and the tribes of Israel his companions"—with the southern tribes—"Judah and the children of Israel his companions"—under one leadership. This would seem to refute the opinion of R. Akiba (Mishnah *Sanhedrin* 10:3) that "the ten tribes are not destined to return." There is some evidence that included among the returnees with Zerubbabel· and Ezra were members of these tribes, indicating that they preserved their identity as Israelites in the Assyrian captivity over several generations. See also *Sifra* to Lev. 26:38.

9. The Talmud explains *mikdash me'at* as referring to the houses of worship and study which the Jews established in Babylon (*Megillah* 29a). Though it is beyond the scope of this study to discuss the exact period in Jewish history when synagogues were first established, there is no doubt that they were a vital factor in preserving Jewish identity in the Diaspora.

10. See also the statement of King David when fleeing from Saul beyond the boundaries of Judea: "For they have driven me out this day from being joined to the inheritance of the Lord, saying, Go serve other gods" (I Sam. 26:19).

11. Cf. Maimonides, *Guide of the Perplexed*, vol. 3, chap. 32, where he explains that the commandment to offer animal sacrifices was only a concession to the prevalent mode of worship. The commandment "to serve the Lord with all your hearts" (Deut. 11:13) refers to prayer (*Taanit* 20a).

12. Cf. the rabbinic explanation: "*I did not command* the son of Mesha king of Moab to be sacrificed; *nor did I speak* to Jephtah to sacrifice his daughter; *neither came it into My mind* that Isaac son of Abraham be sacrificed" (*Taanit* 4a, and slightly different version in Midrash *Tanhuma, parashat Vayera*, sec. 40).

13. Some scholars ascribe chaps. 56–66 to a "Trito (Third)-Isaiah, "who presumably prophesied in Judea at the time of the Return to Zion (last quarter of the sixth cent.). See, however, S.W. Baron, *Social and Religious History*, vol. 1, p. 342, n. 3: "The weight of evidence now favors the basic unity of Isaiah 40–66. Nor have the voices arguing for the unity of the whole Book of Isaiah been completely silenced."

14. In classic Jewish literature, the first experience of Exile for the Jewish people was the bondage in Egypt; and the going out of Egypt under Moses was an act of *ge'ulah*, or Redemption. Thus Nahmanides (Ramban) begins his commentary to the Book of Exodus with the statement: "This book is devoted to the theme of the

First Exile and the Redemption therefrom." In Exod. 6:6, God's promise was "I will redeem you [ve-ga'alti]"; and in prophetic and rabbinic liturgical literature God is praised as the Go'el Yisrael, the Redeemer of Israel. The Torah, however, invariably uses the expression, "I Who have taken you out [hotzeiti] of the land of Egypt"; as, for example, in the opening verse of the Ten Commandments (Exod. 20:2). The prophets, when forecasting the future Redemption, compare it with the Redemption from Egypt (Isa. 11:16; Mic. 7:15), but more often use the expression "going up" (aloh) from Egypt, and speak of God as "the One Who brought you up [ha-ma'aleh] from Egypt"; a reflection of God's promise to Jacob on his way down to Egypt: "I will go down with you to Egypt, and I will also bring you up" (Gen. 46:4). It is from this Hebrew root that we have the current name, aliyah, for immigrating to Israel, and the immigrant is called an oleh (plural, olim).

The oft-repeated statement in the Pentateuch that "I am the God Who took you out of the land of Egypt," coupled with the command to remember the going out of Egypt daily (Deut. 16:3), plus the annual celebration of the Festival of Passover, which impresses even more deeply in the mind of the Jew this historic event which occurred at the formative stage of Israel's peoplehood, have all contributed to the complete overshadowing of the Return to Zion in the days of Cyrus, for which there is today no commemorative festival in the Jewish calendar. Thus it is the Redemption from Egypt which has served the Jewish people in its millennial exile as the example and the hope for the future—and hopefully, the final—Redemption.

15. Cf. Ps. 55:18, Berakhot 26b and 31a for the origin of prayer three times a day. Also Bereishit Rabbah 68:11, the statement of R. Samuel b. Nahman: ". . . corresponding to the three times that the day changes [from night to morning to afternoon]."

16. The Book of Esther (2:7) says, "And he [Mordecai] raised Hadassah, she is Esther." The name Mordecai is, no doubt, of Persian origin (Marduk), but it is a moot question whether Esther is the Persian equivalent of Hadassah (myrtle) or unrelated to it (Esther is a form of the Persian Istahar). See the rabbinic discussion (Megillah 13a) as to the meanings of these names. The Sages probably attempted to counter this tendency to adopt non-Hebrew names and languages by asserting that the children of Israel merited redemption from Egypt because—among other things—"they did not change their [Hebrew] names and did not change their language." See M. Kasher, Torah Shelemah, vol. 9, p. 9, for the various sources.

17. "R. Haninah said: 'The names of the months came up with them from Babylon'" (J. Rosh Hashanah 1:2). See also Ramban to Exod. 12:2 for an explanation.

18. Tosefta Sanhedrin 4:7, J. Megillah 1:9, Sanhedrin 21b—22a. Z. Yavetz, Toldot Yisrael, vol. 3, supplementary sec., pp. 14 ff., explains that Ezra changed the script in order to differentiate the Torah in the hands of the Jews from the one held sacred by the Samaritans, who retained the Canaanite script. Coins struck later on by the Maccabean kings bore the ancient script, which by that time had become archaic; this was prompted by nationalist pride.

19. The vision of the Wicked Woman seen by the prophet Zechariah (5:5—11)

is interpreted by the Sages as a symbol of the evil of idolatry, which was overcome and banished from Israel (*Yoma* 69b).

CHAPTER 4

1. In appreciation of Cyrus's proclamation, his capital, Shushan, was portrayed in relief over the eastern gate of the Temple Mount (Mishnah *Middot* 1:3). Cf. Rambam, Commentary to Mishnah, ad loc.: "When they [the exiled] went up from Shushan to build the Temple, the king commanded them to portray the city of Shushan in the Temple, so that the fear of the king should be upon them and they should remember the days of their dwelling there, and they would not rebel against the king."

2. It is difficult to accept Baron's contention that at this period the influence of the prophet weakened, and "the priestly class gained prestige in the eyes of the people" (S. W. Baron, *Social and Religious History*, vol. 1, pp. 149–50). It is sufficient to cite Zech. 3, where the prophet has to contend against the Satan standing at his right hand to accuse Joshua the high priest. The fact of the matter is that the prophets found it necessary to call upon the priests to restore their fallen prestige by returning to their chosen vocation; cf. Mal. 2.

3. Compare the statement in the Talmud (*Zebahim* 62a): "Three prophets returned with the Israelites from the Exile. One of them testified as to the exact site of the Altar; another testified as to its prescribed dimensions; and the third testified that all the sacrifices might be offered upon this Altar even though the Temple was not yet rebuilt." The Sages customarily group the last three prophets together (e.g., *Sotah* 48b), though the first two preceded the third by a generation. In *Abot D'R. Nathan*, chap. 1, these three are classed in a category by themselves, separate from the prophets in general.

4. Some historians claim that the first governor appointed by Cyrus for Judea, the Sheshbazzar mentioned in Ezra 1:8, was the son of Jehoiachin, but that he died shortly after assuming office and was succeeded by his nephew Zerubbabel. Others maintain that Sheshbazzar was the Babylonian name of Zerubbabel.

5. This prediction was eventually realized in two respects: in the size of the Temple structure as enlarged by Herod, and in the number of years it stood; cf. *Baba Bathra* 3a.

Incidentally, the prophet uses the term *aharon*—literally, "last"—for the Second Temple, which gave the early Christians a scriptural basis for their claim that the Second Temple was to be "the last," and with its destruction there was no hope for the rebuilding of a Third Temple, thus sealing forever the doom of the Jewish people as a nation. However, as has been pointed out by Elijah Gaon of Vilna, the word *aharon* in the Bible—as, for example, in Exod. 4:8-means "the one after" or "the latter," but not "the last."

6. See above, p. 21. It seems that there was a temporary struggle for power between Zerubbabel and Joshua, and therefore the prophet intervened. He decided,

in accord with the tradition established by David and confirmed by the Sages, that the king takes precedence over the high priest. Less than a century later, in the absence of a political leader from the House of David, the high priest assumed the position of both political and religious leader; see above, chap. 3, n. 2.

7. See the author's *The Light of Redemption* (Jerusalem, 5731), chap. 1.

8. The people realized that the modest structure they had built was far from the glory of the First Temple. In fact, at the dedication of the Second Temple we are told that "many of the priests and Levites and heads of fathers' houses, the old men that had seen the First Temple standing on its foundation, wept with a loud voice" (Ezra 3:12) because it was so unimposing in comparison with the previous structure. Furthermore, they knew that they were lacking one of the most important components of the First Temple, the Urim and Thummim (Ezra 2:63). See the statement in *Yoma* 21b that five things which were present in the First Temple were missing in the Second.

9. Cf. Rambam's statement at the end of *Hilkhot Melakhim:* "The Sages and Prophets did not long for the days of the Messiah that Israel might exercise dominion over the world, or rule over the heathens, or be exalted by the nations, or that it might eat and drink and rejoice. Their aspiration was that Israel be free to devote itself to the Law and its wisdom, with no one to oppress or disturb it, and thus be worthy of life in the World to Come."

10. Rashi in *Yoma* 9b says that it was half.

11. S. Klein, *Eretz Hagalil,* chap. 1.

12. In making such comparison, certain balancing factors should be borne in mind. Firstly, modern means of transportation have telescoped distances. Secondly, the geographical pattern of the area—whereas the ancient province of Judea was somewhat in the shape of a square, the modern State of Israel (before 1967) was largely an elongated but narrow coastal strip, and furthermore included the large area of the almost uninhabited Negev.

13. Cf. *Baba Bathra* 119b: "Eretz Yisrael is an inheritance from our fathers [i.e., the Patriarchs]"; and Mishnah *Kelim* 1:6: "Eretz Yisrael is holier than any other land."

14. To reconcile this with the statement in Num. 14:5 and Josh. 15:4, some would read *nahal* instead of *nahar*, and identify it with Wadi El Arish in the Sinai Peninsula. The "river of Egypt" is the Nile.

15. *Shebiit* 9:2.

16. See discussion in J. *Demai* 2:1 whether the majority of the inhabitants of Eretz Yisrael were Jewish or non-Jewish.

17. See D. Urman, "Jewish Inscriptions in the Golan," *Israel Exploration Journal*, vol. 22, pp. 16−23.

18. Cf. *Hagigah* 3b: "The olim from Babylon left many cities unconquered so that the poor could receive their tithe during the Sabbatical year [i.e., since these cities were ruled as being outside Eretz Yisrael, the land could be tilled and produce fruit in the Sabbatical year from which the poor could take their share]." Also, *Hullin* 6b−7a: "Rabbi [Judah ha-Nasi] permitted [the fruits of] Beth Shean [to be eaten

without removing the tithes]." Cf. J. *Demai* 2:1 (22c), where it is said that Rabbi permitted the fruits of many other cities.

19. See P. Neeman, *Encyclopedia of Talmudic Geography* (Tel Aviv,5732), vol. 2, pp. 432–33.

20. *Abodah Zarah* 21a, *Gittin* 8a–b, Tosafot *ad loc.* s.v. *kibbush.* Cf. *Sifre* to Deut. 11:24: "Only after you conquer Eretz Yisrael will you have the right to conquer outside the Land. However, once you conquer outside the Land, the mitzvot are applicable there. But then you may ask, 'Why are not the mitzvot applicable in Aram Naharayim and Aram Zovah [Syria] conquered by David?' The Sages said: 'David did contrary to the Torah; he conquered those lands before conquering the Jebusites near Jerusalem.'" See also Rambam, *Hilkhot Terumot* 1:2–3.

21. Cf. *Sifre* ad loc.: "*Every spot,* etc. If this verse comes to teach us the boundaries of Eretz Yisrael, are they not already given [in the second half of the verse]? What then does *every spot,* etc., come to teach? Moses said to them: 'Every place outside of these [already specified] places which you will conquer is yours.'"

22. Mishnah *Kiddushin* 1:9.

23. Ramban ad loc. Cf. *Sifre* to Deut. 11:17: "God said, 'Even if I exile you from the Land to outside the Land, be distinguished [from your non-Jewish neighbors] by observing the mitzvot, so that when you return to the Land they will not be new [i.e., strange].'"

24. *Sefer ha-Mitzvot,* no. 153.

25. Bk. 2, secs. 8–14.

26. Ramban to Lev. 26:16, commenting on the verse "I will make the land desolate, so that your enemies who settle in it will be desolate over it" (Lev. 26:32), says: "These are good tidings, that our land is not hospitable to our enemies . . . for since we have departed from it, it has not welcomed any nation; and all those who have attempted to inhabit it have failed."

27. Cf. J. *Kilayim* 9:4 (32c), where the Sages differed concerning this practice: R. Bar Kiria and R. Lazar were walking in the street and saw coffins which were being brought from *hutz la-Aretz* to Eretz Yisrael. R. Bar Kiria said to R. Lazar: "What are they accomplishing? Concerning them I cite the verse 'You have made My inheritance an abomination, [Jer. 2:7] in your lifetime; 'You have come and defiled My land,' in your death." R. Lazar retorted: "As soon as they reach Eretz Yisrael a clod of earth is placed on their coffin [and they are pardoned], as it is written, 'His land makes atonement for His people' [Deut. 32:49]." Here we find the origin of the custom today to place a bag of Eretz Yisrael soil in the coffin of those interred in *hutz la-Aretz.*

28. See, however, the midrashic interpretation in *Yalkut Shimoni* ad loc.: "What kind of *men of valor* are these who are exiled? These are men of valor in the disputations of the Torah." See also *Gittin* 88a, where "the craftsmen" are interpreted to be the craftsmen of the Halakhah; and Rashi to *Succah,* bottom of 44a, in name of *Seder Olam.*

29. Apropos, Babylonian Jewry did not appoint an exilarch *(resh galuta)* during the entire period of the Second Temple, maintaining officially their subservience to

the authorities in Jerusalem (S. Asaf, *Tekufat ha-Geonim*, p. 25). See also *Succah* 20a: "In the beginning, when the Torah was forgotten in Israel, Ezra went up from Babylon and established it; when it again became forgotten, Hillel the Babylonian went up and established it; when it again became forgotten, R. Hiyya and his sons went up and established it."

30. For a talmudic description of Alexandria in all its glory, see *Succah* 51b.

31. Babylonian Jewry also had several translations of the Torah into Aramaic, known generally as Targum, the first one in the days of Ezra, and a later one by Onkelos, which became the official one accepted by the Sages (*Megillah* 3a); but it was always secondary to the Hebrew original (cf. Mishnah *Megillah* 4[3]:4); whereas in Greek-speaking Egypt the Greek translation superseded the original Hebrew. In Alexandria, the day the Septuagint was completed was declared a holiday and every anniversary was celebrated; whereas the Sages in Babylonia compared it "to the day in which the Golden Calf was made," and declared it a fast day (*Soferim* 1:7). However, in Eretz Yisrael, where Greek was more widespread, Rabban Simeon b. Gamaliel ruled that scrolls of the Torah could be written in Greek (Mishnah *Megillah* 1:8), and Rabbi (Judah ha-Nasi) said: "In Eretz Yisrael why speak Syrian; speak either the Sacred Tongue [Hebrew] or Greek" (*Sotah* 49b). See also J. *Megillah* 1:9 (71b): "There are four convenient languages: Greek for poetry, Latin for battle, Syrian for dirges, and Hebrew for conversation." See also Rambam, *Hilkhot Tefilin* 1:19: "Greek has already been submerged from the world, corrupted and lost; therefore we write all sacred scrolls only in Assyrian" (i.e., the square script which Ezra adapted from the Assyrian for the Hebrew Bible, and which is in use to this day).

32. See *Niddah* 69b: "Twelve questions the men of Alexandria asked of R. Yehoshua b. Hananiah, three of wisdom [i.e., of Halakhah], three of Aggadah, three of no consequence, and three of wordly ways [*derekh eretz*]."

33. See Tosefta *Pe'ah* 4:6 that one could establish his priestly lineage in Eretz Yisrael, in Syria, and in Babylonia; whereas in Alexandria, says R. Simon b. Elazar, this could have been done only "in early times when there was a Court there." Significant also is the fact that messengers to advise the *golah* of the proclamation of the New Moon by the Court in Eretz Yisrael were sent to Babylonia but not to Egypt, where the Jews apparently fixed the calendar themselves. Cf. Rambam, *Hilkhot Kiddush ha-Hodesh* 5:10; also J. *Erubin* 3:9, where it seems that R. Abbahu (second half of third cent. C.E.) went to Alexandria to advise them about the calendar.

The Sages attributed the downfall of the Alexandrian community to the fact that they transgressed the biblical injunction "You must not go back again to Egypt" (Deut. 17:16; *Succah* 51b). The attitude of the Sages to the Alexandrians can be seen in two instances of the Yom Kippur service, in which they attribute to Alexandrians the crude conduct ascribed by the Mishnah to the Babylonians (*Yoma* 66b and *Menahot* 100a). For other differences in the attitudes of the Sages toward Babylonia and Egypt, see Mishnah *Yadayim* 4:3: "The regulations concerning

Egypt are of recent origin, those concerning Babylon are of ancient origin; those concerning Egypt were instituted by the Elders [Second Temple period], those concerning Babylon were instituted by the prophets [First Temple period]."

CHAPTER 5

1. Most scholars agree that Malachi is not the personal name of the prophet—thus, for example, his father's name is not mentioned, as is customary with the other prophets—but a pseudonym that simply means "My [i.e., God's] messenger" (cf. Mal. 3:1). Various opinions are expressed in the Talmud (Megillah 15a) identifying Malachi with prominent personalities of the period, such as Ezra or Mordecai. One thing is certain; his message was directly reflected in the activity of Ezra.

2. For the rabbinic interpretation of Elijah's function to "turn the heart of the fathers to the children, etc.," see Mishnah Eduyot 8:7: "R. Yehoshua said: 'I am in receipt of a tradition from Rabban Yohanan b. Zakkai, who heard from his teacher, and his teacher from his teacher, as a ruling to Moses from Sinai, that Elijah is not coming to declare what is unclean or clean; nor to pronounce [persons of doubtful lineage] removed from or brought nigh [to the priesthood]; only to remove those who were brought nigh by force, and to bring nigh those who were removed by force.' R. Simon says: '[He is coming] to decide matters in dispute.' The Sages say: 'To make peace in the world.'" See also Maimonides' Commentary to the Mishnah, ad loc., and Encyclopedia Talmudica (Eng. edition), vol. 2, pp. 271 ff., s.v. Eliyahu.

3. Megillat Taanit records two days, the seventh of Iyar and the fourth of Elul, as semi-holidays, for on them "the wall of Jerusalem was dedicated." In addition, the sixteenth of Adar is recorded as the day "on which they began to build the wall of Jerusalem." The Book of Nehemiah records: "And the wall was completed on the twenty-fifth day of Elul in fifty-two days" (Neh. 6:15). The elaborate ceremony of dedication is described in Neh. 12:27–43, but no specific date is given. The baraita in Megillat Taanit comments: "Twice does this Megillah record the dedication of the wall of Jerusalem; once when Israel came up from the Exile [i.e., in the days of Nehemiah], and once when the Greek kings breached the wall and the Hasmoneans closed it up." For the various theories concerning these dates, cf. H. Lichtenstein, HUC Annual, vol. 8, pp. 280, 301, 307.

4. This became a precedent for the ruling that a platform be erected in the Court of Women for the public reading of the Torah on the occasion of hakhel (Deut. 31:10–13; Mishnah Sotah 7:8). From this in turn was derived the ruling that a platform be erected in every synagogue upon which the Torah is read (Rambam, Hilkhot Tefillah 11:3; RAMO, Shulhan Arukh, Orah Hayyim 150:5). Hence, when one is called to the reading of the Torah he is said to have an aliyah, i.e., a going up to the platform for the reading.

5. A section of this resume is incorporated in the daily shaharit service.

6. Cf. *Seder Olam Rabbah,* chap. 6: "Up until now the prophets would prophesy with the Holy Spirit; from now and henceforth, incline your ear and listen to the words of the Sages."

Various terms have been employed to designate a Sage. In the Book of Nehemiah (8:7), those who taught the Torah were called *mevinim,* i.e., "they who caused the people to understand." Following the title which distinguished Ezra, *ha-sofer* (the scribe), the expounders of the Torah in subsequent generations were called *soferim,* and their enactments and interpretations of Scripture are referred to as *divrei soferim* (for explanations of this term as it is employed by Maimonides in his *Mishneh Torah,* see Y. Y. Neubauer, *Ha-Rambam Al Divrei Soferim* [Jerusalem, 5717]). In the Jerusalem Talmud, the term *sofer* (Aramaic, *safra*) refers to a teacher of young children. Later, the Sages were called *hakhamim,* and young scholars were called *talmidei hakhamim,* "disciples of the wise," an expression applied to scholars in general. In the course of time, when a scholar became qualified to make authoritative decisions the title of "rabbi" was conferred upon him. Occasionally, the Mishnah employs the biblical nomenclature for members of the Court, i.e., *zekenim* or "elders"; e.g. *Yoma* 1:3.

7. Cf. the statement of the Men of the Great Assembly: "Raise up many disciples" (*Abot* 1:1).

8. For a cursory comment on the various explanations of this phenomenon, see E. E. Urbach, *Hazal Emunot Ve-De'ot* (Jerusalem, 5729), p. 504 and nn. 65, 66.

9. This searching of the Torah is called in the Bible *lidrosh* (Ezra 7:10), and the teachings derived therefrom are known as *midrash.* In the course of time, midrash was divided into two categories: *midrash halakhah,* halakhic rulings fixing the manner in which the mitzvot of the Torah are to be complied with; and *midrash aggadah,* homiletic expositions of biblical passages whose primary purpose is moral edification. An academy where such "searching" was conducted and its results taught was known as *beit ha-midrash,* and it was regarded as having greater sanctity than *beit ha-kenesset,* a place of assembly for public prayer (*Megillah* 26b—27a).

10. Compare the version in *Megillah* 3a: "That a prophet *will not* in the future innovate anything from now on."

11. In the parallel passages in the Jerusalem and Babylonian Talmuds, there are differing versions as to the number of participants in these deliberations, some putting the number at one hundred twenty elders. Most probably, the original version was, "eighty-five elders, and with them [read *imahem* instead of *meihem*] thirty-five prophets," thus making a total of one hundred twenty. The number eighty-five corresponds to the number of elders who signed the covenant drawn up by Ezra and Nehemiah (Neh. 10).

12. See also J. *Berakhot* 1:4 (3b): "To what can a prophet and an elder be compared? To a king who dispatched two of his agents to the province. With respect to one of them he wrote: 'If he does not show you my seal, do not trust him'; with respect to the other he wrote: 'Even if he does not show you my seal, trust him.

Thus concerning a prophet it is written:'And he shall give you a sign or a wonder, [Deut. 13:2]; whereas with respect to elders it is written: 'According to the law which they shall instruct you' [Deut. 17:1]."

13. Nevertheless, even in Torah leadership lineage (yihus) is taken into consideration. Cf. Berakhot 27b, when R. Elazar b. Azariah was chosen to replace Rabban Gamaliel as head of the Sanhedrin even though R. Akiba was superior to him in scholarship, because "R. Akiba does not have the merit of distinguished forbears [zekhut abot] whereas R. Elazar b. Azariah is a scholar and is wealthy and is the tenth generation from Ezra."

14. Cf. their statement (Abot 1:1): "Make a hedge about the Torah"; namely, additional regulations in order to ensure the observance of biblical law. See, however, Abot de-Rabbi Nathan for a qualification of this activity.

15. Kenesset Ha-Gedolah is also translated "the Great Synagogue." (I do not understand why it is translated "the Great Community" in the English rendering of Abot in the Siddur of the Rabbinical Council of America.) The duration of the Kenesset Ha-Gedolah is a matter of dispute among historians, depending largely upon the identification of the Shimon ha-Zaddik mentioned in Abot 1:2 as one of its remaining members. He was either the high priest who flourished at the end of the fourth century B.C.E. or the high priest who lived at the end of the third century.

16. See above, n. 11.

17. For sources and ramifications, see Encyclopedia Talmudit, vol. 10, pp. 95 ff., s.v. hefker beit-din. For a retroactive confiscation, see Tosafot Kethubot 3a, s.v. teinah.

18. See S. W. Baron, The Jewish Community, vol. 1, p. 169, for the usual text of the herem.

19. See, for example, Mishnah Yoma 7:1 and Rashi, ad loc., for the benedictions recited by the high priest on Yom Kippur after the sacrificial service. One such version is still retained in the conclusion of the Avodah benediction recited when the priests rise to bless the congregation on the Festivals. See also TUR Orah Hayyim, sec. 188, regarding the changes in the text of benedictions necessitated by changes in the situation of the Jewish people.

20. Hilkhot Tefillah 1:4.

21. See Tosafot Berakhot 3a, s.v. ve-onin. Other examples, Yekum Purkan and Berikh Shemei.

22. A possible reference to the collecting of the various books of the Bible into the canon of Scripture may be found in the verse in Ecclesiastes (12:11): "The words of the wise . . . masters of collections." The third division of the Bible, the Kethubim (Writings, or Hagiographa), was canonized later, as it includes some writings of the post-Ezra period. The final canonization of the Hagiographa was completed in the period of the Tannaim, who still argued about the inclusion of some of the books; see Mishnah Yadayim 3:5.

23. See Mishnah Kelim 15:6 and Mishnah Mo'ed Kattan 3:4, where reference is made to the copy of the Sefer Torah placed in the Temple Court (sefer ha-azarah)

which served as the standard text. Some read *sefer Ezra* instead of *sefer ha-azarah*.

24. See the author's *Study of the Nature and History of Jewish Law*, pp. 18–20.

25. See Tosafot, ad loc., s.v. *kedei*, why Mondays and Thursdays were chosen. Following this *takkanah* and the one concerning courts of law, each Monday and Thursday became known as a *yom ha-kenisah*, a day of assembly, when the Jews from the villages would come to town; cf. Mishnah *Megillah* 1:1. Also, these days were selected as days for fasting; cf. Mishnah *Taanit* 2:9.

26. *Soferim* 16:10 speaks of 175 sections, or *sidrahs*, into which the Pentateuch was divided, which indicates that the reading cycle was completed once in three and a half years, or twice in a Shemittah cycle of seven years. Rambam, *Hilkhot Tefillah* 13:1, writes: "The custom which is widespread in Israel is to complete [the reading of] the Torah in one year. . . . Some complete it in three years, but this is not a widespread custom." For further details, see *Jewish Encyclopedia*, s.v. "Triennial Cycle."

27. TUR *Orah Hayyim*, sec. 145, and *Shulhan Arukh, Orah Hayyim* sec. 285, par. 2. Cf. J. *Nedarim* 4:3(38c), where *mikra* and *targum* are placed in the same category.

28. J. Kapah, *Halikhot Teiman* (Jerusalem, 5728), p. 68.

29. See above, n. 25. Also, Tosafot *Kethubot* 3a, s.v. *she-batei*.

30. *Midrash Rabbah* to Eccles. 1:13.

31. Mishnah *Gittin*, chaps. 4–5. See also *Baba Bathra* 8b: "The inhabitants of a city are authorized to regulate the units of measurement, prices, wages, and to establish penalties for violations."

32. See Tosafot *Arakhin* 31b, s.v. *hithkin*, for discussion whether this ruling also nullified the law of Shemittah, which prohibited work in the fields every seventh year. A similar disputation raged when Jewish agricultural settlements were established in Eretz Yisrael at the end of the nineteenth century, and opinions are still divided to this day as to what measures have to be taken nowadays in order to comply with the laws of Shemittah.

33. Thus the obligations of a husband to his wife are derived from the law of the Hebrew maidservant (Exod. 21:10; *Kethubot* 47b); and the obligation of an employer to grant a bonus to an employee leaving his service (severance pay) is derived from the verse "When you set him [the Hebrew slave] free, do not let him go empty-handed; compensate him liberally from the good with which the Lord your God has blessed you" (Deut. 15:13–14).

CHAPTER 6

1. The first modern Christian scholar to analyze this period in an unbiased manner was the late George Foot Moore of Harvard in his *History of Religions*, vol. 2 (New York, 1928).

2. See V. Tcherikover, *Hellenistic Civilization and the Jews* (Philadelphia,

1959), pp. 358 ff.; H. Leon, *The Jews of Ancient Rome* (Philadelphia, 1960), pp. 250–52.

3. See S. Belkin, *In His Image* (New York, 1960), pp. 15–19.

4. See especially the section known as *malkhuyot* in the *Mussaf Amidah* for Rosh Hashanah, and the statement of R. Yohanan, "A blessing which does not include *malkhut* is not a blessing" (*Berakhot* 40b).

5. See our discussion about the phenomenon of royalty in Israel in chaps. 1 and 2.

6. Zech. 9:9 and 14:9. Cf. also Isa. 40:11–12, which predicts that "the Lord will come . . . and will pasture His flock like a shepherd," with Ezek. 37:24, "And My servant David will be king over them, and one shepherd will be for all of them," using the same figure of speech for God's rule and David's rule.

7. Margolis and Marx, *History of the Jewish People* (Philadelphia, 1938), p. 153.

8. *Berakhot* 6a: "The Holy One, blessed be He, dons Tefillin."

9. *Baba Metzia* 59b. See also M. Silberg, *Talmudic Law and the Modern State* (New York, 1973), p. 64.

10. This is so only according to the Babylonian Talmud, whose decisions we follow today. According to the Jerusalem Talmud, the conclusion of the benediction for the building of Jerusalem includes the phrase "God of David" (J. *Berakhot* 4:2; J. *Rosh Hashanah* 4:6).

11. Cf. the conclusion of the first benediction of the *Shemoneh Esreh*, "God the Shield of Abraham."

12. Cf. *Abot* 1:2, statement of Simon the Just: "On three things the world stands, on the Torah, on the [Temple] Service, and on deeds of lovingkindness." The Sages interpreted "And Jacob was . . . a dweller of tents" (Gen. 25:27) to mean that he dwelt in the tents of learning (*Ber. Rabbah* 63:15). See also Rashi to Gen. 28:9, that Jacob spent fourteen solid years of study in the Beit ha-Midrash of Eber.

13. See the discussion by the late Chief Rabbi I. H. Herzog in the journal *Talpiot*, vol. 7 (New York, 5718), on the powers of a king which exceed those of a regular *beit din*.

14. *Mishpat Kohen* (Jerusalem, 5697), pp. 337–38.

15. *Sefer ha-Hinukh*, mitzvah 507.

16. *Pesahim* 57a. I understand the phrase "the Court cried out" to mean that the people who were gathered in the Court demanded.

17. S. Schechter, *Studies in Judaism, Second Series* (Philadelphia, 1908), pp. 65–66.

18. *Antiquities*, XI, sec. 326; *Megillat Taanit* to the twenty-first of Kislev, quoted in *Yoma* 69a. For a discussion of the historical circumstances at the time of this incident, see A. Kasher in *Beit Mikra*, vol. 20 (Jerusalem, 5735), pp. 187–208.

19. Actually, this high priest's name was Yadoa, but the Talmud likes to ascribe all good things to Simon the Just, perhaps to compliment the high priest Simon the Hasmonean, whose leadership was so exemplary.

20. No doubt referring to the high priest as he emerged from the Inner Sanc-

tuary of the Temple on the Day of Atonement. This verse is the basis of the liturgical poems of the Yom Kippur service which rhapsodize the appearance of the high priest on this holiest day of the year.

21. See the strictures of the Ramban in his commentary to Gen. 49:10 against the later Hasmoneans for assuming the royal title.

22. *Megillat Taanit* for the third of Tishri, quoted in *Rosh Hashanah* 18b. See also Tosafot *Baba Bathra* 162a, s.v. *lefi*, where the assumption is that *moshel* (ruler) does not refer to the high priest but to the foreign ruler, an assumption that does not follow from our discussion of the position of the high priest. See also Mishnah *Yadayim* 4:8, where many read *im hashem* ("with God's name") instead of *im Mosheh.*

23. Margolis and Marx, loc. cit.

24. Rambam, *Hilkhot Kelei ha-Mikdash*, 4:20, 5:1.

25. II Macc. 4:7–10.

26. The Talmud (*Abodah Zarah* 9a) compresses the period of Persian rule to thirty-four years, and hence reaches a total of only four hundred twenty years for the period of the Second Temple, which actually lasted almost six hundred years. The Talmud's calculation was, no doubt, due to the lack of literary records which could definitely be assigned to the second century of the Persian period, and to the antedating of the second half of the Book of Daniel.

27. See *Shabbat* 149b, where the Talmud interprets "your people are as they that strive with the priest" (Hos. 4:4) to mean that the priests strive amongst themselves.

28. According to A. Buchler, *Ha-Sanhedrin* (Jerusalem, 1974), this Court was the *Beit ha-Din ha-Gadol*, referred to by many as the Sanhedrin, which supervised and rendered decisions in all religious matters including the Temple Service, and was not identical with the political Sanhedrin, which was a separate Council with powers of punishing criminals.

29. See also *Yoma* 39a, bottom of page.

30. For references, see Baron, op. cit., vol. 2, p. 342, n. 43.

31. *Berakhot* 25b, *Shabbat* 88b–89a, *Nedarim* 10a, J. *Kiddushin* 4:12 (66b): "Man will be called to account for not enjoying the things available to him."

32. *Yebamot* 20a "Sanctify yourself in [refraining from] what is permitted to you." See also *Sifra* to Lev. 19:1.

33. Mishnah *Sanhedrin* 5:1, *Sanhedrin* 8b, *Makkot* 7a.

34. *Sanhedrin* 46a: "The Court may punish without it being prescribed by the Torah . . . in order to make a fence for [i.e., to protect] the Torah." See also *Sanhedrin* 75a and 82a.

35. *Kiddushin* 39b, 40b; *Erubin* 22a.

36. This seems to be contrary to the assertion of Maimonides that those resurrected will live a long, healthy, mundane physical life but eventually will die. Maimonides, however, maintains that *hayyei olam*, everlasting life, refers to the purely spiritual life of the souls of the righteous in *olam habo*, the world-to-come,

which Maimonides insists is the supermundane domain of the *nefesh*, the intellect which survives after death. See *Hilkhot Yesodei ha-Torah* 4:9.

37. There is a variant reading, "serve . . . not on condition that they receive a bounty"; see discussion in *Tosafot Yom Tov*, ad loc.

38. Mishnah *Sanhedrin* 10:1.

39. The second benediction of the *Shemoneh Esreh* praises God as "the One Who resurrects the dead," among other deeds. The twelfth and thirteenth benedictions speak respectively of the punishment of the wicked and the reward of the righteous. These two principles are the eleventh and thirteenth articles of faith *(ani ma'amin)* postulated by Maimonides.

40. See Maimonides' Commentary to the Mishnah, *Sanhedrin*, chap. 10.

41. *Hilkhot Melakhim* 12:2.

42. For further clarification of the Oral Law, see my *Nature and History of Jewish Law* (New York, 1966), chap. 2.

43. *Yalkut Shimoni* to Hos. 8:12: "He who has My mysteries is My son; and what are My mysteries, the Mishnah." See also *Gittin* 60b, J. *Pe'ah* 2:4 (17a), J. *Hagigah* 1:8 (76d).

44. For an explanation of this term, see *Encyclopedia Talmudit*, vol. 8, pp. 365 ff. The ceremonies referred to in the text are the libation of water on the Altar *(nisukh ha-mayim)* and marching round the Altar with willow branches. Also, the beating on the ground of the willow branch *(hibbut aravah)* on the seventh day of the Festival; i.e., Hoshanah Rabbah (Mishnah *Succah* 4:5−9).

45. See discussion in both Babylonian and Jerusalem Talmuds following the Mishnah in *Hagigah* cited in the text. Most historians of the Halakhah agree that the *halakhah* preceded the *midrash*. See also, *Encyclopedia Talmudit*, vol. 2, pp. 105 ff., s.v. *asmakhta 1*. Someone characterized the true scholar as one who "combines two attitudes: an awe of the text founded on the assumption that everything already exists in it; and the presumptuousness of imposing the truth upon ancient texts."

46. Tosefta *Sanhedrin*, end of chap. 7; introduction to the *Sifra*.

47. Cf. discussion of the Tannaim in the Mishnah, *Pesahim* 6:1.

48. Cf. "There is no session of the Beit Midrash which does not produce a *hiddush*"; *Hagigah* 3a. For the history of these academies, see N. Drazin, *History of Jewish Education* (Baltimore 1940), pp. 35 ff.

49. *Bamidbar Rabbah* 21:2, *Berakhot* 58a. See also B. deVries, *Mehkarim* (Jerusalem, 5728), chap. 11.

50. J. *Hagigah* 2:2 (77d), *Erubin* 13b.

51. Tosefta *Eduyot* 1:1, J. *Yebamot*, end of chap. 1 (3b).

52. *Shabbat* 23a. Cf. Rambam, *Hilkhot Berakhot* 11:3: " . . . so that the meaning of the formula of benediction is as follows: . . . Who sanctified us with His commandments by commanding us to hearken to those [i.e., the Sages] who commanded us [to perform the particular ritual]."

53. The expression "had heard" is appropriate in view of the fact that the

halakhot were as yet not codified in a written code of law. Nevertheless, masters of the law would write down for their own information new oral traditions which they had heard. These writings were called *megillot setarim*, hidden scrolls; see *Shabbat* 6b and *Baba Metzia* 92a, with Rashî's explanations.

54. For the various explanations of this term, see H. D. Mantel, *Mehkarim be-Toldot ha-Sanhedrin* (Tel Aviv, 1969), pp. 157 ff.

55. Its location, whether on the north or the south side of the Temple, is a matter of dispute. For a detailed discussion, see A. Buchler, *Ha-Sanhedrin*, chap. 1.

56. Mishnah *Sanhedrin* 1:6.

57. Mishnah *Yoma* 1:3.

58. *Kiddushin* 66a.

59. Rabbenu Nissim of Gerona, *Derashot ha-Ran*, chap. 11.

CHAPTER 7

1. Mishnah *Taanit* 4:6, *Taanit* 29a. Maimonides, Commentary to Mishnah, *Rosh Hashanah* 1:3, says that during the Second Temple "they would fast on Tishah B'Ab even though it was optional [see R.H. 18b] because many tragedies occurred on that day." J. N. Epstein, *Mavo le-Nusah ha-Mishnah* (Jerusalem, 5708), pp. 1012−13, adduces other rabbinic sources to substantiate this opinion.

2. For a more detailed analysis of the situation, see G. Elon, *Toldot ha-Yehudim b'Eretz Yisrael* (Tel Aviv, 1954), introduction, and S. W. Baron, *Social and Religious History*, vol. 2, chap. 11. For the financial assistance rendered by the Diaspora to the central institution in Eretz Yisrael, see especially Elon, op. cit., pp. 156 ff.

3. Mishnah *Yadayim* 4:6; *Megillat Taanit* to the eighth of Nisan, quoted in *Menahot* 65a.

4. *Succah* 28a, *Abot* 2:8.

5. Mishnah *Rosh Hashanah* 4:1. The Babylonian Amoraim Rava and Rabbah assert that the reason for not blowing the shofar on the Sabbath is a rabbinic restriction "lest one might—forgetting the Sabbath—carry the shofar four cubits in the public domain [which restrictions did not apply in the Temple]" (*Rosh Hashanah* 29b). The Jerusalem Talmud, however, bases the ruling of the Mishnah which permits the blowing only in the Beit ha-Mikdash on Scripture. If so, the ruling of Rabbi Yohanan that the blowing be permitted in Yavneh demonstrates his desire to have Yavneh, at least in some respects, assume the prerogatives of the Temple. Rambam (*Hilkhot Shofar* 2:8) asserts that Rabbi Yohanan permitted the blowing only in a *beit din* whose members are officially ordained (*semukhim*) and which is authorized to proclaim the New Moon. Since no such *beit din* has existed for centuries, in no place is the shofar now blown on the Sabbath, though several rabbis at one time or another suggested that it be blown in Jerusalem. It is reported that Rabbi Isaac Alfasi blew the shofar on the Sabbath in his court (most probably in

Lucena, Spain, where he had migrated from North Africa), but his disciples did not continue this practice (Rosh, ad loc.).

6. Mishnah *Rosh Hashanah* 4:3−4.

7. *Abot de-Rabbi Nathan*, chap. 4.

8. Reform Judaism at first eliminated all prayers for a return to Zion, asserting that it is the mission of the Jewish people to remain dispersed among the nations so that, presumably, the latter will learn and adopt the universal principles of Judaism. Events of the present century have proved how illusory this hope has been, and consequently most Reform Jews are now ardent Zionists, though their attitude toward the rebuilding of the Beit ha-Mikdash on its ancient site is not clear. Conservative Judaism prays for the return to Zion, but does not petition for the restoration of the sacrificial service, deeming such service an unseemly manner of worship. Several Palestinian Amoraim asserted that in the future all sacrifices will cease except the thanksgiving offering (*Vayikra Rabbah* 27:12). See also above, chap. 3, n. 11.

9. The rebuilding of Jerusalem and the rebuilding of the Temple are considered as one unit, and they are used interchangeably in the sources. Thus, for example, according to the Jer. Talmud (*Berakhot* 4:3 [8a]), the prayer for the rebuilding of Jerusalem recited on Tish'ah B'Ab should be added to the benediction for the restoration of the Temple Service; whereas the custom was adopted to include it in the benediction for the rebuilding of Jerusalem (*boneh Yerushalayim*; see RIF, end of *Taanit*). See also Tosafot *Shabbat* 63a, s.v. *ain bain*. the assumption that the rebuilding of Jerusalem and Mikdash, coupled together, are sine qua non in the days of the Messiah.

10. *Hagigah* 5b, *Pethihta Eikhah Rabbati*.

11. Zech. 8:19, *Rosh Hashanah* 18b.

12. Rabbi Simon ben Gamaliel, who met his death at the time of the *hurban*. Apparently, he did not share in the peace efforts of Rabbi Yohanan, but supported the war party.

13. Though the center of Jewish life was still in Eretz Yisrael, Jews after the *hurban* considered themselves in a state of Exile as long as the Redemption did not come to pass. What the Redemption (*ge'ulah*) implies we shall discuss in a later chapter.

14. See *Taanit* 29a for another version of how Rabbi Gamaliel was saved.

15. *Eduyot* 7:7: "Rabbi Gamaliel went to obtain authority [*reshut;* cf. *Abot* 2:3] from the ruler in Syria."

16. Simon ha-Pekuli. He is not mentioned elsewhere in the Mishnah. Cf. J. *Berakhot* 2:4 (4d): "Even *he who* regulated this prayer did so in a fixed sequence." Incidentally, J. Heinemann, *Ha-Tefilah Bitekufat ha-Tannaim* (Jerusalem, 5726), p. 17, after citing various talmudic sources (though he fails to cite the above source), concludes: "Almost each one of the above sources ascribe the fixing of the prayers to a different generation. . . . We may therefore affirm that the origin of fixed prayer began hundreds of years before the *hurban* and reached the point of crystal-

lization and editing in the generation after the *hurban*." I do not think he has grasped the matter sufficiently. Only twice was it necessary to make a full revision and fix anew the text of the *Amidah* (the statutory prayer): once at the time of the Return to Zion, when it became necessary to revise the prayer following the transition from a situation of *hurban-galut* to a situation of *ge'ulah;* and second at the time of the second *hurban,* when the transition from *ge'ulah* to *hurban* called for a corresponding revision in the text of the *Amidah.* Hence, both the Jerusalem and the Babylonian Talmuds report the fixing of the prayer both by the Men of the Great Assembly and by Rabbi Gamaliel. Cf. TUR *Orah Hayyim,* sec. 188, "The third [i.e., the third benediction in *Birkat ha-Mazon*], *boneh Yerushalayim,* was instituted by David and Solomon. This is not to say that the benediction was not recited before them, but they regulated the text in accord with the change for the good accrued to Israel; for certainly the same prayer was not recited before the conquest [of Canaan] and the building-up of the Land as after the conquest and the building-up. Just as we do not recite the same text fixed by David and Solomon, since we petition for the return of the kingdom and the building of the Temple, and they prayed that the peace of the Land and the Kingdom and the Temple continue." So also Ramban, quoted by the *Beit Yosef* in sec. 187: "the language of prayer is recited according to the times."

17. Cf. the statement of Rabbi Yishmael with reference to the *minnim* (*Shabbat* 116a): "These persons who place enmity and hatred and dissension between Israel and their Father in heaven."

18. See Elon, op. cit., pp. 179 ff., and S. Lieberman, *Tosefta Kipshuta,* vol. 1, p. 54.

19. *Sanhedrin* 11a.

20. The Babylonian Talmud says that he was eighteen years old at the time; the Jerusalem Talmud (*Berakhot* 4:1 [7d]), sixteen years old. The basis for these assertions is the statement by Rabbi Elazar (Mishnah *Berakhot* 1:5): "I am *like* one who is seventy years old," which can also be understood as "I am *about* seventy years old"; cf. J. ibid. (3d).

21. The statement of Jesus as found in the New Testament (Matt. 5:17). A variant reading in the Talmud says: "I have not come to subtract from, *but rather* to add to the Law of Moses."

22. It is interesting to note that the very first disciplinary regulation of the Zadokite (or Damascus) Document prescribes that any person who proceeded against another Jew in a Gentile court should be put to death.

23. Mishnah *Sanhedrin* 1:5, Tosefta *Hagigah* 2:9. See also above, p. 86.

24. J. *Sanhedrin* 1:1 (18a), *Abodah Zarah* 8b. See also S. B. Hoenig, *The Great Sanhedrin* (Philadelphia, 5713), p. 111, for an examination of the sources re the date of the removal of the Sanhedrin from the Temple area.

25. *Gittin* 57a. There the reading is "a distance of a mile"; in *Eikhah Rabbati* 2:5, "a distance of four miles." We have written "forty miles," which is closer to the truth and most probably the original version.

26. For details of their reception in Usha, see S. Klein, *Eretz ha-Galil,* pp. 74 ff.

27. Referred to in the Talmud simply as Rabbi Yohanan, without the patronymic. He was an untutored youngster when he first entered the academy of Rabbi Judah (*Hullin* 137b), but attributed his knowledge of Torah to the privilege of having seen the *nasi* from a distance (J. *Betzah* 5:2 [63a]).

28. "Edom is Esau" (Gen. 36:1). Since according to the prediction given to Rebecca (Gen. 25:23) her two sons represented two peoples who were destined to be eternal adversaries, "and one people will be mightier than the other people," the Rabbis designated Israel's adversary of their day, Rome, as Edom (see *Megillah* 6a and *Sanhedrin* 12a, the epistle sent to Rava). By a similar transference of names from their biblical origin to the contemporary scene we see how France came to be known as *Tzarfat* and Spain as *Sepharad* (Obadiah, v. 20). The prophecy of Obadiah deals exclusively with the great enmity between Israel and Edom. Jews living in Moslem countries were said to be in *Galut Yishmael* since the Arabs were descendants of Yishmael.

29. Historians question the presumed identity of Antoninus with the emperor Marcus Aurelius; see Baron, op. cit., vol. 2, p. 400, n. 19.

30. *Megillah* 5a—b, *Eikhah Rabbati* 2:5.

31. *Abodah Zarah* 11a, *Baba Metzia* 85a, inter alia.

32. *Kethubot* 104a, *Baba Bathra* 8a.

33. See H. Albeck, *Mavo le-Talmudim* (Tel Aviv, 1969), pp. 8—9.

34. See Mishnah *Eduyot* 1:4—6.

35. For an explanation of these terms, see Albeck, op. cit., chap. 1.

36. See my *Nature and History of Jewish Law*, p. 62, for a discussion of encyclopedias of the Talmud.

CHAPTER 8

1. See above, chap. 7, n. 13.

2. See above, p. 101.

3. This incident must have taken place about thirty years after the previous one. The Rabbi Judah here is Judah II; Rabbi Hiyya is Bar Abba, whereas the one previously mentioned is the colleague of Judah I and usually referred to as Rabbi Hiyya Rabbah in order to distinguish him from Bar Abba; Rabbis Ami and Asi were amongst the foremost disciples of Rabbi Yohanan. When they received their rabbinical ordination, the people sang out, "May all candidates for *semikhah* be like these" (*Kethubot* 17a).

4. I have followed here the talmudic interpretation of Rabbi Judah's statement, It is not exactly clear what specific role the *hakham* played in the Academy.

5. Though he also is referred to in the Jerusalem Talmud simply as Rabbi, or Rabbenu, and one must be careful to recognize whether the reference is to the grandfather or the grandson. See especially J. *Shabbat* 1:4 (3d).

6. In *Sanhedrin* 14a the reading is: "the governor's lady."

7. See also *Hagigah* 14a, where the phrase "man of distinction" (Isa. 3:3) is ap-

plied to Rabbi Abbahu because of his successful efforts on behalf of Jewish rights.

8. See J.N. Epstein, *Mavo'ot le-Sifrut ha-Amoraim* (Jerusalem, 1962), pp. 282 ff., for a discussion as to whether a section of the Jerusalem Talmud was edited in Caesarea.

9. Cf. the version in *Soferim* 16:4. Also, my article on "The Function of the Drashah in Israel," in *Shanah be-Shanah* (Jerusalem, 5734), pp. 182 ff.

10. See J. N. Epstein, *Mavo'ot le-Sifrut ha-Tannaim* (Jerusalem, 1957), pp. 365–66, as to when the change took place.

11. Actually, not always was Rosh Hashanah celebrated for two days in Eretz Yisrael, probably not until the eleventh cent.; see commentaries to Alfasi (RIF), *Betzah*, p. 4. Here is another instance, in addition to the Saadia–Ben Meir controversy, where the Geonim of Babylonia were able to impose their view upon the small and impoverished community in Eretz Yisrael.

12. See my *Nature and History of Jewish Law*, p. 19.

13. For details of the controversy, see H. Malter, *Saadia Gaon* (Philadelphia, 1942), pp. 69–88.

14. See also *Erubin* 21a, that the rabbis would frequent the synagogue in which Daniel prayed.

15. For the many sources and versions, see *Otzar ha-Geonim* to *Sanhedrin*, Mossad Harav Kook ed. (Jerusalem, 1966), pp. 33 ff.

16. For the meaning of this title, see *Arukh ha-Shalem*, s.v. *Gaon*. Legend has it that the title gaon was conferred upon the teacher who was versed in the sixty tractates of the Talmud, sixty being the numerical value of the word *gaon*; see *Beit ha-Behirah*, introduction to *Abot* (p. 52 in edition of *Makhon ha-Talmud ha-Shalem* [Jerusalem, 5724]).

17. In the Sabbath morning prayer *Yekum Purkan*. For the meaning of the word *kallah*, see *Arukh ha-Shalem*, s.v. *kol* (p. 227). There has been a revival in modern Israel of the *yarhei kallah*, where people in all walks of life are invited to spend a period of ten days studying Talmud and listening to lectures.

18. See also *Kethubot* 106a, that for the lecture of Rav Huna it was necessary to have thirteen speakers (Amoraim) circulate to different sections of the auditorium because of the large attendance, and when the scholars would rise from the academy of Rav Huna and shake out their cloaks, the dust would darken the skies and in Eretz Yisrael they would say: "They have risen from the academy of Rav Huna the Babylonian."

19. The concluding phrase of this prayer, which in some prayer books reads *bizekhut tefillat Rav* and in others, *bizekhut tefillat rabbim*, is a corruption of *Berakhot tefillat Rav*, indicating the source of the prayer (*Berakhot* 16b).

20. See H. Tikuchinsky, *Takkanot ha-Geonim* (Tel Aviv–Jerusalem, 5720).

21. S. Assaf, *Tekufat ha-Geonim* (Jerusalem, 5715), p. 62.

22. See also *Shabbat* 45a and *Betzah* 4b and 6a, the fear that the kingdom may pass an evil decree forbidding the free exercise of the Jewish religion.

23. For an extended discussion of this ruling, see S. Shilo, *Dina de-Malkhuta Dina* (Jerusalem, 5735).

24. See above, chap. 7, n. 27.

25. Sherira Gaon is the author of the famous *Iggeret*, a history of rabbinic scholars from the days of the Mishnah, through the period of the Talmud, to his own day, toward the end of the period of the Geonim. It was written in response to a request from the community of Kairouan for information about the necessity for composing the Mishnah, and why there are so many opposing opinions in the Talmud.

26. S. W. Baron, *The Jewish Community* (Philadelphia, 1942), vol. 2, p. 3.

27. Rabbenu Tam's statement is quoted by the ROSH, *Sanhedrin*, end of chap. 3. Rashba's responsum is in vol. 1, no. 729.

28. Quoted by A. H. Freiman, *Seder Kiddushin ve-Nissuin* (Jerusalem, 1964), p. 68.

29. For a further discussion of this tale, see Z. Yavetz, *Toldot Yisrael* (Tel Aviv, 5692), vol. 10, pp. 238 ff.

30. See M. Margaliot, *Ha-Hilukkim bein Anshei ha-Mizrach u-Benai Eretz Yisrael* (Jerusalem, 5698).

31. Maimonides tempers this harsh judgment by specifically excluding "those born into such [heretical] opinions and raised according to them; they are like forced converts, and they should be judged like an infant captive among gentiles, all of whose transgressions are done unwittingly." Cf. a similar statement with reference to the Karaites in *Hilkhot Mamrim* 3:3.

A modern halakhic scholar, the late Rabbi Karelitz of Bnai Brak *(Chazon Ish)*, argued that such harsh measures were effective in olden times when communal discipline could be enforced; in modern democratic societies such measures would only lead to greater opposition to the religious authorities and therefore should be abandoned.

32. See Margaliot, op. cit., p. 13.

33. See H. J. Leon, *The Jews of Ancient Rome* (Philadelphia, 1960), chap. 1.

34. Quoted in a *teshuvah* of Rabbenu Tam.

35. Tosafot *Abodah Zarah* 15a, s.v. *eimur*. See also Tosafot *Abodah Zarah* 2a, s.v. *assur*, and ROSH, ibid., sec. 1.

36. Of course there were Jews in England in the Middle Ages. We are referring here to their resettlement under Cromwell after an absence of four hundred years.

37. An interesting example of such a community is the one that existed for over a millennium in Yemen. For a description of its way of life, see J. Kapah, *Halikhot Teiman* (Jerusalem, 1969).

38. For a detailed description of the activities of the council, see Baron, op. cit., vol. 1, pp. 325 ff., and Yavetz, op. cit., vol. 13, pp. 64 ff. In the classic literature, *parnas* referred to the spiritual as well as to the lay leader; cf. *Yoma* 86b: "Two beneficent *parnassim* . . . Moses and David," and *Taanit* 9a: "Three beneficent *parnassim* . . . Moses, Aaron, and Miriam." See also the discussion in *Arakhin* 17a re the relationship between the *parnas* and his generation.

39. See, for example, the controversy between R. Moshe Isserles and R. Shlomo Luria in *Teshuvot ha-Rama*, nos. 6 and 7.

40. Cf. the quotation on p. 150 in Z. Yaron, *Mishnatho shel ha-Rav Kook* (Jerusalem, 5734). For a summary of the problems generated by these phenomena, see my *The Light of Redemption* (Jerusalem, 1971), pp. 25−28.

41. An alternative translation of this dictum is: "The study of the Torah *leads* to them all."

42. For a discussion of this subject, see E. Berkovits, "An Integrated Jewish World View," in *A Treasury of Tradition* (New York, 1967), and Yaron, op. cit., chap. 9.

43. For an illuminating essay on the formation and growth of the Yishuv, see B. Z. Dinur, "The Historical Foundations of the Rebirth of Israel," in *The Jews*, ed. L. Finkelstein (Philadelphia, 1949), vol. 1, pp. 454 ff.

44. Chaim Weizmann used to say that the term *Jewish State* was like the *Shem ha-Meforash*, the Ineffable Name of God, to be pronounced only on the most sacred occasions.

45. Cf. Yaron, op. cit., p. 187, n. 37, for Rabbi Kook's objection to granting women the right to vote.

CHAPTER 9

1. Cf. Josephus, *Wars of the Jews*, bk. V, chap. 1 (p. 288 in Masada edition): Bemoaning the civil strife in Jerusalem at the time of the siege by Titus, Josephus exclaims: "O Jerusalem, you no longer are the dwelling-place of God, nor could you remain 'the lot of His inheritance,' for you have become a burial ground for your children, and your Temple has been turned into a field for the dead."

2. Cf. Tosafot ad loc., s.v. *lo*.

3. Cf. the rabbinic comment re number of times Torah has warned concerning the *ger*: "In thirty-six places the Torah has warned against [mistreatment of] the stranger" (*Baba Metzia* 59b).

4. *Hilkhot Yom Tov* 6:18.

5. Cf. Rambam, *Sefer ha-Mitzvot*, no. 1, difference of opinion between Maimonides and Nahmanides, the former construing this verse to be the first of the commandments, whereas the latter construes it only as the introduction to them.

6. Most commentators explain "my father" in the verse to refer to Jacob. Rashbam, however, maintains that it refers to Abraham.

7. *Sifre* ad loc. quoted in the Passover Haggadah. Cf. the statement in *Shemot Rabbah* 1:1, that the Jews in Egypt did not change (i.e., Egyptianize) their names and language.

8. Cf. Y. Herzog, *A People That Dwells Alone* (New York, 1975), esp. pp. 124−33.

9. Interpretations differ as to the scope of this injunction against *hukot ha-goy*; whether it includes purely social customs and habits of dress, or only those customs associated with the Gentile mode of worship. See *Sifra* ad loc.

10. Since it was difficult to maintain the ban against Gentile bread and oil, later authorities rescinded the ban; cf. the source indicated in the text. Similarly, the ban against food cooked by a non-Jew had to be circumvented since many Jews employed non-Jewish maids in their household; cf. *Shulhan Arukh, Yoreh De'ah*, sec. 113, par. 4, esp. gloss of Ramo.

11. In the benediction preceding the Shema; the Festival Kiddush and Amidah; the benediction preceding the study of Torah.

12. Yehudah Halevi: "These religions [which came after Judaism] are merely a preparation and introduction to the hoped-for Messiah" (*Kuzari* 4:23). Maimonides: "The teachings of the Nazarene and the Ishmaelite [Mohammed] serve the divine purpose of preparing the way for the Messiah . . . for they have spread the words of the Scriptures and the law of truth over the wide globe" (*Hilkhot Melakhim* 11:4). The foregoing quotation from Maimonides was expurgated from the printed editions, but is found in most manuscripts and in the Rome edition. For the full text, see Yale Judaica Series, vol. 3, p. xxiii (New Haven, 1949).

13. Cf. Rambam, loc. cit., for clarification of the Noahide laws.

CHAPTER 10

1. J. *Berakhot* 2:4 (5a), *Eikhah Rabbah* 1:57.

2. H. J. Schonfield, *The Passover Plot* (New York, 1966), p. 12.

3. Mishnah *Sanhedrin* 10:1.

4. Cf. *Pesahim* 56a, where the Sages say that Jacob wanted to reveal to his sons "the End of Days," but the *Shekhinah* (the Divine Presence, which confers the power of prophecy) departed from him.

5. Cf. Ps. 37:37, where *aharit* means "a future."

6. See M. Kasher, *Haggadah Shelemah* (Jerusalem, 5715), pp. 94–95, for sources.

7. See I. Ben-Zvi, *The Exiled and the Redeemed* (English ed. Philadelphia, 5718), pp. 40 ff. and 209 ff.

8. Cf. Rambam *Hilkhot Melakhim* 11:1, 12:2.

9. Cf. *Yalkut Shimoni* to Exod. 12:40 and Ps. 45:3, also *Shemot Rabbah* 25:16.

10. Maimonides apparently has adopted this reconciliation of the opinions of Rabbi Eliezer and Rabbi Yehoshua. He repeatedly records the statement of Samuel that "there is no difference between this world and the days of the Messiah except [the redemption from] subjugation to the kingdoms" (*Hilkhot Teshuvah* 9:2 and *Hilkhot Melakhim* 12:2) which, according to the Talmud, corresponds to the opinion of Rabbi Yehoshua; and nevertheless he asserts that "Israel will be redeemed only if they repent," corresponding to the opinion of Rabbi Eliezer (*Hilkhot Teshuvah* 7:5; cf. discussion of *Lehem Mishneh*, ibid. 8:7). But he adds: "The Torah has already assured that Israel will eventually repent at the end of their Exile,

and they will immediately be redeemed, as it is said, 'And it shall be when all these things will come upon you, etc., you will return to the Lord your God, and the Lord your God will return your captivity, etc.' [Deut. 30:1–3]."

11. Cf. *Sifra* to Lev. 26:6, and Rambam, *Hilkhot Melakhim* 12:2.

12. Micah, a younger contemporary of Isaiah, echoed Isaiah's words in his own prophetic message, chaps. 4 and 5.

13. Cf. *Megillah* 17b: "Wars are the beginning of the Redemption."

14. See, however, chap. 5, n. 2.

15. See above, pp. 39f.

16. This phrase is the concluding sentence in some versions of the memorial prayer for the dead *(El Malei Rahamim)*.

17. *Pesahim* 119b. Cf. *Sanhedrin* 99a: "To what does the verse 'The eye has not seen' [Isa. 64:3] refer? This is the wine kept in its grapes from the Six Days of Genesis"; and *Baba Bathra* 74b re the Leviathan and the Behemot. This messianic feast is described in the liturgical poem *Akdamut* recited before the reading of the Torah on the Festival of Shavuot.

18. An excellent example can be found in N. Ausubel, *Treasury of Jewish Folklore* (New York, 1948), "Joseph della Reyna Storms Heaven" (pp. 206 ff.).

19. See. G. Scholem, *The Messianic Idea in Judaism* (New York 1971), pp. 37 ff.

20. For an extended discussion of these last two movements, see ibid., chap. on "Redemption Through Sin."

21. In the *Kuzari*, see esp. bk. I, sec. 115. The quotation from Maimonides is in *Hilkhot Melakhim*, final chap. In his *Iggeret Teiman* he dwells at length on the cause of Israel's suffering in Exile, and comforts the people that God has by no means abandoned Israel, and urges them to maintain their Torah way-of-life. For the arguments of Nahmanides, see H. D. Chavel, *Kitvei Ramban* (Jerusalem, 5723), pp. 279 ff. and 308 ff.

22. E. Hoffer, *The True Believer* (New York, 1951), p. 34 in paperback edition.

23. Cf. Rashi, bottom of *Rosh Hashanah* 30a, and Tosafot *Shevuot* 15b, s.v. *ein binyan*. Maimonides thought otherwise. He included in his *Mishneh Torah* the rules and specifications for the Beit ha-Mikdash "which will be built in the future" *(Hilkhot Beit ha-Behirah* 1:4), implying that it will be built by human hands. See my *Sefer Athalta di-Geulah* (Jerusalem 5731), p. 23, for a further confirmation of the difference of opinion between Rambam and Rashi re the building of the future Temple.

24. See above, chap. 9.

25. According to one version (*Sanhedrin* 93b), the Sages killed Bar Kochba when they found his claim to be the Messiah King false. They interpreted the word in Isaiah 11:3 *ve-hariyho* ("his smelling") literally; to wit, that the Messiah will be so inspired by the Lord that he will be able to judge a person's guilt or innocence merely by his sense of smell, and since Bar Kochba was unable to do so he was killed. (I wonder if there is an adumbration here of the story of Jesus.) According to another version, Bar Kochba met his downfall because when he went out to battle

he would say, "Master of the Universe, don't help me and don't destroy me." Furthermore, he suspected Rabbi Elazar of Modin of conspiring with the enemy and killed him (J. *Taanit* 4:5 [68d]).

26. Rashi explains Rabbi Yehudah's disapproval "because there in Babylonia there are Yeshivot which are continually spreading Torah."

27. Tosafot *Kethubot* 110b, s.v. *hu omeir*.

28. Maimonides' visit to this sacred site has some relevance to a disputed matter nowadays; namely, whether Jews are permitted to visit the Temple Mount. According to his own ruling (*Hilkhot Beit ha-Behirah* 6:14 and 7:7), the sanctity of the Temple site endures to this day despite its ruin, and therefore ritually unclean persons —and today every Jew is ritually unclean since we do not have the ashes of the *Parah Adumah* (Red Heifer, see Num. 19)—are restrained by the Halakhah from visiting the Temple Mount. Indeed, it is in accord with this ruling that signs are posted today at the entrance to the Temple Mount warning Jews not to enter. (See, however, RABD, ad loc., who disagrees with Rambam as to the severity of this restriction.) We do not know how Maimonides reconciled his act with his own ruling.

29. See Scholem, op. cit., pp. 176 ff., for a rather strained defense of his theory that early Hasidism "neutralized" the Messianic idea as an actual historical force for imminent Redemption. See also above, p. 124.

30. See *Teshuvot Hatam Sofer, Orah Hayyim*, nos. 15 and 16.

31. For a description of the manner in which the *kollelim* functioned, see B. Z. Gat, *Ha-Yishuv ha- Yehudi B'Eretz Yisrael* (Jerusalem, 5723), chap. 4. For the dispute that arose between the Ashkenazim and the Sephardim re the distribution of the funds collected in Europe for the Yishuv, see M. Solomon, *Three Generations in the Yishuv* (Heb.) (Jerusalem, 5702), pp. 23 ff.

32. *Vayikra Rabbah* 5:4.

33. J. L. Blau and S. W. Baron, *The Jews of the United States*, vol. 3, pp. 917—19.

34. Cf. *Teshuvot Hatam Sofer*, no. 203: "Contributions for Jews living in Eretz Yisrael are not in order to assist them in fulfilling the mitzvah of dwelling in Eretz Yisrael, but for ourselves to fulfill the words of the Torah, for if Jews were not to dwell in Eretz Yisrael the Torah would, God forfend, be dissipated" (cf. Rambam, *Sefer ha-Mitzvot*, no. 153).

CHAPTER 11

1. *Hadash* is the new grain which may not be reaped or consumed until the *omer*, the meal-offering of barley, is offered in the Beit ha-Mikdash on the sixteenth of Nisan (Lev. 23:9—14). In the absence of the Temple Service, it is the day itself which makes the new grain permissible (*Menahot* 68b). Whether the prohibition of *hadash* obtains outside Eretz Yisrael is a matter of dispute; see *Talmudic Encyclopedia*, vol. 12, p. 626.

2. In addition to being abhorred by the link in Czarist Russia between the Church and the reactionary policies of the government, secular Zionists were motivated by the desire to "normalize" the situation of the Jewish people. They argued that Jews would not be subject to anti-Semitism once they became "a nation like all other nations" in their cultural as well as political identity. Such cultural homogeneity with the enlightened civilized world could be achieved only by forsaking the traditions of Judaism which made Jews so different and peculiar in the eyes of the goyim. Of course, such an ideology was—and still is—self-contradictory. A Jewish nationalism which is not based upon the continuity of Jewish history, a continuity which is based primarily upon Israel's religious traditions, is an anomaly incapable of sustaining itself.

3. A view expressed by Nahman Syrkin, one of the early protagonists of Socialist Zionism, which was the ideology of the Poalei Zion organization.

4. Typical is the statement issued by the German Rabbinical Assembly (Reform): "The efforts of the so-called Zionists to erect in Palestine a Jewish national state run counter to Judaism's messianic hopes as expressed in Scripture and later religious sources. Judaism imposes upon its adherents the obligation to serve with devotion the country to which they belong, and to promote its national interests wholeheartedly and with all their strength." See above, p. 139.

5. Compare this to mekhirat hametz, the selling of one's leavened food before Passover in order to avoid the Torah's command, "Seven days shall there be no leaven found in your houses" (Exod. 12:19).

Objections to Rabbi Kook's ruling are based both on halakhic and on ideological grounds. The Halakhah forbids selling land in Eretz Yisrael to non-Jews (Abodah Zarah 20a: "It is written, 'and give them no quarter' [Deut. 7:2], implying that we may not give them any resting-place in the land"). Tosafot, ibid., maintains that this prohibition applies to all non-Jews, whereas Rambam (Hilkhot Akum 10:13) confines this ruling to the "seven nations" which occupied Eretz Yisrael at the time of Joshua. Ideologically, it is paradoxical that we should sell land to non-Jews at a time when we want to redeem as much land as possible from them through purchase. Nevertheless, it is now the accepted practice for the Chief Rabbinate to arrange a bill of sale of all Jewish land to an Arab for the year of Shemittah. The agricultural settlements of Agudat Yisrael do not accept this heter, and avoid doing any kind of work on the land that is prohibited by the Torah.

6. Rabbi David Cohen, known as the Nazir because of his refusal to cut his hair and his strict vegetarianism. Rabbi Goren is his son-in-law.

7. Of course, agricultural laws are discussed in the Babylonian Talmud, but not in a thorough and systematic way, and not with the application to the situation at the time of the discussion, as in the Jerusalem Talmud.

8. For the halakhic sources, and for a graphic description of the latest milking machines, see the journal Torah u-Madah, vol. 1 (Iyar 5731).

9. For a poetic description of the early settlers, see Malca Shapira, Midin le-rahamim (Jerusalem, 1969), pp. 276 ff.

10. Maimonides was an outstanding exception; he included in his Code the

laws of a Jewish state in all its ramifications, though he necessarily was limited—as far as our modern life is concerned— by the scope and mode of thought of his times. An example of the narrow scope of a rabbinic code for an independent Jewish state, written but two generations ago, is the *Arukh ha-Shulhan ha-Atid* by the eminent talmudic scholar Rabbi Yehiel Mikhel Epstein, whose Code for the future state consists primarily of a pilpulistic commentary on the Code of Maimonides.

11. *Hilkhot Talmud Torah* 1:10.

12. For a detailed survey of the developments of the Jewish school system in early times, see N. Drazin, *History of Jewish Education* (Baltimore, 1940).

13. Cf. Mishnah *Erubin* 1:10: "Four things were permitted to an army camp, etc." See also Tosefta *Erubin* 3:5–7.

14. The halakhic basis for such opposition is the rabbinic interpretation of Deut. 22:5, "A woman must not put on man's apparel"; implying that a woman is not permitted to go to war bearing arms (*Nazir* 59a; cf. Targum Onkelos to verse). Of course, the major objection to women being drafted in the army is based on the fear that women in the service leads to sexual promiscuity.

15. Cf. *Menahot* 29b: "He would infer from every stroke of the Torah mounds of rulings." See also *Yebamot* 16a.

CHAPTER 12

1. Max Nordau, Herzl's closest collaborator, said: "In the case of most Zionists, anti-Semitism was only a stimulus causing them to reflect upon their relation to the nations, and their reflection has led them to results that must remain for them a permanent intellectual and spiritual possession even if anti-Semitism were to vanish completely from the world" (quoted in S. W. Baron, *Modern Nationalism and Religion* [New York and Philadelphia,1940], p. 340).

2. See, however, Baron, op. cit., p. 234.

3. Cf. *Shemot Rabbah* 15:18: "The great among the nations will see a lowly Israelite and will desire to kneel before him, etc."

4. *Bamidbar Rabbah* 2:12.

5. End of *Hilkhot Melakhim*.

6. Cf. the midrashic interpretation of Deut. 26:6: "*And the Egyptians dealt ill with us*, as it is said [Exod. 1:10]: 'Come let us deal wisely with them'" (*Sifre* ad loc., quoted in the *Haggadah shel Pesah*). The Midrash here interprets *va-yarei'u* to mean "they made us bad," i.e., they said that we were a bad people.

7. N. Bentwich, *Josephus* (Philadelphia, 1940), pp. 206 ff.

8. *Hilkhot Beit ha-Behirah* 6:16.

9. See the chapter on Jewish identity in my *The Light of Redemption*.

10. *Shemot Rabbah* 1:33. Cf. Rashi ad loc.: "that no man is destined to issue from him to be converted [to Judaism]."

11. In 1962 the Chief Rabbinate dealt at length with this question, concluding that the Benei Yisrael are Jewish, but before they may marry an investigation has to

be made concerning the marriages of their parents and grandparents (Cf. Mishnah *Kiddushin* 4:4, where there are even more stringent rules concerning the marriage of a *kohen*). In view of the fact that the Benei Yisrael were not aware of many halakhic rules, the question revolved mainly about the possibility that some of their forebears might have consummated halakhically forbidden marriages; cf. I. Herzog, *Teshuvot Heikhal Yitzhak*, vol. 1, nos. 13, 14.

12. I have pointed out elsewhere (*Beyond the Moon*, p. 365) the distinction in the prophet's phraseology between *ve-hayu la'ahadim* (v. 17) and *ve-hayu ehad* (v. 19), the former indicating the first stage in the unification of the two divisions of the Jewish people, in which each group does not lose its particular identity within Klal Yisrael, and the latter indicating the final stage, in which there is a total merging of the two divisions. For the present, it is desirable that Sephardim and Ashkenazim maintain their distinctive traditions and halakhic norms, but ultimately there must emerge one halakhah and one life-style for all Jews.

13. See also *Temurah* 16a, also *Shabbat* 104a, that no prophet can proclaim any new law (i.e., on the basis of a Divine revelation). See above pp. 55ff.

14. *Hilkhot Mamrim* 2:1.

15. Rashi explains that Rav Ashi and Rabina edited the discussions of the Amoraim, which stretched over a period of three centuries, from the beginning of the third to the end of the fifth, in no way implying the cessation of authority to expound Scripture for halakhic purposes. There are a few isolated instances where a later authority based his decision on the scriptural text.

16. Introduction to the *Mishneh Torah*.

17. See *Talmudic Encyclopedia*, vol. 6, pp. 698 ff., for the various interpretations of this principle. This writer is inclined to follow the opinion of Rabbenu Menahem ha-Meiri as set forth in the *Beit ha-Behirah* to *Betzah* 5a.

18. For the denigration of later generations as compared to the earlier generations, see *Sotah* 49a, *Berakhot* 20a and 35b, *Shabbat* 112b. See also *Shulhan Arukh*, *Yoreh De'ah*, sec. 243, RAMO to pars. 2 and 8, and *Pithei Teshuvah*, ibid., par. 3.

19. For a full discussion of this problem, see *Ha-Mishpat ha-Ivri U-Medinat Yisrael* (Jerusalem: Mosad Harav Kook, 5729). For the interaction between the Halakhah and civil law, see M. Elon, *Ha-Mishpat ha-Ivri* (Jerusalem, 5733), vol. 1, chap. 4.

20. See above, p. 234, n. 16, quotation from *TUR* and *Beit Yosef*. Cf. also *Taanit* 14b, "R. Yehudah said (in connection with prayer for rain), 'In these times, all is according to the years, all according to the places, all according to the time.'"

A change in phraseology should also be instituted for the *ketubah*, the marriage contract, which in Israel today is a hodgepodge of various traditions. The late Chief Rabbi Herzog had proposed the insertion of a clause that provides that a daughter inherit an equal share with a son, but he failed to receive any support for such an innovation from the *roshei yeshivot*. In this instance as in others, the *roshei yeshivot* did not follow the example of the Sages, "who were intent upon protecting the interests of the daughters of Israel" (*Kethubot* 2a).

21. Examples are the taking of medicine on Shabbat, the prohibition of *s'tam yeinam*, which renders wine touched by a non-Jew forbidden, and *yom-tov sheni shel galuyot*, which imposes upon Diaspora Jews an extra day of Yom Tov.

22. One example is in fixing the legal status of women. The rabbinic ruling that a woman's testimony is invalid (they did make some exceptions to this rule) is based upon their interpretation of the verse "the two men shall stand" (Deut. 19:17) as referring to the witnesses, with the use of the masculine *anashim* (men) excluding women; see *Sifre* ad loc., *Shebuot* 30a, Rambam, *Hilkhot Edut* 9:2. Not always is the use of the masculine form interpreted to exclude women; see *Baba Kamma* 15a and the commentaries ad loc., also end of n. 20 above. Another example would be an up-to-date classification of what constitutes a *melakhah* prohibited by the Torah on Shabbat. The categories set down by the Rabbis do not comprehend all the modern devices of commercial, industrial, and agricultural enterprise.

23. A possible example would be if the Knesset were to pass a bill permitting euthanasia. The Chief Rabbinate could advise the Knesset in preparing legislation concerning abortion.

24. Cf. *Abodah Zarah* 2b: "The Holy One, blessed be He, offered the Torah to every people, but they refused to accept it."

25. Quoted in Zvi Yaron, *Mishnato shel Harav Kook* (Jerusalem, 5734), p. 319. See especially ibid., n. 63, re the name *Medinat Yisrael*.

26. Rashi ad loc.

27. From the Israel government's *Annual* for 5712, in an article entitled "The Spiritual and Pioneering Goals of Israel."

28. Maurice Samuel, *The Great Hatred* (New York, 1940) esp. p. 39: "It [anti-Semitism] is the expression of the movement to put an end to the Christian episode in human history. . . . It is the conspiratorial, implacable campaign against Christ the Jew." Compare Solomon Schechter's characterization of the Higher Biblical Criticism of the Wellhausen school as an expression of "higher anti-Semitism."

29. Cf. *Sotah* 14a: "How does one walk after the Lord; by walking in the way of His attributes."

30. Cf. *Shabbat* 63a and 151b, the statement of the Amora Samuel.

31. Cf. *Sifre* to Deut. 15:4 (quoted by Rashi) for the rabbinic reconciliation of the two verses.

32. *Hilkhot Mat'not Aniyyim* 10:7.

33. The Talmud interprets *ger* to mean the proselyte who accepts upon himself all the mitzvot of the Torah *(ger tzedek)*, whereas *toshav* refers to the non-Jewish resident of Eretz Yisrael who has accepted the seven Noahide mitzvot; see *Sifra* ad loc. and *Abodah Zarah* 64b. In a paper I prepared for my M.A. (Harvard), I pointed out that *ger* most probably refers to the non-Jew who came to live within the Jewish community, and *toshav* refers to the old inhabitant who remained within the non-Jewish community. For the interpretation of the modern critics, see E. A. Speiser, *Genesis* (New York, 1964), p. 170, n. 4. The new translation of the Torah (Philadelphia: 1962) Jewish Publication Society, p. 230, gives an interpretation of this verse totally at variance with the traditional one, and to my mind totally unwarranted.

34. Concerning burial, Rashi notes: "Not in the same burial grounds, but they [i.e., their corpses] are taken care of if found killed together with Jews."

35. *Hilkhot Teshuvah* 9:1.

36. Quoted in S. W. Baron, *Modern Nationalism and Religion* (New York and Philadelphia, 1960), p. 222.

INDEX OF BIBLICAL REFERENCES

INDEX OF RABBINIC REFERENCES

GENERAL INDEX